*A Scholar in Action*

# EDWIN F. GAY

*Sponsored by*
*The Friends of Edwin F. Gay*

Fabian Bachrach

EDWIN F. GAY

# *A Scholar in Action*

# EDWIN F. GAY

By

HERBERT HEATON

HARVARD UNIVERSITY PRESS

Cambridge · Massachusetts

1952

*Distributed in Great Britain by*
*Geoffrey Cumberlege*
*Oxford University Press*
*London*

*Library of Congress Catalog Card Number 52–5397*
*Printed in the United States of America*

# PREFACE

THIS STUDY was to have been a brief interpretative memoir, which the Friends of Edwin F. Gay invited me to write. Since my own intimate acquaintance with him covered only the last few years of his life, even such a limited task called for many interviews with those who had known him well, and also for the inspection of whatever records had survived. These records proved to be embarrassingly abundant. The papers in Gay's own files ran from grade school reports and high school diaries all the way through the years, with few thin or blank patches, down to a questionnaire on Russo-American relations on which he penciled his comments about a month before he died — in all a span of well-nigh seven decades.

Here, and in other manuscript collections, was material for a biography rather than a memoir; and the subject merited the former rather than the latter. For Gay's story, as it took shape, was not only unusual at many points, such as his refusal of any academic post until, at thirty-five, he felt sufficiently qualified in scholarship to be a competent teacher; it is also an important part of the history of American higher education, in the widest sense of that term, during the first half of the present century. He was a great teacher, who put the study of economic history on its feet and taught it how to walk and work. Beyond that, he was one of a small band of pioneers, innovators, academic statesmen, who transformed the equipment and outlook of American scholarship, initiated a new era in social studies, and opened up new fields of research. During World War I he was chiefly instrumental in breaking the shipping bottleneck and in making available more vessels for transporting the

American Expeditionary Force to Europe. Then for a while he managed a New York newspaper. Thus he touched American education, politics, and journalism at many high points, and everywhere he left his mark.

In the chapters which follow I have dealt chiefly with the scholar in action, as dean, public servant, newspaper president, or as promoter and guiding spirit in research institutions or projects. But the story would be incomplete without some account of the long apprenticeship served by the scholar in the making and of his work when he became a practicing master of his craft.

Many who were Gay's friends and colleagues have supplied me with information and read the manuscript in whole or part. The officers of Harvard University, of the National Bureau of Economic Research, and the Social Science Research Council have allowed me to examine their records. Mr. Thomas S. Lamont gave me access to his father's papers relating to Gay's years as president of the New York *Evening Post*. Gay's daughter, Mrs. Godfrey Davies, allowed me the free run of her father's files, and has been a gentle constructive critic of my script. The Honorable Herbert Hoover, Mr. William L. White, and the Director of the Franklin D. Roosevelt Library have granted me permission to quote letters. Dr. Arthur H. Cole and my wife have been my ever-present help in time of trouble.

Herbert Heaton

University of Minnesota.

# *Contents*


| | | |
|---|---|---|
| | INTRODUCTION — THE MAN AND HIS WORK | 1 |
| I | A SCHOLAR IN THE MAKING, 1867–1902 | 13 |
| II | HARVARD, 1902–1917 | 58 |
| III | WARTIME IN WASHINGTON, 1917–1919 | 97 |
| IV | THE NEW YORK "EVENING POST," 1919–1923 | 139 |
| V | HARVARD AND THE SQUIRREL CAGE, 1924–1936 | 186 |
| VI | IN AND OUT OF THE IVORY TOWER, 1936–1946 | 226 |
| | INDEX | 253 |

*A Scholar in Action*

**EDWIN F. GAY**

# INTRODUCTION

## THE MAN AND HIS WORK

When Edwin F. Gay joined the faculty of Harvard University as Instructor in Economic History in the fall of 1902 he was thirty-five years old. He had a wife and two young children. Yet this appointment, on the bottom rung of the academic ladder and for only one year, was his first job.

In offering it President Eliot may well have felt he was acting on faith rather than facts. For Gay was virtually an unknown quantity. He was not a Harvard man. Only one member of the faculty knew anything about him, though what he did know was good enough to justify the recommendation that Gay be given a trial run. There were probably not a dozen people in the United States, apart from relatives and "in-laws," who were aware of his existence. He was almost a foreigner, or at least an expatriate, having spent nearly sixteen of his thirty-five years in Europe. Since early 1890, when he went to Germany to begin his graduate studies, he had been back home on only four very brief visits. Now he was returning to a land that knew him not.

When he died in 1946 a legion of friends, colleagues, disciples, and acquaintances paid tribute to the man and his work. They belonged to many walks of life in America and abroad. Their occupations not only covered the gamut of American academic activities, but in addition included high executive office in almost every branch of commerce, finance, industry, transportation, law, journalism, literature, and public administration. Their interests were those which did much to mold the economic, political, and intellectual life of the United States during the first half of the twentieth century. Two of the men have served as American ambassadors in London, and two others have come to rank as "elder statesmen."

A few university teachers have won such widespread esteem of scholars and men of affairs by devoting their lives entirely to fruitful labor in classroom, seminar, office, and library. Gay had chosen that kind of cloistered career for himself, though only after long deliberation and much soul-searching wherein he wondered whether it was the highest use to which he could devote his life. To prepare himself for it he used the whole of the modest legacy from his father's estate in financing more than twelve years' postgraduate study in Germany, Switzerland, Italy, and England. There he ranged widely in his reading of history, political economy, and philosophy; learned how to do a difficult piece of research; and immersed himself in the literature, art, music, politics, religious debates, and social problems of western Europe.

This long apprenticeship gave him a breadth and depth of knowledge which contributed much to the reputation he won as one of Harvard's great teachers. Students who knew him only as lecturer gained from his class such new vistas of history and such an insight into the way a master sought, analyzed, and presented his material that in retrospect they counted the course one of their most valued intellectual experiences. Those who went further, following under his guidance the road to a doctor's degree, learned the high standards of rigorous work he demanded, but they also discovered the infinite pains he would take and the individual attention he was ready to give to their problems. The result was that Harvard became one of the two or three best places in the world for the systematic study of economic history and the training of economic historians.

If Gay had remained "a simple professor," taking in his stride the committee and minor administrative duties that lay along the path, he would have found the life of scholar and teacher full enough of work, of rich achievement, and of grateful remembrance by those he had taught. In 1908, however, he was confronted by President Eliot with a request he saw no way of refusing and became dean of the newly created Graduate School of Business Administration. He thereupon started a new life, or rather in large measure a double life, for in shouldering the new duties he did not shed all the old. It was a challenging assignment, partly because he knew almost nothing about modern business, and also because university education for business—especially at the graduate level—was so little developed that there were few guides or precedents. He had to conceive the broad purposes of the School, translate them into courses and teaching methods, seek the coöperation of businessmen and labor leaders, and pass the hat when income fell short of expenses.

In this combination of promoting, policy-making, administration, and public relations he became a scholar in action. As the School gradually won wide repute its builder became known far beyond Harvard Yard as a person of inventive mind and unbounded energy who did things or got them done. Consequently men who wanted help in developing a new idea, in finding the answer to a new question, or in undertaking a novel piece of work began to seek his aid. They continued to do so throughout the rest of his life. When, in 1942, in his seventy-fifth year, he informed a friend that he had been "drawn reluctantly into an unexpected job," back came the retort, "After all, you have made a lifelong career of being drawn reluctantly into unexpected jobs." On occasion the reluctance hardened into refusal, but usually it quickly melted away if a project promised to combine intellectual challenge with public service. He found it well-nigh impossible to say no.

There was no reluctance to be overcome when he was called to Washington during World War I. His immediate task was to provide the policy-makers with statistics which would guide them in restricting imports, reducing exports, using ships more economically, and thereby increase the supply of tonnage available for war service. Soon he was helping to shape the policies, then fighting hard to get them carried out. He discharged this triple duty with such speed, skill, and courage that he was drafted to aid other war agencies and to serve the White House. He became known as one of the "kings" of Washington, and when the war ended was showered with offers of all kinds of high positions — business, governmental, educational, and international.

He chose one that seemed to afford the widest scope for furthering the international coöperation, informed economic policies, and good government which the war years had convinced him the United States needed if the country was to prosper at home and play its proper part in the world. Turning his back on the teaching and "deaning" that awaited him at Harvard, he accepted the invitation to take complete charge of the New York *Evening Post*, a paper of great age and high repute but lately badly run down and near ruin. He hoped to restore its prestige and through its columns translate a liberal progressive creed into terms appropriate to a changed and chastened world.

The *Evening Post* years (1919–1923) began as high adventure and ended in financial disaster. The rapid recruiting of many additional men for the editorial staff, the initiation of a literary supplement which later became the *Saturday Review of Literature*, the calls on scholars and business experts for occasional contributions, the fight for the League of Nations and for other causes, all were magnificent. But they were immensely costly, and they failed to attract many more readers or win increased patronage from advertisers. They combined with the rising price of labor and of materials to burden the paper with deficits which broke its back. After two signal successes — the Business School and the Washington work — the scholar in action went down to defeat, yet in this defeat establishing standards that have had a continuing effect on other papers.

When the end came half a dozen universities sought to gather Gay back into the fold. Harvard succeeded, and in the fall of 1924 he returned to his first love as professor of economic history. There he stayed until 1936, carrying a full load of teaching, guiding graduate studies, and participating in the increasingly varied activities of a rapidly expanding university. The return to Harvard was not, however, a complete one, a clean break with the recent past. Though he had shed a newspaper, he did not sever three other ties knit during the New York years. Two of them were with institutions as deeply devoted to the advancement of knowledge as was any university.

The first was the National Bureau of Economic Research, created in 1919 as an alliance of academics and men of affairs to undertake research on the workings of the American economy. Gay had been one of its founders and served as its first president. When the *Evening Post* passed out of his hands he was invited to share with Professor Wesley Mitchell in the active direction of the Bureau's investigations, and did so until 1933. The second was the Council on Foreign Relations, which emerged in 1921 as another joint venture by scholars and men in business or public affairs. Gay had welcomed its appearance because he believed it would help to give the United States that understanding of international problems which was so woefully lacking in 1918–19. He became its first secretary-treasurer and retained that office until 1933, when he became a vice-president; served on its directing board from 1921 to 1945; was the moving spirit in launching its quarterly journal, *Foreign Affairs*, in 1922; and in 1927 became chairman of its research and publishing committee.

The third tie was with Washington. The war years had convinced Gay of the need for improved and better-informed government agencies. He tried in 1919 to salvage for peacetime use some of the statistical machinery built during the war. His effort was unavailing, but when Mr. Hoover, a wartime acquaintance, became Secretary of Commerce Gay was frequently called on to aid in reorganizing or extending some part of the federal services.

The years 1924–1932 were therefore piled high with external work on top of the Harvard duties. The National Bureau and the Council drew heavily on Gay's time during semesters and still more during vacations. He was continuously engaged in shaping their policies, promoting research and publishing programs, drawing up budgets, supervising operations, reading manuscripts, and raising funds.

Washington continued to seek his counsel throughout the Hoover regime. Meanwhile he became deeply involved in plans for coöperation among social scientists in the promotion of research. The Social Science Research Council, formed in 1923 for that purpose, put him on its key committee. He played a leading role during the formative years of that Council's existence, helping to promote and appraise research projects and submitting a number of his own.

For a while this hard labor, this shuttling between Cambridge and New York City, with occasional journeys to Washington, Chicago, and other points and three transatlantic trips to attend international conferences, earned rich reward. American scholarship rode high on the wave of business prosperity. It was able to indulge its insatiable curiosity about countless aspects of domestic and international society. Funds were forthcoming from foundations, corporations, or private purses for research and publication, no matter how ambitious the project. When, however, depression struck in 1929 the exhilarating work of promoting scholarly ventures gave place to exhausting efforts to finish what had been begun, even to keep alive the institutions born during the twenties. Funds were now short, budgets had to be pared to the core, research plans were still-born or died from lack of nutrition.

In these years of gloom Gay looked back on his working life and felt a sense of disappointment, frustration, partial failure. He saw it as "a distracted and dislocated career" which had started out on a chosen and carefully prepared line of scholarship but had been switched off in other directions. "It is one of my serious regrets," he wrote in 1935, "that I ever undertook the deanship of the Business School." That step, he believed, had led him inexorably on to the distractions and divided loyalties; had prevented him from attaining full stature in any sphere of endeavor; and in particular had made it impossible for him to write a single book. The time and circumstances seemed ripe for him to abandon the ceaseless round of promoting and directing other people's research in order to do a bit of his own. Only in that way could he, who had been responsible for stimulating and guiding the production of so many additions to the literature of economic history, make his own direct contribution.

In early 1933, resigning the more arduous of his offices at the National Bureau and the Council on Foreign Relations, he went on sabbatical leave for eight months in Europe. There he spent much time in the British Museum, collecting material for a volume on the Industrial Revolution. Those months rekindled his zest for research, but the fire was quickly extinguished when he returned to America. He was still too deeply involved in too many activities in Harvard or New York to have any spare time for writing. In 1936 he therefore determined to break these ties. He accepted an invitation to join the staff of the Huntington Library in San Marino, California, in the hope that on the other side of the continent he could "retire to some activities dear to [his] heart."

This hope was only partially fulfilled. The Library was a rich mine of English medieval and early modern manuscripts. Gay dug deep into them and extracted an account of the vicissitudes through five generations of an English landed family. But the Library was not a hermitage. The West soon sought him out for addresses, advice, and aid. More distracting still, the East refused to leave him alone. In eight years he made ten trips to the Atlantic seaboard, spent about eighteen months there, but was able to devote less than four of them to his own research. Not only did old associates seek him out; calls came for help in planning new research ventures, and when war came to America he called on himself to undertake the task of developing a scheme for the study of postwar policies and problems by university groups. If his eastern friends could have had their way he would have spent all his time with them, and had it not been for his wife's failing health he probably would have been content, even eager, to do so. When her sickness grew grave and his own health was shaken by illnesses contracted on his journeys, his advice remained on call by airmail special to the end of his life.

Such were the ingredients of Gay's career: nearly three decades of effective teaching; the planning and building of a pioneer graduate school to train men for business; a vital contribution to the winning of World War I; a valiant effort to save a venerable metropolitan newspaper; and a leading laborious role in shaping institutions through whose investigations America has come to know itself much better. It was a creditable record of constructive achievement. It touched and influenced the American mind at many points during four decades that can well be dubbed dynamic. To many men of his own generation and of the next one it brought enrichment of their lives, reorientation of their careers, the opening of opportunities, and the advancement of their fortunes. It placed scholars, businessmen, institutions, even the country at large, in debt to his vision, inspiration, and zeal. It won for him such a wide circle of friends and admirers, such expressions of individual and group gratitude, such evidence of dependence on his judgment, and such testimony to his indispensability as ought to gladden the heart of any man.

To his work in many walks of life Gay brought a rich combination of qualifications. In the first place, he felt a strong obligation to devote whatever talents he possessed to the service of others. What he did for his students far exceeded the call of duty in professional aid and personal solicitude. He did not avoid the drudgeries of office any more than he sought them, whether they meant copying out musical scores for a high school orchestra, doing the chores of a college newspaper, reading the thousand pages of proof of a National Bureau book, or conducting in his own handwriting at the age of seventy-five much of the correspondence that launched the scheme for the study of postwar problems.

In the second place, he developed, fairly early in life, a belief that research would unlock the past, give understanding to the present, and perhaps suggest the possible shape of things to come — or of things that ought to come. At twenty-three he looked a little enviously on the achievements of the natural scientists, by whose labors "the great laws of life are becoming known." He was confident that the great laws of social life, of historical development, and of economic behavior could also become known if a sufficient number of scholars worked at the job hard enough for many generations. In that faith he tried to make sure that his own generation had a chance to contribute its quota to the task of revelation.

In the third place, his range of knowledge in many fields, his ability to see the whole landscape of which the fields were part, and his sense of the "altogetherness of everything" gave him breadth as well as depth of understanding. What this meant to his teaching we have already noted. It enhanced his value to committees and conferences in a period when scholars belonging to different "disciplines" were seeking common ground for coöperation. One such coöperator said of him: "He is an exceedingly important part of the bridge between the social sciences and the humanities." This was true as well between the experts on ancient, medieval, and modern civilizations. Meanwhile his journeys into the wider world of affairs taught him lessons which are not part of the usual education of a scholar. Consequently, to continue the testimonial quoted just above, "His wisdom in all practical matters, as well as in matters of principle, is remarkable." He was, in short, a perfect committeeman, an ideal chairman.

To these attributes were added considerable talents as promoter and organizer, and smaller skill as administrator, also great powers of physical endurance that recognized no limit to working hours and days. He also had a full measure of courage that never shirked an unavoidable fight, that refused to believe "Safety First" was a fit rule of life, that would not admit defeat till denial was no longer possible, then wrote off each rebuff or failure with the question, "Well, what do we do next?" Finally, there was a personal forcefulness which made him drive himself as much as he drove others, which inspired in colleagues and subordinates an enthusiastic loyalty to the man and his work, and gave them a sense that their work — whether a piece of individual investigation or a humble job in a large organization — had value and purpose.

That he had the defects of his qualities was, perhaps, to be expected. The urge to be of service left him with "a poor capacity for cutting off importunities of various kinds," led him to take on too many tasks, and consequently made him at times what a colleague called "a messy manager." His desk was never clear. Some of the plans and projects which he envisaged for himself or for others were too grandiose to be practicable with the talents, time, and resources that were available. Some of the methods and policies by which he sought to achieve an objective were impulsively conceived on too lavish a scale, overelaborate, ruthless, and doomed to failure. Finally, the qualities which made him "a full man" also helped to make him a divided man.

We have already seen what he thought of that division. His judgment of himself was no secret to those who knew him well. When he died, one friend of forty years' standing wrote: "Edwin F. Gay was essentially the scholar in action; in him the call to scholarship and the call to action created a conflict that endured throughout his mature years." In similar vein three of his colleagues described him in the minutes of the Faculty of Arts and Sciences of Harvard University:

> This conflict between his ideal of single devotedness to scholarship, which was always escaping him, and the busy life of affairs into which he was continually being led was the dominant characteristic of [his] career. To it he ascribed his failure to carry out most of the major projects of writing about which his mind continuously played. To it his friends must ascribe the faulty perspective which prevented his finding any sense of accomplishment in his numerous significant contributions to the life of his university and of the world outside.

Gay's colleagues could have gone further and pointed out that his conflict was not unique. It was shared by any number of his contemporaries, eminent scholars who fought a losing battle against the encroachments of administrative duties within their own universities or of compelling interests outside. The American urge to embark on new enterprises and to mobilize kindred spirits for joint ventures has levied a heavy toll on the undertakers and chiefs of staff. Wesley Mitchell once ruefully remarked that the Social Science Research

Council was an organization for the suppression of research in so far as its members were concerned. Of the score of historians, including Gay, who agreed in the twenties to write one volume apiece for a series of historical studies on the making of modern Europe, less than half have completed their assignments at mid-century. Even the editor has not finished his book.

In Gay's case the obstacle to "productive scholarship" was only in part a lack of time. It was partly the nature of the theme on which he hoped to write, for the Industrial Revolution is a subject with no set metes and bounds and the mass of material he felt obliged to examine was inexhaustible. But it was probably even more the nature of his mind. His interest in whatever he studied was a road with many alluring sidetracks and no terminus. His desire for full comprehension was born of the intellectual pleasure that came from acquiring sufficient knowledge to solve a problem to his own satisfaction. When he had done that, he would rather go on to seek the answer to another question than settle down to the drudgery of expounding in print for other people the solution of the first. Time after time an editor to whom he had promised a book emphasized the importance of his beginning to write instead of getting too deeply involved in marginal secondary problems. Always Gay agreed, but it was obvious that he did not heed and "was having a perfectly grand time running down questions which had long interested and bothered him."

He therefore found it almost impossible to stop reading and start writing for publication. Even the few articles which embody his research on limited topics were begun with difficulty and finished only just on the dead line. Of them, as of the handful of addresses which got into print, he was far from proud. His verdicts on them ran in such comments as "this dreadful presidential address," "a poor little thing," "a rather slight performance," or "this blessed paper, twice rewritten, is not the article I set out to write . . . I hope rather that [the editor] does not accept it." Since he was so critical of his own work, it is very doubtful whether he would ever, under the most favorable circumstances, have produced a *magnum opus*, or even a volume of smaller stature.

Perhaps therefore he served his time and place best by being distracted from his chosen path to do the kind of things he did so well. In doing them he lived an uncommonly rich and productive life. In his generation he had few peers in the sum total of his contribution to the advancement of knowledge in the social sciences from the Pre-Research — or at best the Paleo-Research — Age to its present maturity and to the putting of that knowledge to constructive use in society. Someone else can write the book.

# I

## A SCHOLAR IN THE MAKING

### 1867–1902

EDWIN FRANCIS GAY was born on October 27, 1867, in Detroit. As birthplace for one of the descendants of John Gay, who landed in New England in 1630, Detroit was unusually far west. Seven generations of Gays had been born, lived, and died in or near Boston. A rare adventurer emigrated to Connecticut, Vermont, New York, even Quebec; but most of these exiles returned sooner or later. Massachusetts was a good enough habitation for most Gays.

It might have been good enough for Aaron Francis, born in Boston in 1841, had he not met Mary Lucena Loud. True, there was a streak of youthful restlessness in him, which led him to quit school before he need have done so; but work in his father's account-book manufactory and stationery store on State Street soon made him repent this hasty action and decide it would be wise to return to school, then enter Harvard. His father's death (1859) prevented him from taking that step. Instead it saddled him, at eighteen, with the management of the business, and the support of his stepmother and two younger brothers. He did the job well, made considerable profit during the Civil War years, and might have continued to run the small but flourishing enterprise to the end of his days.

Miss Loud, or rather her father, the Reverend Henry Loud, diverted him from that way of life. Though the Louds were almost as old New England as the Gays, their roots had not struck so deep.

In 1832 Henry's father, a builder and millwright, moved his family to a sparsely settled region in Ohio. Henry, a lad of eight at the time of the migration, learned how to work a farm and as a side-line to operate a little sawmill. Adolescence brought a religious urge and a ready tongue. At eighteen he secured a "license to exhort," then a "license to preach," and his fame as "the boy preacher" quickly spread throughout rural Ohio. After nine years of this strenuous ill-paid labor, he transplanted his wife and four children to Concord, New Hampshire, spent three years there in a theological seminary, then served a series of pastorates in Lowell, Fitchburg, and other Massachusetts towns.

Here he repeated his Ohio success as preacher; but the work began to shake his health, while the stipend was insufficient to pay off the debts incurred for his training and to maintain a family of eight. He therefore sought a way to supplement his income and found it in meeting the Civil War demand for gunstocks. In 1861 he erected a small mill near London, Ontario, in which to saw the walnut and make the stocks. By the end of the war he had paid his debts, accumulated a tidy sum of capital, and resolved to plunge full-time into the lumber business. With two partners he acquired a large tract of pine forest about a hundred and fifty miles north of Detroit on the west shore of Lake Huron, and in 1865 built a mill.

The Louds thereupon moved from Massachusetts to Michigan, and Aaron Francis Gay went with them. He entered the family by marrying Mary Lucena in 1866. He also entered the firm, handing the stationery store over to a brother; and as Loud's original partners dropped out, the business became a family venture — father, sons, and son-in-law. Since Gay's early concern was with the firm's financial and commercial affairs he could do much of that work in Detroit, and lived there until after the birth of the first child, Edwin Francis, in 1867.

By going to the north woods the Louds and Gays solved their income problems, but created a difficult educational one. Au Sable and Oscoda, the base points for the new venture, had been tiny fishing villages from which men went out to catch lake trout. The attack on the forest and the building of the mills increased the population fairly rapidly. The social advance, however, lagged far behind the economic, and it took at least a decade to provide the community with doctor, churches, weekly paper, and school. To fill part of the gap a gifted young teacher, Jane Hosmer, was brought out from Concord. She read diligently to Frank and helped him over the threshold into reading for himself "without awareness of an alphabet to learn or spelling to master." When, in 1874, an "ungraded" country school "with a bearded imitation of a teacher" was established, Miss Hosmer departed and Frank went to it, there to spend four years which were "a blurred and dismal memory" during the rest of his life.

By 1878 the father had decided that the lad and his two young sisters, Mary and Edith, must go where better teachers were available. He was making sufficient money to pay for the kind of education many New Englanders felt was desirable, even essential. In September, therefore, he sent his wife and children, attended by a companion-governess, to Europe. There they stayed for almost three years, divided among Paris, a Swiss summer resort, Florence, Rome, Heidelberg, Hanover, and Paris again. Life ran smoothly until in late 1880 Frank was severely stricken with scarlet fever in Heidelberg. The illness impaired his physique for many years, interrupted his attendance at a series of day schools, and probably caused the family to return home sooner than had been planned.

In later life Gay felt that though there had been some educational value in his first European sojourn, the "formal but broken training" he got in at least five schools contributed "next to nothing" to his development and was, in fact, "a bad break in the 'extracurricular' activity of a normal American boy." The list of subjects studied was so different from that in Michigan that he feared he would fall behind the boys at home. The schools seem to have been poor social centers, lacked facilities for play or sports, and the boys spent little time together outside the classroom.

Life during the European years was therefore in large measure intramural and domestic, with mother as its director and father as remote counselor. Letters from father were filled with exhortation on matters moral, intellectual, and physical. On the first the standards set were high: "Never forget the example of Bayard, *sans peur* and without reproach." "Always remember one thing — that you are a Yankee boy and that you ought to be all that is brave and truthful and honest for the honor and the sake of your country and your mother and father." There was reiterated warning about human frailties, temptations, and "avenues of pleasure . . . that really lead to misery." All this may well have been rather frightening to a lad of eleven or twelve cooped up in an alien secluded environment, and may have contributed something to the bouts of introspection and sin-consciousness that worried his adolescence.

The intellectual aims set by the father for his son were as high as the moral ones. He was striving to improve his own foreshortened education by building up — and reading — a library in his Oscoda home. Bohn's Classical Library, forerunner of the Harvard five-foot shelf, was the foundation. To it he added many-volumed editions of Carlyle, Froude, Bancroft, John Richard Green, Motley, Montaigne, Plutarch, Goethe, Schiller, Emerson, and of the novelists whose works had become classics, especially Dickens, Scott, and Thackeray.

Young Gay had heard his father or mother read some of these works — even the Greek philosophers — and taken a hand at reading them. Now the father impressed on him in every letter the importance of assiduous but selective attention to books.

> Reading is part of the training for life. When men go into training, they don't let them eat cake and drink what will not give them strength. Now while you are training you should read only what will give you strength; and story books, at least some of them, are cake and pie to you mentally, and take strength from you instead of adding it. You ought not to read them.
>
> [Instead] read histories and travels and lives of great men. Learn to consider what quality of mind or heart made them great or brave or

good, and then cultivate those qualities yourself. See where they made mistakes. You will find that errors can be traced to the power of money, or of women, or of ambition.

From such general advice father would pass on to recommend that the eleven-year-old lad make "little abstracts" of each of Plutarch's *Lives of Famous Men*; to ask the twelve-year-old son to read one of Montaigne's essays "and tell me what you think of it"; to suggest that the thirteen-year-old boy study the advice of another father to his son in the *Reflections* of Marcus Aurelius; or to declare his admiration for most, but not all, of Goethe's opinions.

Throughout the letters ran the father's ambition that his son win "a place with the best and first of men," and "be a soloist instead of one of the chorus." While making no attempt to influence the lad's choice of a career he did urge the claims of journalism—with law as second preference—because "in these two professions the widest and most powerful influence can be used." No matter what "call" the son accepted, father was insistent on the need for thorough training:

It should be prepared for by the possession of all knowledge possible, not only in the chosen profession but in all branches . . . It is necessary that you should know everything almost . . . You must work persistently. Genius is good, but persistent persevering diligence that overcomes all obstacles, all hindrances, is better, and if it is allied to genius it makes a man of the first class. Such a man I pray that my boy may be.

These letters had a great influence on young Gay when they were received, and a still greater one when, after his father's death in 1884, they became a treasured legacy as well as a revered guidebook. He reread them many times; he handed them to his fiancée for perusal; at many points his views of the world and his sense of duty to that world reflected the teaching he drew from them.

The guidance exercised by Gay's mother was closer and more direct. She was a woman of considerable intellectual ability, wide interests, firm will, and vast enduring vitality. She was a competent pianist; her appetite for books was insatiable but eclectic; her taste in art was formed and fed as she came to know most of the leading European galleries; and her zest for politics made her an early advocate of women's rights, a keen student of proposals for removing the blemishes from American political or social life, as well as an eager observer of international relations.

One incident will suffice to reveal some of her qualities. In 1897, at fifty-one, she took a trip alone to Europe. Gay, then living in London, went to Antwerp to meet her boat. When he reached the quay at 6.30 A.M. on Sunday, he found she had already gone ashore. After searching for her in all the hotels, he finally ran her down in the cathedral studying Rubens' "Descent from the Cross." For hours they drove around the city, "seeing everything that Baedeker says is worth seeing," paused for a meal and a talk about family news, business, and finances, then at her insistence went to explore the Zoo. Repeatedly throughout the day she rejected Gay's suggestions that she take a rest. After supper, to quote his report, "she said she would like to sit and talk all night; she didn't want to waste time in sleeping — and we might have been at it yet if I had not taken the initiative firmly. We have discussed Greece and Turkey, the tariff, McKinley, silver, and politics generally." Monday was a repetition of Sunday; on Tuesday the mother moved on to Paris and the exhausted son returned to London for a rest.

Such a woman was bound to do all she could to ensure that her children's first long sojourn in Europe (1878–81) be crowded with learning, and as this was her first visit to the Continent she was herself an avid student. Every available moment was devoted to seeing, with open guidebook in hand, whatever was deemed worthy of examination. In Paris the Louvre was done thoroughly — "naked ancients" and all. The process was repeated in every other city. Home lessons supplemented school work, private tutors were engaged to teach drawing and music, and Jane Hosmer was brought over from America to give a hand. There was reading after every meal and in all spare minutes. When Gay was convalescing from the fever his mother read Carlyle's *French Revolution* to him. Looking back fifty years later, he described this experience as one of the educational landmarks of his life:

> I understand that scientific historians do not highly esteem that work; they might hesitate to prescribe it for a boy's reading. But I have reason for deep gratitude to the book, to its author, and to mother's reading of it. That vivid colorful description, read and re-read, gave and kept alive for me the actuality of history, its passionate dramatic values; it led me, for my own pleasurable reading, to other books — Motley, Prescott, Taine, and Buckle; and it was responsible for my later interest in the study of social and economic history.

When the family returned to America in mid-1881, Gay was nearly fourteen years old. His education was rich but patchy. In many respects he was informed far beyond his age, his curiosity had been aroused on a wide range of matters, and he had acquired the habit of jotting down topics that called for further study. He had picked up a good deal of French, some German, a little Italian. He had made considerable progress in drawing — in fact so much that for a time he thought an artist's life would be a desirable career; but his attempts at portraiture, especially "the picture that I made of myself when looking in the looking glass," shook confidence in his artistic ability.[1] Yet the drawing lessons were far from wasted. They give him some understanding of technique and contributed to that informed discriminating appreciation of art which remained an ingrained part of his culture to the end of his life.

In some formal ingredients his training was deficient. His grammar was uncertain, his spelling bedeviled by foreign influences, and his mathematics rudimentary, even though he learned multiplication tables up to 15 "times." As he recalled later, his "peregrinations through foreign schools had always about reached but never quite touched long division." He had to spend the first summer after the family's return in the hands of a private tutor who remedied his shortcomings in mathematics and grammar.

Whether there was another shortcoming, only time could show.

[1] His sister Mary became the artist of the family.

The European environment had been narrow, secluded, circumscribed. The exiles lived in foreign communities, but were not part of them. Attention was concentrated on the artifacts of the past rather than on the activities of the present. Personal contacts outside the classroom were chiefly with servants, tutors, doctors, guides, railroad employees, and shopkeepers. This kind of experience was not the best way of getting to know Europe and its people. More important still, it might prove a poor preparation for the intimate social life of a midwestern high school, a state university — both of them coeducational — and a small town.

In such a town, Ann Arbor, the family now settled down. About two thousand of its nine thousand inhabitants were students in the University of Michigan and another five hundred attended a fairly good high school. It was therefore an excellent bridge between the predominantly private education of Gay's boyhood and the formal training for whatever he decided to do when he reached manhood.

He spent the years 1881 to early 1890 crossing that bridge, most of the time without any idea of where he was going. When he entered high school in 1882 at the age of fifteen he did not know what career he wished to follow, and the family income was such that there was no economic pressure to make an early decision. At seventeen he wrote, "I wish I knew what I was going to be. I don't care very much. I suppose I'll have to wait and see what turns up." When he entered the University in 1886 he was still waiting, and nothing satisfactory turned up till mid-1889.

His program of study therefore lacked any vocational slant. It was made up of the traditional rather than the "modern" subjects. They were taught in the old-fashioned manner, and, if we can believe the remarks in Gay's diary and letters, few of them aroused his "attentive interest." About half his time in school and college was spent, without any enthusiasm or sense of purpose, on Latin, Greek, French, and German. To a youth already widely read in English literature the high school lessons in that subject seemed too formal and elementary. Mathematics attracted him not at all and he fulfilled only the bare requirements. The school work in history — American, Roman, and Greek — lit no fires. In fact, the only school subject that really stirred him to unstinted effort was botany. On many spring mornings he was out by 5.30 collecting specimens; afternoons and Saturdays were given to the same eager search; and during a long summer vacation in New England the hunt continued unabated. His interest in the flora of whatever district he visited endured to the end of his life.

Gay's high school diary is full of such comments as "Am not especially distinguishing myself for scholarship" or "Got through at school with moderate badness." The school report told a different tale, placing him at the top, or very near the top, in most subjects. In the fall of 1884 he was one of the dozen students chosen to make short speeches, read papers, or recite poems at the "Junior Exhibition," an annual gathering held in the school chapel before a "large and select audience" of parents and students. He chose for his subject "The Evils and Benefits of Foreign Immigration," and spent three arduous months preparing this, his first, excursion into political economy. In eight days he "finished all that the University Library has on the subject" — a tribute to his industry or a reflection on the resources of the Library. He prepared six drafts or outlines, inserted "some beautiful figures of speech, metaphors, similes, apostrophes," then cut them out. He drove the household frantic by rehearsing his speech time after time. When the great day came, his "oration" was, according to the local newspaper, "the best of the evening, and one showing thought, brain, and care of presentation. Its delivery was also forceful, as he clearly showed the value to us of the muscle and work of the emigrants."

High school classes ended at midday, leaving much time to be divided between private study, exercise, extracurricular activities, church, and whatever there was to be done at home. The private study sometimes received its due share only by resort to late hours and very early rising. Exercise in moderation was a necessary part of the therapeutic treatment to shake off the after-effects of scarlet fever. There was something wrong with one lung — tuberculosis was feared — and with the muscles of one shoulder. Gay was worried about his pallor and subnormal weight. His mother was disturbed by the lack of balance between his physical and intellectual progress. His Boston uncle, solicitous for his "muscular Christianity," gave him foils, masks, boxing gloves, Indian clubs, and a bicycle. The clubs were swung only intermittently; there was little fun in boxing, for he could not master the rudiments of defense; so only the bicycle got much use. Participation in strenuous team games was ruled out.

Looking back in 1919 on his high school and college days, Gay confessed, "I fear I was rather mopey and sensitive and envious — particularly envious of those who excelled in sport and in physical and social attractiveness." He sought expression for his social urge and escape from envy by throwing himself into nonathletic activities. He was president of his class in its junior and senior years. He represented the school on the University Lectures Committee, serving as secretary. He was secretary, then president, of the Young People's Christian Association, treasurer of the tennis club, as well as managing editor, cover designer, and cartoonist for the senior yearbook. In addition he was secretary and teacher in a Sunday school which served the German and other immigrants living across the tracks in the lower town. Finally, he was cofounder and president of a small orchestra. As such he felt obliged to strengthen the wood-wind section by learning to play the clarinet; also to take on the task of transposing and arranging music for the group — one Sunday afternoon was swallowed up in making a score of "Onward Christian Soldiers"! When engagements to play began to come in, the repertoire had to be expanded, and many evenings were spent "rehearsing our new music — 'Nearer My God to Thee' and all the polkas."

When the family settled in Ann Arbor, father was withdrawing from the Loud firm and embarking on plans for the purchase and sale of timberlands along or across the lower Mississippi. It was hoped that the new enterprise would take him away only infrequently, and that full family life would now be possible. This hope was shattered when he returned, stricken with typhoid fever, from a trip to Louisiana and died in February 1884. He left no will. His property, divided among the four survivors, yielded each of them an income sufficient to defray quietly comfortable living and normal educational expenses, including an occasional journey to Europe — or even a prolonged frugal sojourn there.

Father's death imposed on mother a heavier obligation to see that her son's time was well spent, his health conserved, and his behavior decorous. On these counts she frowned on his participation in evening entertainments. Thus, while the class of which he was president was holding its first party, he sat at home finishing *Vanity Fair* and "getting thinner than ever." She continued to prescribe daily sessions of reading aloud. In 1884 he read to her much of Motley, Schiller (in translation), Dickens, and Thackeray, with Artemus Ward and the *Biglow Papers* as light relief. When she was recovering from an illness, he spent mornings and evenings reading to her — of all things — Benvenuto Cellini's *Autobiography*.

The books read aloud formed only a small fraction of Gay's total reading. During the summer of 1884, for instance, he had a long quiet run of Harriet Beecher Stowe, Bulwer Lytton, Dickens, Fenimore Cooper, with pauses for Barnum's *Forty Years as a Showman* and Plato's *Apology*. There was probably too much living in the world of books. That world was the refuge of a recluse — even his closest friends applied the word "recluse" to him — and the books in turn made him more of one. In his introspective moods — and they were many — he was well aware of the fact. He knew that he had been nurtured from earliest childhood by books rather than by boys, by the characters and events of stories rather than by those of the schoolyard, by reading with his back to the window instead of looking out or going out. He fought, with some success, during high school and college years to escape from "the benumbing of his social nature" and the corresponding "intensification of the ego side." Then the conditions of graduate study abroad plunged him for a time back into solitude and confronted him with an array of books that seemed endless.

The diaries reveal Gay's intense adolescent preoccupation with religion, whether as a goad to self-searching, a road to salvation, or an opportunity to share in the community of public worship. His Unitarian father and Methodist mother had so impressed on him the need for constant striving against man's innate propensity to go astray that his conscience was easily pricked when he surveyed his conduct. The loss of his father stirred him to ponder about life and death, about his obligations and shortcomings. He determined to get a Bible and study it carefully. The edition his Boston uncle procured for him was "just perfect," but as it cost $13 he recognized that he would "have to save money to pay for it." His reading of it soon became fitful, especially when clarinet practice made heavy claims on his spare time. In the spring of 1885 his diary rang the changes on "Read and practised," "Read but did not practice," "Practised but did not read," and "No reading, no practice." How critical or profitable the reading was we have no hint, save one succinct remark: "I can't read parts of Genesis reverently."

Church-going was a much more satisfying duty. As a lad he had enjoyed the exaltation of a hearty service and found the Episcopalian liturgy "rather dull." Sunday was what he described as "my strengthening time of the week. I always make good resolutions, only to be broken." It was also a busy day, with three or four, even at times five, services or school sessions to be attended, and was especially satisfying if he got a chance to speak at one of them. For a time he was not sure that he wished to be formally admitted to church membership, partly because, sobersides though he was, he could not understand why the Church (and his mother) objected to dancing and card games or regarded clarinet playing and music scoring on the Sabbath as sacrilegious. His Sunday School teacher and his pastor gave him sufficient understanding to let him take the step.

Revival meetings were irresistible attractions. When a noted hot gospeler visited Ypsilanti, nine miles from Ann Arbor, three of Gay's classmates rode there in a hired buggy, but he and a friend made the journey by running behind, holding on to the back of the vehicle. When Moody (of Moody and Sankey fame) came to Detroit, Gay and his friend spent the whole day following him around, taking notes on his discourses, stifling their surprise that "he was so fleshy and looked as if he had had plenty of good dinners," but conceding that "you forget him in what he said."

In June 1886, Gay graduated from high school. To celebrate the event he went for nine weeks to western Europe in the company of Dr. Herdman, his physician. In a fast-moving tour through the continental capitals and a more leisurely sojourn in England, he went with Herdman to medical meetings, famous hospitals and laboratories. The experience made him feel, though only vaguely, that medicine might be an attractive career.

In the fall he enrolled in the University of Michigan. There was no thrill of novelty about the step. He had played on the campus, used the Library, ushered at concerts, and as a close friend of "Jim" (James Rowland) Angell, son of the president, he knew the president's house from basement through kitchen and living room to attic. Even the junior college curriculum has a familiar look — Greek, Latin, French, German, Mathematics, and English. The only new studies during his first two years were philosophy and English history. But philosophy was in the hands of John Dewey, who had come to Michigan in 1884 and was already known as exponent of unorthodox concepts. Gay took all the courses he offered — logic, ethics, and empirical psychology — and was a member of the Philosophical Society which met regularly at Dewey's home. He dropped the subject when in 1888 Dewey left Michigan for a year, but resolved to take it up again in Germany and carry it far.

A brilliant teacher of English literature, Charles Mills Gayley, dissipated Gay's dislike of the formal study of books and incited him to "intellectual original work. Working with Gayley was something like the fever of a gold camp in '49," whether the digging was in the works of Walter Scott or of such relatively new writers as Walt Whitman, Dante Gabriel Rossetti, and Matthew Arnold. When the master left in 1889 to take a post in California he urged Gay to choose English literature as his lifework. Gayley's successor, equally impressed, suggested that he take graduate work and serve as "tute" (tutor) in the English department.

In 1888 Gay reached midstream in college; he was almost twenty-one, yet still had found no vocation. That summer he went with four classmates to Europe, settled in Göttingen, and worked hard with a private tutor improving his German. Before sailing he promised his mother he would try to reach a decision concerning at least next year's work. The choice had been narrowed down: it lay between continuing his study of history, literature, and philosophy as preparation for a teaching career, and switching off to science courses that were prerequisite training for medicine. After five weeks' meditation he reported:

> I have as yet come to no conclusion . . . I think about it constantly but everything is dim before me. I want to do some good in the world before I die and to that end I wish to take up that work most fitted me. I want to step into the sphere I was made for — or am I to make it myself? I don't know absolutely which way to turn . . . I don't seem especially fitted by nature for anything, yet I don't like to drift along.
>
> My work from now on in college must bend to some end; and it seems to me as I think it over that, after all, the professor's chair is too easy; that I have wanted to fill it because it didn't mean so much work, and that is rather a sordid point of view. I ought to be at work at something which is to make me work among and with men, and of all the professions the doctor's and the minister's seem to me the noblest. I couldn't take up the ministry; I am not a speaker, and I couldn't bear to preach things which I couldn't practise or in which I couldn't thoroughly believe. I believe there is a *call* to the ministry, and that I haven't received. In some ways I feel that I haven't the tact to be a practising physician, yet a substitute for that might be cultivated. I have been rather waiting all along to have it "come over me," but it doesn't come . . .

It seems to me my choice at present would be between medicine and the study of political philosophy — that is a wider kind of political economy . . . I only hope I will be able to settle it before I return.

He returned resolved to give the premedical sciences a trial run. Physics proved an "ill-fated" choice and he scraped through with a bare pass. He found biology very attractive, spent much time in the laboratory, and became highly excited when he believed he was on the verge of making a revolutionary discovery. Further study revealed he was far from being a pioneer, and at the end of the year the subject was abandoned.

Medicine was thus ruled out as a career. Law was evidently given no thought at all; nor was journalism or politics. Business was explicitly rejected, especially the kind practiced by his father and grandfather. In 1889 he wrote, "I'm afraid I haven't much sympathy with the business push and enterprise which has opened up the lumber supply of the world. My father was one of those Philistines" — the word came from a recent heavy dose of Matthew Arnold — "but I have often heard him say that he didn't want to see me a lumber man."

Whenever grandfather Loud visited Ann Arbor, Gay and he discussed economic problems. The young man extolled "the advantages of Cooperation in its educating influence on working men, arising from the sense of responsibility and self-interest, and compared this with the evils of division of labor." The old man immediately "was all up in arms" and the two "talked at cross-purposes." One said that division of labor and machinery led to higher productivity and better wages. The other retorted that they turned men into machines, or rebels, and that, "all our material nineteenth century advancements to the contrary," it would be better for men "to return to the spirit of such workers as old Nuremberg sent forth, artist workmen with honest pride in their work, whether they tanned hides or carved statues." Through such romantic spectacles, Gay viewed with dislike any kind of business career.

So, by a combination of forces in which exclusion was at least as powerful as interest, he decided at the end of his junior year (mid-1889) to become a teacher of history. He had been reading the subject since boyhood, though without set purpose or syllabus. He had taken only two college courses, in English history and in American constitutional history; but the quality of his work was so good that Richard Hudson, the head of the department, hinted that if he went to Germany for graduate study there would be a junior position awaiting him on his return. With that hint the long search for a vocation ended.

By this time Gay was only one semester from graduation. He crowded it with courses in history, international law, and political economy, and meanwhile made his plans. These were shaped by Hudson's desire to reorganize the Michigan curriculum. He wanted to widen the introductory survey from English to European and to introduce special period courses in Roman, medieval, and early English history. To help in effecting this reform Gay was to make himself master of medieval history, learn enough Roman history to know what preceded the Middle Ages, and pick up sufficient modern history to be aware of what came afterward. Gay agreed that this program was attractive, especially if supplemented with some philosophy and political economy. Like Hudson, he took it for granted that the work could be done in three or four semesters, and that Germany was the best possible place — in fact, the only place — in which to do it.

Gay's college years were even fuller of extracurricular activities than the high school days had been. His physique had improved so greatly that he was able to play a minor part on his fraternity's baseball, tennis, boxing, and running teams. From a political battle between Greeks and Barbarians he emerged elected to one of the leading positions on the student weekly paper. He was chairman of this committee, treasurer of that, and in frequent demand for speechmaking. His speeches suffered at first from the fact that his delivery was, in the words of his uncle, "deficient, rapid, and rather indistinct."

The uncle prescribed a cure: "Pick out words of many syllables. Talk them aloud as you are walking or at leisure, no matter if you are taken for a crank or crazy for doing so. I reckon in a college town they have become pretty well accustomed to cranks and such." Whether Gay tried this remedy is not known; but he did spend part of one long vacation at a Summer School of Oratory, invested fifty cents in *Three Thousand Words Mispronounced*, wrestled with such tongue-twisters as "Some shun sunshine. Do you shun sunshine?" and took singing lessons.

College days brought religious questionings. "Our theology fills me with doubts," he wrote in early 1890, "for I cannot take it all on trust." In vain he sought aid from the experts. "I remember," he recalled in 1899,

> that the lectures I used to hear in Ann Arbor by leading Methodist divines alienated and disgusted me. Men who knew nothing about biology and who had no comprehension of the spirit of modern science, getting up and making cheap witticisms and shallow sneering remarks at its expense, were unconsciously injuring the cause they had at heart.

But he had scarcely got beyond the revolt against what he thought was Christianity when he left for Germany. The rest of the long bitter battle — to discover what he thought Christianity really was — had to be fought out in lonely bachelor quarters in Leipzig or Berlin.

In June 1889, Gay began the first letter in what he hoped would be his "longest correspondence." Louise Fitz Randolph had given him permission to write to her during the long vacation and promised to reply. The two had been classmates throughout high school and college, often as rivals for top place in the examination lists; she had played a decisive part in getting him to forswear whist and waltzes in order to attain church membership; and they had shared some campus responsibilities. As she spent the summer vacation of 1889 at home in Toledo, then went to Boston to keep house for her brother, a graduate student in social work, Gay had to conduct his courtship by mail.

The stream of letters flowed in high flood until marriage in August 1892 stopped it, but was resumed whenever the two were temporarily separated, a frequent condition after their return to America. Hence the correspondence is spread, thickly in some places but with long breaks in others, over fifty-five years. Gay's contributions to it have survived almost intact. As he was a superb letter-writer — at times almost an essayist — they provide a vivid eloquent record of his intellectual, spiritual, and emotional pilgrimage; of his many alternating doubts and certainties, his worries about the character of the world, the part he would like to play in it, and his unfitness for that part; of the plain stubborn matter-of-factness which pulled him out of each slough of self-criticism with some new target for achievement; and, in the early years, of his plans for a married life devoted to scholarly work and public service.

In March 1890, these plans advanced two steps. Gay left Ann Arbor to catch a French liner in New York. He made his way to the boat through Boston, went to State Street to greet his stationer uncle, then hastened to the house where Louise and her brother were lodging. When, two weeks later, he sailed for Europe, he carried her promise to marry him.

The outstanding feature of Gay's years of study abroad is their number. He went to Europe expecting to return within two years, but stayed twelve and a half. Instead of getting his Ph.D. after working for three or four semesters on medieval history, he spent nine in universities — three in Leipzig, five in Berlin, and one in Zurich; then for seven years he studied privately; and finally, after being registered for three more semesters in Berlin but attending no classes, he wrote a dissertation on a theme in economic history, took his examinations, and was granted his degree in the summer of 1902.

This prolonging of the years of preparation was possible because Gay could afford it — as a bachelor by living on the income from his inheritance, after marriage by drawing on his capital. It was caused by a series of decisions and developments, each of which postponed the day for reaching journey's end or altered the destination, and subordinated the acquiring of a degree to the quest of a comprehensive and thorough education.

The first delaying decision came when he realized how immense was the task of equipping himself adequately for the vocation he had chosen. There were many times during the early graduate years when he doubted whether he had picked the most useful calling, wondered whether a life of action would not be more full of service than one of teaching, and asked, "What really is the truest life — to study history or to make history?" The debate always ended with the same conclusion: teaching was the worthiest vocation; he believed he could develop into a good teacher; and history was the subject most worthy of teaching. "The man who had mastered the inward truth of history, whose energies were bent on mastering this truth, would be an inspirer of young men, the bearer of a beacon light to all the world."

When he entered the University of Leipzig in April 1890, he soon realized that "mastering this truth" was going to call for a great outlay of "energies." He felt the invigorating effect of the "atmosphere of philosophical and scholarly enthusiasm which we find here" and was impressed by the provisions for advanced study. But as he got to grips with his work he was dismayed by the revealed inadequacies of his former training, the scrappy superficial smatterings which had frittered away the past years and left him with "such hazy ideals, such unsettled thought, such insufficient special preparation" for the day when he was to be cast on his own resources. As usual he underrated himself, and as usual he reacted by fixing a very high target at which to shoot. Determined "to let no yesterday interfere with today," he charted a course of study that would shift his knowledge of history from a "very treacherous bottom" to a solid deep foundation and allow him to build thereon a broad edifice of general history, surmounted by detailed studies of whatever subject fired his special interest.

At first this chart called for nearly twenty hours weekly in classroom and seminar, with twice as many of private reading. Most of the time was devoted to medieval history; philosophy and political economy got only a lick and a promise of more attention later on. But as he worked on what he called "the ploughing, harrowing, and seed time of our modern world" he became increasingly conscious of "that former period which produced the seed the Middle Ages sowed — the ancient world." "Our modern history," he discovered, "is founded on the union of the three forces flowing from Judaism, Greek rationalism, and Roman order and force."

This discovery was disturbing to one who always had to fight a "tendency to keep continually going back to beginnings." His knowledge of these three forces was "very misty"; he had no time to spare for taking courses that would dispel the mist, yet he could neither understand the Middle Ages properly nor come forward to explore the modern world so long as he was in this fog. Changing the metaphor, he felt there was no use in "carving away on little pieces of the gable ends of history" until he had laid good foundations. He must therefore divert some time from medieval study to reading ancient history.

The price to be paid would be heavy. To his fiancée he wrote:

> You see what this means: the putting off of my thesis; the deliberate preparation; perhaps a longer stay in Germany than I anticipated a year ago. I don't care what the results are, so that they be genuine and I be fitted at the end to do and be something truly helpful in the world. My thesis can wait, my degree can wait, and a position can wait. What cannot wait is that I open my eyes to where I stand and proceed without delay to begin at the beginning and try to remedy a whole life time's smattering education.

So he plunged into reading ancient history, starting with Renan's *L'Histoire du peuple d'Israel* and taking lessons in Hebrew. It soon became apparent, however, that the overtime work was interfering seriously with more important medieval assignments. The Hebrew had to be dropped, then the attack on the ancient world subsided. The objective was not one to be attained overnight even by burning midnight oil. Like another grand plan of those months — the formulation of a philosophy of history — it was something he would "be nearer ten years from now." But the temporary diversion had caused the first postponement of his return to America.

The urge to traverse the whole stream of history was mated to a desire to explore it from bank to bank and to know something of the land that lay beyond the water's edge. "Any man who would take a true man's place in the search for solutions to the social problems our country must face must be prepared with the widest study of the past history of man." This "widest study" must embrace all facets as well as all periods. Yet Gay knew that he must choose some facet or period for special study, for creative work, and for his examination.

His first choice was not economic history. He was aware that "there is a great new field just opening up in this line of work — the Economic History." He believed that "we cannot understand the life of any time without studying its social and economic basis." But he did not place the "great new field" first in importance or regard the social and economic basis as the only factor giving character to the superstructure or determining the behavior of its inhabitants. In late 1891 he read a pamphlet, picked up at the Social Democratic Party's bookstore, describing Marx's economic interpretation of history, and was quick to challenge its thesis:

> There is no doubt that Karl Marx has done great service in calling attention to the fundamental importance of the economic and social basis of national and social life; but it is one-sided to say that ideas have no influence over men. The two, the material and the spiritual life, are as closely interlinked in our social organism as in our individual life . . . and neither factor can be ignored in trying to understand the inner meaning of any historical or individual development. Underneath all the surface history of humanity lies the great mystery of life, its significance and end, as yet only dimly known to us — and here in this mysterious source all truth-seekers are sinking their little plummets.

Gay had already, in early 1891, determined where to sink his little plummet. He had concluded that his mind was most interested in "questions pertaining to the moral development of mankind," in "ethical problems"; and that it was the historical side of such questions — "the development of religious and political ideas, their expression in institutions and history" — which attracted most his "study impulse." He therefore decided to concentrate on the constitutional history of the Middle Ages, give special attention to the story of the Papacy, and write his thesis on the position of the papal legates in England from their first arrival there before A.D. 1000 to their departure with the Reformation. He had also decided to spend three semesters on basic preparation and leave the thesis to be written during a further year's work in Germany, with a trip home in the summer of 1891 to brace him for the extension of his exile.

He had this trip and returned, but not to Leipzig. A faculty feud in the history department there had made conditions uncomfortable, and his adviser urged him to "Go somewhere, anywhere else!" For a moment he toyed with the idea of Oxford, since his research was to be on an English topic; but inquiry revealed that Oxford's facilities for postgraduate work were not the kind he felt he needed. Berlin had them all, so in the fall of 1891 he went there.

That was his second delaying decision, for Berlin proved to be not a researcher's base, but a bigger collection of famous teachers and tempting courses. Gay sampled the lectures of the great church historian, Adolf von Harnack, stayed in the class for three semesters, attended Harnack's seminar, and plowed through his three-volume *History of Dogma*. He entered the medieval course and the seminar of Paul Scheffer-Boichorst, and got stuck in each for three semesters. He thus loaded himself with so much formal work and prescribed private reading that when his first Berlin year ended he had scarcely touched the secondary works bearing on his thesis and had not looked at any of the primary sources. The time did not yet seem ripe for starting research.

Nor did it seem ripe for accepting two calls back to Michigan or one to Northwestern University. He declined all three because they expected more from him than he felt competent to deliver. He could as yet offer "no show of courses nor knick-knacky work." He would know he was committing "the sin of hollowness by seeming to be much more" than he really was, and others would soon know it too. He believed that a teacher should be thoroughly versed in his subject before he accepted an appointment, so that in teaching it his attention could be concentrated on the way he presented his knowledge in the light of the class's needs; also that he should be "far enough advanced to be doing independent work which will keep him fresh and vigorous and furnish material for genuine seminary work with his advanced students. I do not consider myself competent to do that yet." Hence the day of his final return to America must remain undetermined. It would not come until he was satisfied he had attained "thoroughness," "ripeness." It would probably be "some few years ahead," since "life is too short to hurry any more." In that case his former teachers would have ceased to use their personal influence to find a post for him. His recommendations would consist only of his thesis and his German degree. But he had no doubt that he would find a job when he was ready for one. "Those who are fitted to teach and those who want to be taught shall not, I think, find over-great difficulty in coming to each other."

The prospect of more years of study was suddenly made bearable, even attractive, when in early 1892 Louise accepted his suggestion that they be married in the summer and embark on an ambitious plan of study together. Gay had often said it was good for him to have come where he could be alone, where there was leisure to examine his relation to life, to "find" himself, "to think about essential things." He certainly got abundant chance to do all this — and did it. True, he joined the American Church in Leipzig, took part in some of its meetings, and after inordinate labor in preparation gave a talk on the origin and character of the Four Gospels. He jumped at such opportunities to speak, for, as he confessed, "You have no idea how shut up one gets to feel, how distrustful of one's own powers of doing anything unless there is some chance to break out of the cocoon which isolation and books build round one." Yet he made no friendships in Leipzig, but did strike up several acquaintanceships. In Berlin he did not even do that. When he invited Louise to join him he warned her that their life would be "very retired. As you have seen, I have made no friends here and very few acquaintances. It [will] be a life of companionship amid books and quiet study."

The invitation was well-timed, for Louise was graduating at Michigan in early 1892. As a good feminist, she was resolved to have a career of her own, but there was an implicit understanding that it would parallel or complement the work Gay was preparing to do. Her choice of subjects in her senior year had been influenced by the pact to study history, political economy, and social questions together. They read the same book at the same time — a work book such as Rousseau or Bryce's *Holy Roman Empire*, or some "between minute" book, such as Lessing's *Laokoon*, which Gay always had on hand "to be read at those odd moments that come through the day before lectures or while waiting for dinner."

As her graduation drew near and an M.A. program had to be planned, Gay inundated her with suggestions of subjects that would be of value later on in their joint labors. Then he sprung the proposal that they be married the next summer. If they were to be fellow-students and truth-seekers in life, why not begin at once, and what better place than Berlin? He admitted that there was one academic drawback. "I don't think that women are allowed in the lectures at the University. But lectures and seminary work I should think you could follow — not so enjoyably, but still with some profit — through my notes and me."

When his proposal was accepted he followed it up with another. His thesis subject covered too many centuries to be handled by one person. If therefore he investigated the story of the papal legates in England from its beginning with Edward the Confessor to the anti-papal outbursts of Wicliffe's day in the fourteenth century, would Louise be interested in taking up the tale at that point and carrying it on to the end in the reign of Henry VIII? In other words, was she willing to become a late medieval historian? To win her assent he sang the praises of the subject: the work would be in a nearly empty field; it would provide excellent training in critical methods, give insight into the great movements and institutions of the period, throw light on the relations between church and state, lead into the realm of international law, and suggest enough topics for subsequent monographs to keep two workers busy for a lifetime.

This persuasive prospectus achieved its purpose. Louise accepted the assignment. Gay went home in August and returned with his wife in October, all set to prepare for the great research — and consequently, for the third time, to prolong the sojourn in Europe. His part of the preparation called for one more semester's work with Scheffer-Boichorst and Harnack. What Louise did, apart from daily lessons at the Berlitz School to improve her German, depended in part on the University's attitude. Scheffer-Boichorst said she could attend his lectures and seminar, subject to the Rector's consent. When Gay sought it the Rector replied that while he could not grant it he would know nothing and see nothing until officially informed of the lady's presence in a classroom. Louise therefore accompanied Gay to the first lecture and seminar and was very cordially welcomed. At the end of the second lecture, however, the professor informed them that conference with his colleagues had revealed "such a prevailing sentiment against the entrance of women that he felt it necessary to refuse further admission."

This news, though not unexpected, was a damaging blow to the grand plan. The only alternative was for Louise to study privately, aided and guided by her husband. In view of his own shortcomings when he arrived in Germany thirty months before, it was too much to expect that she could by reading remedy similar deficiencies, catch up with him, then go along at his pace. Yet she set out to make the attempt. A program was quickly drafted, including three hours' reading together every morning in the Royal Library, from which she was not debarred; work together at home during the afternoon; then the German lesson; and more reading together after supper — in all, a daily average of about ten hours' hard labor.

While Louise struggled for a year and a half with this grueling schedule, Gay finished his medieval courses and turned, at long last, in the spring of 1893 to the serious study of political economy. He took two courses with that great veteran "socialist of the chair," Adolf Wagner, and two with Gustav Schmoller. Wagner was a tonic, served well stirred and bubbling. It was heart-warming to hear his insistence that Christian ethics must govern economic behavior, that untrammeled individualism was often unethical, that the state must actively and positively protect those who were economically weak or ill-rewarded, and that political economists must use their influence to further wise state intervention — whether by regulation or by operating public enterprises — if the existing economic and social order was to survive. To that creed Gay was increasingly attracted and found himself losing the "kind of fear of the encroaching action of the state" which he had carried with him from America.

It was Schmoller, however, who really fired Gay's attentive interest and enthusiasm. In the first place because he believed that economics could be brought into close interrelation with psychology, ethics, history, and political science to produce a real science of society; that its field was the relations, not merely between man and material goods, but also between men; that the economic order must be regarded as only one integral part of the entire social life and as such was to be evaluated from an ethical point of view.

In the second place, Schmoller was the last notable representative of the German historical economists. The attack begun in the 1840's on the deductive methods and conclusions of the classical economists had long since won the invaders a firm foothold in German universities. After two generations the battle still continued, but had become a stalemate and a little unreal, partly because the classicals had given place to neo-classicals who had improved greatly the tools and methods of deductive analysis. Wagner, for example, was patiently trying in Berlin "to improve upon the classical writers, amending their premises, reconsidering their results in the light of further experience, but retaining their method." Schmoller, however, was still in the thick of the fight; he "threw both methods and doctrines overboard, and devoted himself to the searching out of the development of economic phenomena, [to] making Economics an inductive science,"[2] realistic, factual, and historical.

In this search for facts, past or present, that might provide a sound new basis for economic theory Schmoller and his students were expending great energy when Gay joined them. The newcomer soon felt that here was the intellectual home he had been seeking. Here were the things he believed in: the devotion to history as the key that might unlock many doors; the attempt to see "the interaction of all manifestations of the human spirit, economic, legal, political, social, and intellectual"; the rigorous criticism of evidence; and the hope that from it all would emerge a science of economics which would serve as a sure guide for policies of social betterment.

After attending Schmoller's classes for a semester Gay joined his seminar. There at closer quarters he saw the scholar at work — calm, judicial, slow of speech, methodically proceeding step by step, convincing by the completeness of his treatment, yet tolerant and humble. As Gay recalled him years later, no one could realize more than he the enormous difficulty of the task historical economists had set themselves.

> He was oppressed by the mystery of the creative human spirit that moved behind the interlacing tangle of economic and social changes. Frequently at meetings of his seminar, after he had made one of his exciting suggestive commentaries on some student's paper, he would end, with an interweaving motion of his hands, by saying, *Aber, meine Herren, es ist alles so unendlich compliziert* (But, gentlemen, it is all so infinitely complicated).

[2] M. Epstein, obituary notice on Schmoller in *Economic Journal*, 27: 436 (September 1917).

If a paper seemed to have touched rock-bottom truth in a statistical tabulation he would ask "What does all that mean?" — a query that included the source, sufficiency, and manipulation of the figures as well as their interpretation and relation to other cognate facts and theories. And to those who were seeking salvation for economics by resort to mathematical treatment, with its equations, formulae, and graphs, he would insist that "man's impulses and social reactions normally produce too many variables of conduct for any calculus."

Gay had plenty of time to spare for Schmoller's seminar. By now (October 1893), he had said good-by to the medievalists, limited his historical courses to one on the Reformation, and was doing no research on his thesis. He was not yet thinking of abandoning the medieval or ecclesiastical field for the economic, but only of bringing one more interest within his range of vision. His book-buying had hitherto included scarcely any works on economic history; in fact there were fewer books on that subject on his shelves in 1893 than there were editions of the Bible. When, however, Schmoller invited him to prepare a seminar paper on the history of wages in England from medieval to modern times, he began to order from London such standard reference works as Macpherson's *Annals of Commerce* and Porter's *Progress of the Nation*. He dug into Arthur Young, Eden, Tooke, and similar well-known sources.

From studying the history of wages to exploring the facts and problems of poverty was an easy step. He had long been interested in the social work of General Booth's Salvation Army, which he regarded as almost the sole effort being made by organized Christianity to care for the poor and needy. His eye was now caught by the work of another Booth — Charles — whose *Labour and Life of the People* (1889–1893) had turned a glaring searchlight on the poverty-stricken conditions of a third of London's population. Thus the seminar theme ramified widely over time and space, and two reminders were jotted down in his notebook: "Write to Charles Booth on question of wages," and "Study concept of poverty in New Testament and Old Testament."

In such work, making his first nibble at a piece of research, he spent his last semester, for the time being, in Berlin. Then in the spring of 1894 we find him and his wife registered at the University of Zurich for six courses apiece of lectures and seminars, and in five of them sitting side by side. The reason for the migration is not clear, but it seems that the weather of Berlin had been as uncongenial to Louise as had its academic climate. In Zurich the former was more bracing, the latter "perfectly liberal toward women." There was, however, a secret fear that for Gay the work at Zurich would be a "let-down," robbing him of opportunities for advancing his preparation. Though he insisted that such was not the case, and that "this simple seminary in this simple place" promised more to him than those he had attended elsewhere, it is noteworthy that one course was voted "elementary" and that there was no registration for a second semester.

The sojourn in Zurich was disturbed momentarily by an American caller, bearing the offer of a post at Wesleyan University, Middletown, Connecticut. Gay's reply was the same as that made to the three earlier invitations: he was not yet ready. Failing to shake this decision, the visitor warned him that by the time he felt ready to accept anything all the colleges and universities would be fully staffed. Had the invitation been to Chicago the reply might have been different, as Gay was greatly impressed by the reputation which that new university was winning. But no call came from there, or indeed from anywhere else during the next seven years.

In leaving the Zurich classrooms Gay ended four and a half years of formal study. The next phase was to be informal and private, but thoroughly planned, with a long list of books to be read alone or aloud, and a syllabus to give shape, integration, and purpose to the program. Philosophy was to be studied by reading such classics as Plato, Aristotle, St. Augustine, Hobbes, Locke, Hume, Kant, and Schopenhauer, each in its original language. The history assignment included Gibbon, Mommsen, Ranke, Lecky, and similar giants. The ancient world was now to get serious exploration; the work done already on medieval and modern history was to be brought into focus and synthesis; and economic history had crept up to a place calling for "special" attention.

Having settled in Villeneuve on the eastern tip of Lake Geneva in the fall of 1894, the Gays embarked on this ambitious fast-paced journey through great books, only to be slowed down and almost derailed by a serious deterioration in Louise's health during the winter. A Zurich specialist, after hearing the symptoms — headaches and insomnia — burst out, "That's the *misère* of nervous women studying *philosophie*. They need to rest their brains and instead they insist on using them till they give out." His first advice was that both of them abandon their whole "mode of living," their "plan for intellectual life occupation," and get into "some healthful out-of-door work, such as market-gardening, where [they] could be doing something useful and not be overburdening the brain." Pressed for a less drastic prescription, he admitted that the study need be abandoned only temporarily and could be resumed cautiously when Louise's health was restored. But he insisted that even then the pace must be reduced and that some form of manual exercise or hobby be pursued.

This command was obeyed in part. Throughout the spring and summer of 1895 far less time was devoted to books, a great deal to tennis, to photography, and to cycling in the new "rational garb" on the new "safety" vehicles. When, however, these diversions failed to effect a cure, a Frankfurt nose specialist was consulted. He said the trouble was nasal rather than nervous, and subjected the patient to three months of painful operations and other treatment. By the end of that time she was so exhausted and weak that he prescribed a winter of Italian sunshine as the best restorative.

The Italian tour, begun before Christmas, 1895, lasted till June 1896. At every point along the way, from Milan and Venice, through a long sojourn in Rome, to Naples and Pompeii, the galleries, museums, and buildings were inspected with leisurely thoroughness; the bicycles were put to great use, especially when Louise's health improved considerably; and a small fortune was spent on photographic supplies. There was plenty of reading, for Gay did not intend to miss this chance of learning all he could about Italy's language, literature, art, and long span of history. But virtually all the books were in Italian; the fat German volumes on philosophy and history which had been brought along for study in daily installments remained unopened after the second day of the tour.

The months in Italy formed a great divide in the lives of Gay and his wife. From Capri or Castellamare the problems of medieval constitutional history did not look quite so important as they had in Leipzig or Berlin. The papal legates lost their stature as men worthy of investigation; the double-harness research project was abandoned, and Louise was released from the obligation to spend the best years of her life writing part of their story. It was one that she never should have been asked to shoulder. As Gay's dream of making her in his own image faded away, she gained freedom to be an amateur rather than a professional scholar, to cultivate her interest in art, letters, religion, and feminism. There was still plenty left for her to contribute as a deeply interested and well-informed auditor, a serious critic, a zealot for exactitude in thought and language, yet ever-ready to cry "Well done!" when her husband doubted whether his work was accomplishing anything of value.

The Italian leisure gave Gay an opportunity to reconsider and rechart the course he had mapped for himself five years earlier. The new route led to England. On August 21, 1896, he entered in his diary, "To Reading Room of British Museum. Lunch 5*d*." Now nearly twenty-nine, he had been in Europe more than six years.

The English sojourn lasted until May 1901. There were to have been summer vacations on the Continent, but the birth of the first child in 1898 helped to anchor the family in London. Life *en pension* gave place to a regimen of full domesticity in a furnished apartment. There Louise tried, with some success, to supplement the recipes of *Mrs. Beeton's Cookery Book* with such ingredients of American diet as canned corn, baked beans, chicken every Sunday, Hamburg steak weekly, ice cream in winter, turkey twice a year, even a pumpkin pie at Thanksgiving. She gave her husband lists of groceries to be bought on his way home from the Museum; he shared her grief over the insolubility of the domestic servant problem; and when his sisters wrote to ask what he would like for a Christmas present, one of his two suggestions for "a most acceptable gift supplying a long-felt need" was "a thoroughly competent, honest, energetic, clean, cheerful all-round general servant — an AMERICAN." Relatives from both sides of the family were frequent visitors, and Gay was willingly drafted to take them to see plays, inspect galleries, hear noted preachers or politicians, tour Britain, or scurry on a round trip of the western Continent.

Gay settled in London because he had decided to make economic history, and especially the English story, his field of special study. That this decision had been reached only recently is evident from a letter written in 1897 to his Michigan classmate, Henry M. Bates. The correspondence between the two men had been neglected for some time, and when Bates broke the silence he inquired if church history was still the center of interest. Gay copied the first draft of his reply into his memorandum book. It ran:

> I did not crawl back, for the present at any rate, into the ecclesiastical cocoon, but into the economic one, when I became a bookworm again after sipping the sweets of travel. Both of these, of course, furnish material for the web of life; but (if it is not spinning the figure too fine) I came to see that the economic life and institutions form the strong supporting warp, while the ideas and movements of an age — philosophical, religious, political, literary — make the variegated woof, with patterns more attractive perhaps — and more distracting.
>
> The Church is a highly interesting organism (better, institution), adapting itself to varied social conditions for propagation of some (or certain) valuable forms of popular metaphysics called religion, bound up with ethical ideas or incorporating certain ethical ideas. But my chief interest is in those conditions to which, while helping to form, the Church in the main conforms. Life is short, and whichever cocoon I choose I

must be in it a large part of that short life; then, perhaps untimely wise, be dropped, cocoon and all, in the fatal hot water which ends things for the cocoon — or begins them for the silk-weaver.

One practical consideration apparently helped to change Gay's "chief interest" from the ecclesiastical to the economic. In an undated note he remarks that it seems wise to abandon church history as his "specialty," since there is no likelihood of finding a place where he will be able to teach the subject "free from dogmatic persecution; better to cultivate it privately as integral part of social history and use it wherever possible."

So the papal legates were abandoned and the years spent with Harnack were written off as part of a historian's general education. Now the task was to study production and distribution, "especially from historical side," and to give special attention to one of the "important things for the time being relatively neglected." Though the number of laborers in English economic history was growing, Gay's list of relatively neglected topics was a long one. It included the growth of the great industries (including agriculture), the history of wages, the "urge to income-building," the development of social classes, the nature and development of the "undertaker" — whom today we call the entrepreneur — and the answer to such questions as "Who has most contributed to England's commercial and industrial prosperity — the landlord, the undertaker, or the workman?"

From this array of subjects he chose the history of English agriculture, with special reference to agricultural labor, as a prelude to research on the inclosure of land during the Tudor period "and thence onward as far as have time." It was a timely choice, because twenty years of acute agricultural depression had forced the British to ask what was wrong on the countryside. One popular diagnosis found the root of the trouble in the land system, with its trinity in disunity of great landlords, of large tenant farmers, and of ill-paid hired laborers who seemed to be either sinking deeper into poverty or seeking other occupations. The laborer, so ran the argument, was apathetic or restless because he had no plot of land on which he could work in his spare time and no hope of acquiring a small holding that would transform him into a peasant farmer. He was landless because landlords had deprived his ancestors of the few acres they cultivated and of the commons on which they grazed their few livestock; had thrown these holdings together into fields inclosed by hedges or fences; and had merged the fields into relatively large farms which were leased to tenants who operated them with hired help. Hence the historically just solution of the rural problem was to restore the laborer's access to land.

The controversy posed a challenge to the historian to find out what had actually happened. Here was a superb exercise in critical scholarship, in testing the credibility of contemporary descriptions of events, in unearthing sources of information that would yield quantitative evidence, and in bringing to bear "a fresh keen insight for actual facts and conditions, not befogged by preconceived theories" or by the sentimentality which broods over discussions of the rural way of life. If one took the literary sources — pamphlets, poems, sermons, More's *Utopia*, and the preambles to anti-inclosure statutes — at their face value, one got the impression that Tudor England was swept by an agrarian revolution, as landlords, like "covetous and insatiable cormorants," drove their tenants off arable fields and commons, and converted their estates into inclosed pastures occupied by sheep, a shepherd, and his dog. Plows were put out of use, villages were depopulated, the evicted peasants had no recourse save to beggary or roguery, and the common weal became the common woe.

How much truth was there in this lurid picture of rustic tragedy? Was the revolution a sudden flare-up of the sixteenth century, then of the eighteenth, or was inclosure a continuous process, only more active at some times than others? How many acres were fenced in and converted from arable to pasture, what percentage of the total area of county or country? Finally, was inclosure a necessary improvement, in which some suffered but the many gained as a result of the better use of land and of an increase in the volume of production?

As a first step toward answering his questions Gay settled down to study all the available original printed sources bearing on agricultural history from the Middle Ages to the nineteenth century. From late 1896 to March 1899 he plowed through the British Museum's collection of books, pamphlets, parliamentary debates, reports of royal commissions or select committees, and statutes of the realm. He haunted second-hand bookshops picking up one old treasure after another, so that parts of the living quarters, littered with books and papers in disorderly confusion, moved his wife to coin the word "bookstye." Poetry and fiction were gathered into the net.

This concentrated attention was not permitted to obscure the wider view, the continuing study of history, philosophy, and political economy. The weekly timetable provided for reading the economists from Smith through Marx and Mill to Schmoller, such historians as Ranke and Lecky, philosophers ancient and modern, and new books on metaphysics, sociology, politics, or theological debates. The evenings were devoted to reading together such solid stuff, and only rarely was the training broken with some volume of poetry or the latest novel by Henry James, Anatole France, or Rudyard Kipling.

Thus, as Gay told his sister, he spent nearly three years combining the daily "grinding away" at his mass of agrarian print with

> miscellaneous history, biography, theology, and controversy. The conventional thing, the Carlylese thing, to do is of course to bemoan one's Dryasdust fate, to heap up expletives; but the truth is I enjoy the hodgepodge immensely and hope ultimately to evolve some kind of ordered whole out of it all.

The "ordered whole" was still something to be sought for and thought about. On one occasion he excitedly wrote his mother that he had been evolving some new ideas lately on the philosophy of history for which he had been searching ever since he went to Germany. He did not find it, but he did feel with increasing confidence that the historian would find a useful guide through the centuries if he kept his eye on the ebb and flow of individualism through "cycles of development."

John Dewey had put him on to this track in 1889 when he talked to the Philosophical Society about the conscious beginning of the individualistic tendency with the Reformation, traced its influence on religion, art, and letters, and indicated the evils attendant on it — morbidness, introspection, schools of passionate revolt, and the like. Throughout his study years in Germany Gay had made careful note of the individualistic tendencies in such periods as the later Middle Ages, the age of the Reformation and Renaissance, the English constitutional struggles, and the rise of laissez faire; or, on the other hand, of those anti-individualistic characteristics of the monarchical despotisms of the early modern world and of the movements which were "now so powerfully beginning the breaking of the individualistic sway — the Social Democracy and the centralizing influences at work in the state." The decline of serfdom and the breakup of the medieval village community which he was now studying began to look like one more facet of the "general movement towards individualism not only in social life but in religion, art, learning, and politics, which has characterized the European development of the last five centuries."

History so viewed seemed to run a rhythmic or zigzag course between periods when social controls were powerful and those in which aggressive individuals were in the ascendant. In the former, society built appropriate institutions to protect and further its interests, to safeguard itself against the self-seeker, to maintain stability and ensure security. In the latter, the individual, armed with new ideas, weapons, or technology, energetically asserted his disruptive creative or acquisitive energy, liberated new forces of religion, political power, or productivity, broke what Walter Bagehot called the "cake of custom," and either destroyed the old controls or rendered them obsolete. For a time he was at the wheel, driving fast on a road now devoid of traffic rules. But sooner or later society realized the need for building new institutions that would retain many of the advantages conferred by the innovator, yet curb new manifestations of self-centered individualism and cope with new forms of insecurity that revealed themselves. Thus the cycle of development was completed.

This working hypothesis served Gay both as a historian's tool or "standpoint" and as a guide to better understanding of the contemporary economic and social scene. He went to Europe an economic romanticist, critical of modern industry with its machines and division of labor, and enamored of the spirit of such artist craftsmen "as old Nuremberg sent forth." On landing he was impressed by the attention being given to social problems, the rising tide of socialism, and the "paternalistic" policies central governments were adopting. His German professors had certainly not extoled individualism as an all-sufficing creed. Now in England he studied the writings of the Webbs, the *Fabian Essays*, and the plans for reforming rural society. As he considered this welter of proposals and policies it became apparent that the western world had entered on another of its rhythmic swings toward a new era of social control.

If that be so, it was futile to lament the passing of the medieval craftsmen and of the open-field peasant or to rail at the big farm and large-scale industry. Inclosures, high farming methods, and the coming of machinery, power, and science to industry had liberated great productive forces that lifted the level of life for expanding populations. The task of society was to retain these benefits while removing the individually or socially harmful features engendered in the early stages of transition from old to new. Much had already been accomplished by voluntary groups and by the state, but much more remained to be done. Future measures ought not to be heroic or revolutionary, but come in gradual installments. They should be based on ceaseless study, on "insight into the historical development of social classes and institutions, into economic and technical necessities," and on careful experiment. They should be cautious though courageous, modest in expectation, conscious of the price to be paid and of the difficulties to be met by men imbued with "hard sound sense and brotherly love (that which our religious sect calls Christian)." That in essence was Gay's attitude toward economic and social change throughout the rest of his life.

Though his eyes rested chiefly on Europe, Gay did not forget America, the land to which he would surely return sooner or later. The few surviving letters of his American correspondence show that he tried to keep abreast of events in the United States, and was acutely conscious of the qualities — good and bad — of his native country as well as of its place in the world. Until the Spanish-American War this place had been unimportant, and Gay's intense interest in international affairs had perforce been centered on European diplomacy. The outbreak of that war widened his range and he was as delighted with the event as he was quick to see its implications. He insisted that the Philippines must be taken, because they would give a base for trade expansion in the Far East, because the task of administering them would be good training, but chiefly because overseas possessions would put America into the thick of world politics.

Despite our travel, education, intelligence, energy, we are the most insular of nations, with parochial politics. Action abroad will . . . stir our political indifference to action, our stagnant pool to move . . . As it is we are becoming a quagmire. We have been a small boy long enough. In our Civil War we passed safely through the hobble-de-hoy age. It is time for us to range ourselves as a man among men with other nations. We have been given a continent to grow up in — a big playground, but lonesome. We cannot always remain solitary in the yard, but must come out and face the world, measure and be measured, test our strength and brave our national responsibilities. We have come of age and it will rouse us, steady us, and sober us.

His own sobriety seemed endangered when the news came in December 1898 that the peace treaty had been signed. He had just formulated a "Rule of Life" decreeing that even essential letters be very brief; yet he started one to his mother with the words "So far, good! What next?" and answered the question by writing a twenty-eight-page essay on America's future as "the pivot of international politics." Read today, it seems an uncanny exercise in prophecy true and false. Its thesis is that a world storm is coming "and that we will be involved in it willy-nilly." The birthplace of the storm is St. Petersburg. Russia intends ultimately to conquer all Asia, to evict the British from that continent, and to win thereby the hegemony of the world. Her expansion in population and industrialization is very rapid and she must have Asia as a closed market for her goods. Britain will not be able to resist expulsion from India or to keep the Chinese door open. Her best days are past, she "is going to break, not suddenly but bit by bit, gradually — and the process of decay [has] already set in."

Meanwhile the United States is forging ahead to become the world's greatest economic power as she has already become the leading political power. She must therefore take on the task hitherto discharged by Britain. We can "no longer continue to play the role of jackal to the British lion." True, there is still much strength in the lion and "we are in no hurry to step into her shoes . . . When I think of the British Empire as our inheritance I think simply of the natural right of succession. That ultimate succession is inevitable, but there is no hurry about it." There is, however, need to hurry in formulating "a well-developed policy of our own" to prevent Russia from seizing Asia and shutting America out of that market. Gay therefore framed an eight-point policy for the Far East. Its assumption of leadership, its toughness toward Russia, and its claim to dictate the destinies of the other Great Powers in the Orient would have required such a state of public opinion, awareness of the issues at stake, and military might as the United States did not possess until more than forty years later.[3]

[3] The thesis and arguments in this letter were not all original. Many of them are to be found in the criticisms which some Britons were making of their own shortcomings, which Germans and Americans were voicing, and in forecasts of the shape of the twentieth-century world made by competent students of international affairs. Brooks Adams, brother of Henry Adams, forecast England's decline and the emergence of the United States and Russia as the two great rivals for world supremacy; but the volume in which he gave his reasons for this prophecy (*America's Economic Supremacy*) did not appear until more than a year after Gay wrote his letter, and the arguments were mostly quite different.

There were many similar evening and week-end excursions by the amateur political commentator and diplomat. Some of them were even more aggressive and "manifest destiny" in tone than the one outlined above. They were in part the relaxations of a tired man after the daily installment of research. In March 1899, having finished his reading of the printed works at the Museum, Gay turned his attention to manuscripts, mostly those in the Public Record Office. He hoped to go through them in two or three months and get his degree in August of that year. Actually it took him two years to examine the documents. Some of them were the reports of commissioners who went about England in 1517–18 trying to ascertain how much land had been inclosed and converted from plow to pasture. A British scholar, I. S. Leadam, had recently edited and published these reports, but Gay was dissatisfied with his work and felt obliged to examine the data afresh. He also unearthed more reports, as well as records of many lawsuits in which violators of the laws forbidding inclosure and conversion were haled before the Star Chamber or some other court.

For months Gay worked undisturbed and almost unnoticed. Then summer brought some Americans to the Record Office, including Charles Haskins, the medieval historian from Wisconsin, and Charles Gross, the Harvard medieval constitutional historian. Haskins and Gay took an instant liking to one another, and their friendship lasted until the former died in 1937. Haskins' introduction of Gay to Gross proved to be one of the decisive events in Gay's life. Gross talked about Gay's work to Hubert Hall, one of the senior officers at the Record Office and of the Royal Historical Society, and Hall invited him to read a paper before the Society in June 1900.

Gay thus got his first chance to address a scholarly audience — in fact his first chance to talk to any group since the discourse on the Four Gospels at Leipzig in 1891. The paper may have been his first written work since undergraduate days, as he had taken no examinations in Germany and had not committed his seminar study of wages to writing. He pointed out the shortcomings in Leadam's work, and

Leadam was present to defend himself with skill and vigor. The paper, followed by Leadam's rejoinder and Gay's reply thereto, was published in the Society's *Transactions* for 1900. Gay sent a copy to Gross, who showed it to W. J. Ashley, an Englishman who had been professor of economic history at Harvard since 1892. Ashley wrote Gay asking for a copy, told him he had the better of the argument, and wound up with one of those heart-warming bits of praise he knew so well how to bestow on young men:

> I am exceedingly glad that so competent a scholar as yourself is working on the subject and I shall look for your writings with eager anticipation. When you are next in these parts I shall be very glad to see you if you care to call . . . *P.S.* Our *Quarterly Journal of Economics* would welcome a contribution from your pen and give you any number of copies, although unfortunately it is not in a position to pay for its articles.

Stimulated by this verdict on his first effort, Gay pushed ahead, "working like a beaver" and "hardly stopping for meals." In May 1901 he finished with the manuscripts, moved the family to Berlin, and settled down to prepare his "dissertation." Soon, however, it was decided that Louise should return to America in good time for the birth of her second child, and the whole family reached Toledo, the home of her parents, in late September. Gay immediately hurried back to New York to catch a steamer for Hamburg.

As in 1890, he went to New York via Boston in order to make a special call — this time on Charles Gross. Things had been happening in Harvard. During the summer Ashley had been appointed dean of the new School of Commerce in Birmingham University and returned to his native land. There was no time to find a suitable successor before the next academic year began and no one in sight comparable in stature to Ashley. Gross told President Eliot that Gay was worth trying out and Eliot agreed to look him over. Unfortunately the President was away from Cambridge when Gay arrived, but Gross spoke quite encouragingly about the prospect of a job.

Back in Germany, Gay worked on his notes, but progress was so slow that there was no hope of getting his degree by November. Schmoller recommended that he postpone the final effort until next semester, whereupon he dashed back to America — after having been in Germany only six weeks — to remain with his wife until after the birth of the child. His stay, the longest since he had left for Germany in 1890, was made noteworthy by the arrival of a daughter, the very slow recovery of his wife, and an interview with President Eliot. Gross urged him to come to Cambridge once more and he was eager to do so. With his degree almost in sight the long trail was nearing its end. Twelve years had eaten up most of his inheritance, he was now a family man, a job was becoming essential, he could no longer say he was unready, and Harvard was the best place in the country for an economic historian.

The fateful interview lasted so long that Gross, who had taken Gay to the President's office and then waited for him in the anteroom, asked when he emerged if he had been having a Ph.D. examination. It had been much worse than that. Eliot subjected him to very searching questions and jotted down the important answers. The first line of these notes reads "1630 — John Gay," the second records the birthplace of Gay's father, the sixth the address of his parents-in-law, and the seventh says "Has some money; has lived on it." As Gay reported to his mother, the President seemed as much interested in his pedigree as in his personal record. He omitted neither health nor "religious persuasion and bent, if any; not that it made any difference to him personally, but it had a certain weight outside." He asked about teaching experience, inquired who could speak with knowledge about Gay's work, and boiled the answers down to the depressing conclusion that "it practically resolves itself to this, that Professor Gross is the only one who knows you and speaks for you. You have two possible sponsors from outside (President Angell and Professor Schmoller), who cannot know your work very intimately, and you have had no previous experience in teaching."

Having painted the sky so dark, Eliot said he would keep Gay in mind, provided he was willing to consider a provisional post at the lowest level. Gay replied that he was willing, gave the President a London mailing address, and retired. Six weeks later, still in the dark, he sailed for Europe, feeling that "Providence and President Eliot will have to settle the matter between them." The President took the responsibility and wrote offering an instructorship in economic history for 1902–1903 if Gay felt "ready to accept such a position." From London Gay promptly accepted the offer, then hastened to Germany to complete his getting ready by taking the prescribed three steps to the doctor's degree.

He almost fell down on the first one, the writing of his dissertation. His aim was to present a critical revision of the whole inclosure question, to show that the literary evidence must be treated with "mistrustful caution" as "contemporary hysterics," then to present tables which would indicate, county by county, the acreage inclosed and converted from arable to pastoral use, the percentage of each county affected, and the number of "houses of husbandry" that had "decayed," of persons displaced, of plows rendered idle. The dead line for handing in the typed manuscript, in English and in German, was June 15. It took Gay, aided by a statistician and a borrowed calculating machine, till mid-May to complete the tables. On June 15 the manuscript was far from finished, but Schmoller kindly extended the time to June 30, and the writing was pushed to completion. One stenographer could not read Gay's handwriting, so he was compelled to go to the man's house and dictate the text to him. On the evening of June 28 the translator reported that he was not half way through his job of turning the English version into acceptable German. Schmoller granted yet another week's grace, though this reduced his time for reading the document to two days.

The product of this "little spurt of work" gave scant satisfaction to its author. When printed under the University's rule requiring all dissertations to be printed as soon as they had been approved, it filled only sixty-five pages, nearly half of them with footnotes. It bore signs of hasty writing. More seriously, it was only a fragment of what could have been written. The critique of the contemporary literary evidence was there, as was the restatement of the character and continuity of the inclosure movement. But there had been no time left for setting out the quantitative results of the research; there was not a single statistical table and scarcely a line of argument based on the computations and calculations. Consequently Gay was glad that it was to appear first in German dress in a very small edition. He would greatly improve and expand it for publication in English and meanwhile could limit the number of German copies that went out to the world of scholars.[4]

Schmoller's opinion was very different. He invited Gay to round the dissertation out, add an exhaustive study of his figures, and generally prepare it for publication in the *Staats- und socialwissenschaftliche Forschungen*, a series of volumes in which Schmoller printed the work of his best students. Gay agreed to do so in token of his personal obligations to Schmoller and his "general obligations to German scholarship." But that task would have to wait till he had adequate leisure — and he never had it.

The remaining steps to the degree presented no difficulties. In late July he took his oral *Examen rigorosum*, passed it *summa cum laude*, and was informed that his dissertation had been adjudged *insigne*. These were the highest possible marks of distinction, rarely given in Berlin and almost never before won by an American.[5] There remained now only the "Promotion." To the end of his dissertation a candidate must append three "theses" which he stood ready to defend in the hall of the University against all comers, but especially against three "opponents" who had been given the theses beforehand. If he acquitted himself satisfactorily he was regarded as being fit to become a "Doctor" — one able to teach (*docere*); he took the oath to uphold the honor of his profession and was invited by the presiding dean to come up to the highest platform, from which only doctors were

[4] In this he certainly succeeded. The printed dissertation, entitled *Zur Geschichte der Einhegungen in England*, is in very few libraries, and was unknown to Tawney, Gonner, and other scholars who worked on the subject in later years.

[5] In view of his long period of preparation for the test, Gay did not feel that he deserved much congratulation on his achievement.

allowed to speak. There he voiced his thanks to his auditors, and the ceremony was over.

To the historian in Gay this performance linked the present with the days when Peter Abelard, Duns Scotus, or Thomas Aquinas had defended their theses in such a conclave. To the realist, eager to get home to his family and his first job, it was a vexatious farce — or at best a well-rehearsed comedy. Schmoller's secretary consented to be one of the opponents and to find two more. Gay met them several times to coach them in their parts. On the appointed morning (August 9) the mock dispute took place. Each opponent asked his prepared questions; Gay made his prepared replies; the dean invited Doctor Gay to the higher dais; he said his word of thanks and "That was all — save a little dinner to my three opponents."

Two days later he left Berlin for London, Liverpool, and New York. This was his tenth Atlantic crossing since, more than twelve years before, he had prepared "to make a journey into a far country, invest [his] talents, and return — perhaps a 'tute.'" He was now thirty-five; his initial status at Harvard would be somewhat better than that of a "tute"; but whether he had invested his talents wisely only time could tell. It was true that the years had permitted his scholarship to become wide and deep; that he had given much thought to the interrelationships among history, economics, politics, religion, and philosophy; and that he had developed a discriminating taste in literature, music, and the arts. But he still had to discover whether he could teach and also whether he could play his full part on a campus or in the wider community. The married years, like the bachelor days, had been secluded. There is little evidence of friendships formed, of more than casual acquaintanceships, or of rubbing shoulders with people apart from the kinsfolk. The arrival in Cambridge was therefore an emergence from the wilderness of solitude and study into a society where services had to be rendered. As such it had the elements of a leap in the dark.

## II

# HARVARD

## 1902–1917

I SHALL BE HAPPY INDEED to be home and to settle down at last. This Ulysses is tired of wandering." In that mood Gay came back to America. Yet settling down was bound to have its tiring as well as its testing aspects. There was a home to be made, or rather a temporary lodging, since the one-year appointment might not lead to permanent tenure. There were lecture courses to be given, students to be aided and advised, and in such work he would learn at long last whether he was suited for the career he had chosen. There was the ordeal of walking among colleagues, some of them veterans, others no older than he but of much higher rank.

The home-making proved no easy task. Gross had obtained for Gay a year's lease of a furnished faculty house which he described as "old but convenient and comfortable." The tenant quickly discovered that only the first adjective was correct and that the landlord had removed much of the essential equipment "commonly appurtenant to a furnished house." Making it habitable called for "not only an unexpected outlay of money" on carpets, curtains, bedding, table and toilet china, cleaning, and "some very tedious plumbing," but also for "a considerable expenditure of time and strength at a very inopportune season." To render the season still more inopportune and the welcome to America more chilly, a long coal strike made fuel very scarce that winter. New customers received a low priority rating on the dealers' lists, and it was Christmas before Gay got the promise of enough fuel to warrant his thinking it safe to bring his children and still invalid wife from Toledo to the new home. Actually the winter was almost over before they came, and he spent his first semester in cold solitude.

Perhaps he needed the solitude, for the unwonted task of preparing lectures absorbed well-nigh every waking hour. His main work was what he over-described as an "encyclopaedic course on the economic history of mankind from Adam to Adam Smith." The university calendar labeled the first half of it "Medieval Economic History," the second "Modern Economic History of Europe (from 1500)," and announced that the class would meet "Tuesday, Thursday, and (at the pleasure of the instructor) Saturday at 9." As the new "instructor" was too conscientious to avail himself of the "pleasure" proviso, he went through the "everlasting grind" of producing three lectures a week. In the second semester he also offered two lectures weekly on nineteenth-century German economic thought and stood willing to direct research students in work on "Select Topics in English Economic History."

This was a fairly heavy program for a beginner. It was made heavier for Gay by the fact that while he had devoted more than a decade to reading he had very rarely been under compulsion to focus and arrange his knowledge for presentation to others. As he discovered when he began preparing the German lectures, "I have read off and on in the last ten years quite a little that is helpful to me in working up the course; but it is one thing to read with a merely general interest and another to read for the purpose of teaching." Further, he had been out of university life for eight years and had enjoyed no recent opportunity to watch teaching craftsmen at work. Finally, he had never taken a course that covered the ground he now had to traverse. Nowhere in his educational travels had he listened to any series of lectures dealing systematically with a period of economic history.

If he was to make three, then five or more dead lines a week, he must sacrifice everything to the work on his lectures, and Schmoller would have to wait a bit longer for the promised manuscript. "I wish there were thirty-six hours to each day," he wrote his wife. "But I shall pull through all right. I always catch my train, you know." He pulled through, but often by staying up "till the gray of the morning working on today's dectures." To the end of his career he failed to lighten appreciably the burden of preparation. He never wrote out a cut-and-dried set of notes or accumulated what an English contemporary called a collection of phonograph records that could be used year after year. There always had to be some new preparation, rearrangement, or fresh approach each time a subject was presented to a class.

Even before his first courses had taken acceptable shape he began to think about adding to his repertoire. By December 1903, he had courses "cut out for several years ahead." Some were for graduate students, but one of them, suggested by President Eliot, was to cover the economic history of Europe in the nineteenth century, and was expected to be far more "popular" than any of the others could ever be. He gave it for the first time in 1906, and in that year also took over from Professor F. W. Taussig the course on American economic and financial history. Thus his work spread over more time and territory, and, while he tried to keep alert his interest in the earlier centuries, he was drawn deeper into the story of the Industrial Revolution and its ramifications since 1750 in Europe and America.

By 1906 he was spending eight hours a week in Harvard classrooms and repeating many of his courses to the women at Radcliffe. The repetition seemed as unnecessary to him as it had seemed "ludicrous if it were not pathetic" to his predecessor, Ashley. Whenever he got a chance he voted "with conspicuous emphasis" in favor of admitting the women to Harvard classes, but was usually in a minority of three or four against a hostile four-score. Like Ashley he found the payment for the Radcliffe lectures a meager but necessary addition to his salary, as he did also the money earned by teaching in summer school; but these supplementary sources of income ate into time and energy. Summer school cut a big slice out of the middle of the long vacation and proved itself to him, as it has to countless others, an enemy of creative scholarship.

By Christmas, 1902, he felt confident that he was holding the attention and interest of his students. By that time he also had learned, through T. N. Carver, chairman of the department, what the students thought of his work: they said it was so stiff and heavy in its demands that "whenever you see any of us going around with circles under our eyes, you can know we are taking Gay's course." There were very few of them at first; the medieval story and the German economists did not attract much attention. When, however, he began his courses on modern Europe and the United States the enrollment in what later became known as Economics 2a and 2b mounted above the hundred mark. Graduates and undergraduates alike took "Ec. 2." To some of them, in retrospect, it stands out as one of the great experiences of their Harvard years. They recall the story, widely believed, that Gay used to tear up his notes at the end of each session so that he would have to prepare new ones next year. The report sounds legendary, since there were no notes worthy of preservation; but it gives point to the students' awareness that they were not being cheated by the rehashing of stale stuff and were listening to a man who was constantly growing as scholar and teacher.

That reputation soon began to attract graduate students to him and his field. By 1905 six men were doing research under his direction. For handling them he took Schmoller's "orderly preciseness and directness of personal interest" as guide. "If I could only transfer some of Schmoller's qualities into my work as teacher I would be happy." He tried to do so at every stage, from the first conference with a new graduate student to the publication of the finished study — and beyond into later plans for teaching and research. The orderly preciseness expressed itself in the insistence on stiff basic preparation, real competence in the use of foreign languages, and ability to treat sources critically. For the rest, each student was an individual, to be given whatever encouragement, guidance, criticism, deflation, or restraint seemed necessary in his particular case.

If a man came with a plan and subject for investigation, Gay encouraged him to talk at length in order to assess the worth of student, theme, and viewpoint. If his interests had not yet settled on a suitable field of research Gay made various suggestions. Many of them reflected his belief that commerce was "the plastic element in economic development"; that German scholars had erred in overemphasizing "industrial stages"; and that it would be more revealing to trace changes in methods of distribution and the widening of the market area than to concentrate so much on the way production was organized or the place — cottage or factory — in which it was carried on. Hence he urged the need for research in this important neglected area, and some of his students answered the call. There was, however, no attempt to steer all the undecided into the same field. Many other pastures were pointed out as fertile and in need of a pioneer laborer or of more intensive cultivation.

When the men got into them — in Spain, France, England, or wherever else it might be — their letters combined jubilant reports of material unearthed, fears that they would be unable to examine it all, and pleas for guidance or advice. Gay's long replies shared their excitement, gave them detailed advice, and told them not to be overwhelmed by the amount of work to be done. "Your experience," he wrote to one of them, "is indeed familiar. I went through weeks and months of it in London; but gradually one becomes somewhat hardened, does what one can, and smothers the poignant regrets and dissatisfaction which are bound to arise."

When the student returned to write his thesis Gay worked carefully through the various drafts, trying to balance between guide and judge. He invited one author to come to his house and use his new typewriter for making the final copy. If the verdict on the finished manuscript was satisfactory, he labored almost as hard as did the writer to get it into print, going through the script with the fine comb of an editor, sometimes correcting the galleys, and on at least one occasion reading the page proofs and checking the index. When funds were needed to defray publishing costs, he enlisted the aid of

Taussig, that redoubtable extracter of money for aiding deserving scholars, until he gradually learned how to do his own begging.

By such unstinted aid he stifled his own regrets over the suspension of his own research work. There was some consolation in seeing most of the theses written by his men get into print. Four of the first nine volumes in the *Harvard Economic Studies* were the work of his students, as were a few of the books in the companion *Harvard Historical Studies.* The authors' gratitude found expression on the dedication page, in paragraphs of warm thanks in prefaces, and in personal letters. When he had completed ten years at Harvard, some of his students felt the time was ripe and the record rich enough for a volume of essays as a testimonial to his teaching. He promptly squelched the idea:

> I hope you will allow it to go no further than the stage of contemplation. In other words, I should really feel embarrassed at this stage of the game if you should raise a monument to my memory. Perhaps after I have taught twenty-five years or retired from my professorship, it would be nice to have you young men soothe my declining years, but at present I should much prefer not to have it done.

The young men did not forget, and a *Festschrift* volume was presented to him twenty years later.

The esteem of his colleagues seemed, to him, to come very slowly. He arrived in Harvard somewhat nervous about the reception he was likely to receive. Apart from the President, the only men who knew him — Gross and Haskins[1] — were in the history department. His position, junior and temporary, was in the economics department, yet the economists had played no part in choosing him. When he visited Cambridge for his interview, he met neither the veteran F. W. Taussig nor the recently appointed younger men, Carver and Ripley. Apart from a very brief encounter with Carver in Berlin in the summer of 1902, he was a complete stranger to all his associates.

Perhaps he magnified trifles, but a remark to his wife in early 1903 reveals that his first experiences were not happy: "The past half year

[1] Haskins moved from Wisconsin to Harvard in the fall of 1902.

. . . seems to have gone all right and to have made a favorable impression, and I think the coolness of my colleagues toward me or toward my line of work — whichever it was — has largely diminished; it may be too soon to say vanished. Anyway, I have had no other signs of it." By the beginning of his fourth year he felt more at home, for "three hours at Harvard Hall to meet new students and confab with one's associates passed more rapidly and pleasantly than in previous years. It is increasingly evident that I am beginning to become 'one of them.' The cordiality was marked and pleasant."

How far the coolness and slow thaw were figments of Gay's self-depreciation, it is hard to say; but his closest friends were conscious of his prolonged feeling of being an "outsider." This was in spite of the fact that by Christmas, 1902, he was informed the department wanted him to stay and before his first year ended he was raised to the rank of assistant professor of economics with a tenure of five years. In recommending the promotion Carver wrote to Eliot: "His scholarship is of the very highest type and his success as a classroom lecturer is unqualified, as shown by his work this year."

His years as assistant professor (1903–1906) were strenuous, partly because of the new courses and partly because of the claims of interests outside the classroom. He never found time to expand his dissertation for publication in Schmoller's *Forschungen*, but atoned a little for this breach of promise by presenting his statistical findings on the extent of inclosure, and his map showing the areas affected, in the Harvard *Quarterly Journal of Economics* (August 1903). He also sent a paper to be read before the Royal Historical Society and to be published in its *Transactions* for 1904. There the printing of his research ended; the material was never assembled, reorganized, and put into a book.

A few reviews written during those years reveal Gay's wide knowledge of the French, German, and English literature in his field, as well as the rigorous critical standards he had learned to apply, whether to his own work or that of others. He rode roughshod over Doren's book on the Florentine woolen industry, dubbed much of it secondhand, negligent, superficial, rhetorical, and hoped that later work would be "better ballasted with facts and figures." Though he found George Unwin's study of industrial organization in Tudor and Stuart England "admirable in temper and spirit" and counted it "one of the most significant contributions of recent years," he regretted that the central thesis rested on inference rather than on fact and was based on "exiguous entries" separated by many a "sad gap" for which there was "a total lack of information." He detected the defects in the statistical technique of Thorold Rogers' *History of Agriculture and Prices* and forecast that "doubtless at some distant day a new history of prices in England must be written with a broader documentary foundation and a wider outlook," little dreaming that twenty-five years later he would play a leading role in initiating such a price history project with an international outlook.

In 1905 he was drawn into the first of his long series of extramural ventures. A group of historians met in New York to consider the establishment of an American center of historical research in London. A committee was chosen and Gay, as its secretary, prepared the questionnaire and explanatory statement which went out to some eighty scholars. The general idea was to have a director stationed in London, who would steer students to the sources, provide a social center to which they could flock when they felt lonely, and arrange for transcribing documents needed by historians back home. Prussian, Austrian, and French institutes were doing such work in Rome. British archivists, notably Hubert Hall, gave generously of their time and knowledge to American investigators; but they were busy men, and students, even when armed with letters of introduction, often hesitated to tax their patience. It was therefore high time American historians "shouldered some share of responsibility for assistance and, where necessary, for competent guidance." It was hoped the Carnegie Foundation would provide money for the venture.

When the replies revealed that most historians approved the proposal, Gay called his committee together to consider the next step. There was no such step, probably because funds were not forthcoming. The incident had, however, given him his first contact with a wide range of American scholars; also his first experience in planning projects that were beyond the scope or interest of any one institution.

In 1906 he began to gain experience of another kind. He was promoted to the rank of professor and during Carver's absence on leave served as acting chairman of the department. In 1907 the word "acting" was deleted. He had done no such work since the "activities" of high school and college days, but quickly got back into his stride, even when the walking was on rough ground. Of the seven men in the department, only Taussig had been there since before 1900. His two years (1880–1882) as secretary to the president and a quarter century's work in the department had accustomed him to getting things done by methods which did not always conform to the canons of departmental deliberation. The early days of Gay's chairmanship were therefore marked by "a strong feeling of tension underneath"; but there were plenty of tasks on which the two men could work together harmoniously.

It was now no longer possible for Gay to tell himself that he was not "one of them." Any last lingering doubt was dispelled when he was invited to be one of the dozen founding members of the Tuesday Evening Club. This group was gathered together by Jerome Greene, secretary of the Harvard Corporation, to dine, talk shop, and consider methods for improving educational policies. Its members had such a way of being converted fairly quickly into secretaries, deans, or departmental chairmen that in 1910 one versifying member wrote of it:

The Tuesday Evening Club has nearly done
The noble work for which it was begun.
How nice it is to see these bright young faces
Adorning all administrative places!

How simple Eliot's task and Lowell's too —
In choosing Deans they'd nothing more to do
Than look about the Tuesday Evening Club
And take the first unoccupied young cub.

As an explanation of Gay's appointment to the deanship of the new Graduate School of Business Administration in early 1908 this doggerel would be the wildest poetic license. The departmental chairmanship had brought him into fairly close official contact with President Eliot and revealed a combination of qualities — resourcefulness, thoroughness, firmness, and sense of humor — in dealing with the problems that cropped up. Yet he was not the President's first choice when the long and at times desultory discussions about university education for business came to a head in March 1908, with the official decision to establish the new School and give it a trial run of five years.

The President had his heart set on William Lyon Mackenzie King as first dean. At thirty-four King had already chalked up a varied career: Toronto journalist, Canadian dominion commissioner to inquire into whatever scandal or trouble arose, instructor in political economy at Harvard for a year (1900–01), and since then an indefatigable resourceful Deputy Minister of Labor at Ottawa. Taussig and Greene had considerable difficulty in convincing Eliot that it would be impolitic to choose as the first dean a man who was not an American and who in addition had no business experience of any sort. Eventually, however, King was left undisturbed to proceed to the leadership of the Canadian Liberal party and to the longest tenure as prime minister in the history of the British Commonwealth of Nations.

With King ruled out, Eliot, on February 19, 1908, offered the post to Gay. "I asked time to consider my decision," wrote Gay in his diary. "The president was good enough to speak highly of my administrative ability when I urged my lack of experience for this task.[2] I spoke also of its postponing still farther any writing by me, and the President thought the postponement would not be longer than two years."

[2] According to another version, Eliot met Gay's self-depreciation with the remark: "I know all that, but I've noticed you have an inventive mind."

When the interview ended on that note of hopeful forecast, Gay went off to think the matter over. His first reaction was:

> I do not wish to undertake this work. It will interfere with my work of research, already seriously interrupted. It diverts my energies to administrative problems which do not particularly attract me and for which I have had no preparation. It will probably do this for more than two years; it may lead me on to other administrative work — though I hope and trust that I may be preserved from permanent lodgement in a Deanship! . . . But unless I can suggest to the President an acceptable candidate for the post, I fear I must answer "yes" to the President's invitation or challenge.

Five days later he wrote:

> I have accepted the President's invitation with reluctance. I told him that his offer seemed to open to me an opportunity for service which perhaps I ought to accept, and I would take it on the chance that this might be the best service I could do in the next four years.

It may be well to pause for a moment's examination of the considerations which played around this momentous decision. That the deanship would interfere with or postpone research and writing was certain; but the duties of an ordinary professorship had already done this, and probably would continue to make leisure a scarce commodity. His old interest in inclosures was dead. His new interest in the Industrial Revolution was growing apace, but he would need many years of relative freedom for continuous research, with at least one long sojourn in Europe, before he could feel ready to start writing.

The plea of administrative inexperience lost some of its force in the light of his effective work as departmental chairman; that of ignorance of business and of businessmen had more weight. His friend H. M. Bates only exaggerated when he said that in 1908 Gay did not know a quarter from a $100 bill. He had never studied the structure or operation of any modern industry, branch of commerce, or contemporary economic situation. His acquaintance with businessmen and business life was almost nonexistent. Whether, as the President assured him with a shake of the head, this ignorance might be a compensating advantage by allowing him to approach study and teaching with a fresh, wider, and detached viewpoint as well as a stronger social sense, only time could show. There was a risk that it would not, or at least that the viewpoint would be bookish; and there was the certainty that some businessmen would question Gay's qualifications. As he said to Bates: "Fancy me, who never did a day's business in my life, going out to Chicago to tell the rich Harvard alumni they need more education in business."

In accepting Eliot's "challenge" because it seemed to open "an opportunity for service," Gay answered the kind of "call" for which he had been hoping during the preceding two decades. As we have already seen, he had experienced considerable trouble in satisfying himself that a teacher's career was the highest form of social service and at times daydreamed of a life of action. Now he was confronted with an opportunity to combine scholarship and action in a virtually unexplored field. To fashion, build, and manage a school which would train men for business as for a profession; to bring his wide range of knowledge to bear on planning and guiding that training; to inculcate an awareness of the social obligations and consequences of business enterprise; and to do this for a country that was traveling fast toward economic maturity and political preëminence—here indeed was a call to active service that could not be declined.

Seven years earlier Ashley, then in his forty-first year, had accepted a similar call. He put aside a career as teacher and writer of economic history, although he was a recognized leader in his field and could look forward to two or three more decades of pleasant productive labor. He felt that part of the mission of a modern university was to provide a home for the professional education of businessmen, and believed that studies which were frankly utilitarian in their purpose could be infused with the humanistic spirit and the scientific approach.[3] Now it was Gay's turn. And if a still small self-doubting voice whispered that the task was too large for him, then, as he said to Bates, he was going to prove to himself that he had "the guts to do

[3] See Anne Ashley, *William James Ashley: A Life* (1932), pp. 90–97.

it." To which Bates had no reply, save to regret that contact with businessmen was already contaminating his vocabulary.

To his mother, Gay's announcement of the new "very considerable responsibility" ended on a personal note. The job "means practically no increased money reward, but I cannot help thinking that father would have been glad that I am entrusted with this work."

So, in his forty-first year, Gay became the scholar in action. The action had to be rapid, for if the School was to open its doors in October, plans for general policy, finance, staff, and courses must be drawn at once, preliminary announcements had to be made in the spring, and detailed bulletins of information be distributed by midsummer. There were virtually no principles or practices to guide the action, save the insistence that the School be conducted on the graduate level in order to place it alongside the schools of medicine, divinity, law, and applied sciences.[4] This proviso made it well-nigh impossible for Gay to learn much from the experiences of other universities in America or abroad. Their work was nearly all pitched at the undergraduate level.[5]

He therefore had to start from scratch, go ahead at full speed in the dark, hoping that dawn would soon break. "I know nothing about men suitable as teachers," he confessed, "and very little about what should be taught in such a school." He could have added that he knew little about raising funds; but he did not have to worry about this matter, since Eliot and Taussig had persuaded sponsors to guarantee the School an annual income of $25,000, apart from student fees, for five years.

By mid-July he had "managed to make a start of organization." He had tried his hand at budget-making, basing his figures on fore-

[4] Dr. Eliot seemed to think that the task of the School was to provide suitable training for what a contemporary called "the typical Boston trustee." Gay took pains to win him to a wider view.

[5] The Wharton School of Finance and Commerce, founded in 1881, had blossomed out with a four-year undergraduate course in 1894 and added facilities for graduate study soon afterwards. The Tuck School at Dartmouth offered one year of graduate work. In general, however, the emphasis in most university business schools was on undergraduate instruction.

casts ranging from his own expectation of not more than fifty students in the early years and of two hundred by the end of the fifth year, up to the five hundred predicted by some enthusiasts. He had hatched a name for the degree—"Master of Business Administration"—and when the President's office asked how this ugly label could be Latinized for use on the diploma he gave a pat reply:

The Latinized form of our proposed degree would be *Magister in Negotiis Administrandis*. . . There is a stately tradition which recommends the use of the Latin diploma. But despite this tradition . . . I have decided to recommend to the President that the diploma be written in English. This is not merely because of the lack of correspondence between the English degree and its Latinized form, but because the use of plain English seems not inappropriate to our new School of Business.

He had made some progress in recruiting a permanent staff and in finding businessmen who consented to give one or two lectures on their special interests or activities. Some of the regulars, such as William Morse Cole (Accounting) and O. M. W. Sprague (Banking), he took over from the economics department. The others he had to hunt for, scouring Boston, New York, and Philadelphia, shooting at almost any suitable or possible name that he could think of or that others might suggest.

The disappointments were many. Mackenzie King, when asked if he could be considered as a member of the staff of the new School or of the old economics department, confessed: "My most cherished desire at one time was such a connection, and I can truly say that at the moment its charms are none the less real and dear to me"—but not sufficiently endearing to make him desert Ottawa. The managing editor of an engineering magazine reluctantly said no, because he could not abandon his editorial work in New York. An insurance expert had to withdraw his promise to lecture because his executive committee had, on second thoughts, decided the work would take too much of his time. Judge Gary, president of the United States Steel Corporation, was too big and too busy to be lured as visiting lecturer into a Cambridge classroom. His aide did admit, however, the deirability of doing everything possible to establish confidence on the part of the faculty and students of Harvard in the policies of the Corporation; and on this as well as other grounds Gary authorized is comptroller to give two lectures on the management of surplus ccounts by "U. S. Steel."

By the time the School opened, Gay had mustered enough faculty nen and visitors to make an impressive showing. Some of the names on his visiting roster caused certain members of the University Corporation to feel disquietedly solicitous about Harvard's good repute and to suggest that it might be desirable to have each name submitted or formal consideration and approval. The suggestion was gently sidetracked by the administrative officers, and Gay was left free to see whether some courses, such as Corporation Finance, could be handled satisfactorily with a bevy of businessmen as lecturers and a staff member to keep the wheels turning.

Experience was to prove to him that this "somewhat hazardous experiment" led to many disappointments. He was discouraged by the inadequate teaching ability of some eminently successful captains of industry or commerce, their combination of reminiscences and generalities, and their frequent need to cancel or postpone their visits. He did, nevertheless, find several men sufficiently willing and competent to be invited for a second appearance. They included a cabinet officer, federal and state judges, high officers in railways, banks, manufacturing or commercial concerns, accountants, and lawyers. Some of the outstanding men in these fields gave a skilled and friendly hand until the School was able to build its own permanent staff.

The most arduous and foresighted part of Gay's hunt for teachers was the ensnaring of Frederick Winslow Taylor and his little band of associates. If the term "scientific management" had been coined by 1908 — which seems doubtful — it was unknown to the general public and to economists. Since the early eighties a few mechanical engineers had been seeking more rational and efficient methods of production. One of them, F. W. Taylor, a gang boss at the Midvale Steel Company's plant in Philadelphia, had started his search after an countering workers' resistance to his attempt to raise output by making them work harder. Patiently he and others studied the factors which determined output. They investigated such matters as the best speed for running a machine tool when cutting metal, the improvement of transmission shafts and belting, the designing of standardized machines, the moving of materials, plant layout, and the functions of the foreman. In addition they experimented with various kinds of piece-rate and bonus systems, analyzed costs, and looked into what was soon to be called industrial fatigue. But their findings were known only to readers of such technical journals as the *Transactions of the American Society of Mechanical Engineers*, and had not yet been gathered together in an integrated system or labeled "scientific."

How Gay learned of their work is not revealed in his papers. In June 1908 he called on "F. W. Taylor, the Philadelphia genius," asked him to let one of his men join the School's permanent staff, and invited him to give a few lectures. The genius was uncompromisingly hostile to both requests. Gay then approached Carl G. Barth, who was Taylor's right-hand man; but Barth declined the invitation to join the staff on the ground that "Taylor does not think my chances of being useful in your University are comparable with my present usefulness in the industrial world. Nor does he believe I would be happy working under the kind of administration Harvard University shares with similar institutions."

Refusing to take this as a final answer, Gay persuaded Taylor to visit Harvard in order to appraise conditions. Something in the atmosphere of the Yard caused him to thaw out. Before he left he announced that while no one could be spared for full-time work he would give an occasional lecture and advise all his colleagues to do likewise. Gay thereupon rushed off an invitation to Barth, and received the following reply: "I have just telegraphed you 'Yes,' as there is evidently no way of escaping it, and I do admire your persistency so long as you feel that way about me."

Gay was fortunate also in unearthing two men whose practical knowledge of business life made them invaluable additions to his full-time faculty. Paul T. Cherington, a member of the staff of the Philadelphia Commercial Museum, had a master's degree at the Wharton School of Finance and Commerce, and in addition a wide knowledge of American economic resources, commercial organization, marketing, advertising, and kindred subjects. The other man, W. J. Cunningham, boasted "no academic antecedents whatever." He had worked on a railroad since boyhood, "obtaining his technical education in the school of experience and diligent study," and was now in the statistical office of the Boston and Albany Railroad. That his teaching would be "practical" was evident from the start, for one of the first requests Gay had to make after the School opened was that Eliot would approve the "paying of a moderate sum for the use of a pony engine in the railroad course."

Thus the feverish work of preparation went on throughout the spring and far into the summer, through days that were often so soggy that the chief report to the family, away on vacation, ran in such terms as "I have wilted three collars and two shirts today." By mid-August a booklet was out, giving an account of courses and regulations; but countless other details had to be settled, and it was early September before Gay could get away for three weeks' vacation.

There had been no such strenuous months since those of 1902, when he was putting on that other "little spurt of work" to complete his dissertation. As Eliot said of him, he "transferred himself body and soul to the new School, put all his time and strength into it." But the body was beginning to insist that he recognize there was something awry. The doctors called it "catarrhal appendicitis." Though its symptoms were mild and slow in developing, there had been the lurking fear throughout the months of school-building that matters might come to a head too soon. Now that preparations were completed, Eliot urged him to take a good rest and then, while he was feeling the benefit of it, to have his operation immediately. Since the "good rest" was occupying most of September, Eliot's conclusion was that "the best moment [for the trip to hospital] might fall on the first of October." Forget about the School for a while, was his advice.

"Inhibit it . . . as a subject of thought and conversation. . . If you have to leave the running of the School to others for the first month or two, never mind. Your friends can take good care of it during your temporary absence."

It was too much to expect that Gay would accept this official invitation to "cut class." He was on hand to welcome the twenty-four regular and thirty-four "special" students who enrolled for the first semester. He presided at the first meeting of his administrative board, and discussed with the fourteen full or part-time instructors such eternal questions as the best method of determining students' grades. Then, with that satisfactory end of the beginning to cheer him up, he went to hospital.

For almost ten years, from the day he accepted the deanship until his departure at the end of 1917 for war work in Washington, the Business School was in the forefront of Gay's mind. Economic history had perforce to take second place. He continued to give the big lecture course on Europe and America since 1750, with the aid of a young assistant; also to advise graduate students; but most of his other courses were handed over to junior men, given only infrequently, or abandoned. The deanship not merely banned all thought of research, but cut grievously into teaching and reading.

This was inevitable, for the nurture of the School was a full-time task, an experiment conducted without the aid of well-tested techniques in an environment notoriously skeptical concerning ends and means. There was no assurance — apart from the reluctance of universities to commit infanticide — that the experiment would be continued beyond five years unless it proved itself an undeniable success. The years were therefore full of challenge, of laying foundations in the hope they would prove solid, of improvised expedients as well as planned experiments, of constant critical appraisal from within as well as without, and of ceaseless work. "No gardener," Gay wrote in 1910, "ever tended a fragile plant more carefully than I need to keep an eye on all the details of our infant School." As one plows through the records of those years, one wonders how many, or rather how few, dinners he ate at home.

While this book is not the place to describe in detail the early history of the School, some account of Gay's contribution to its growth and design is essential. In late 1911 he wrote, "When I started I felt something of an architect, but I feel now as though I were becoming a mere hod-carrier." The description is so over-modest as to be untrue. There was work for him to do not merely as architect, but also as interior decorator, as dietitian planning and testing courses, as guardian of high scholastic standards even though this meant a heavy "casualty list," as teacher expounding his views on the social functions of business, and as a keeper of the purse who had to wonder how it would be replenished when the days of assured income came to an end.

Gay's plan for the School soon came to rest on "two main ideas that interlocked." The first was his definition of "business" as the job of *making things (utilities) to sell at a profit — decently* and his concept of the qualities requisite for success in business. These he decided were courage, since all business was speculative and fraught with risk; judgment, since a man must know when to act courageously; and "sympathetic tact, a certain kindness of spirit which unites the other two elements, which purifies courage by removing its grosser belligerency and tempers judgment by the understanding heart."

To fortify these essential qualities, possessed by many — perhaps most — young men, was the function of the School. Consequently the second "main idea" was that "the great opportunity of a graduate school was to experiment and to learn what the *content* and *form* should be for the training of mature students primarily for 'making' or 'selling.' " It would try to strengthen courage by dispelling the fears ignorance inspires; to train judgment by working with and on knowledge of men and affairs; and to widen sympathy by providing an understanding, or at least a consciousness, of the problems, strivings, and movements of the society in which the businessman operates. It could thus hope to inculcate a rational "method of attack on business problems, and a habit of intellectual respect for business as a profession, with the social implications and heightened sense of responsibility which goes with that."

From this concept of the School's purpose the next steps were to frame a curriculum that would provide the necessary content and to develop a suitable method of teaching. The curriculum, conceived in terms of two years' work, required the study of three core subjects — Accounting, Commercial Contracts, and Economic Resources of the United States (later transformed into Marketing) — and of two "electives," of which Industrial Organization, Corporation Finance, and Banking were the most popular. In the second year the student took his choice from eight fields of more specialized work, such as railroading, accounting, banking, insurance, investments, foreign trade, and municipal administration.

The plan was more easily drawn than carried out. Many students did not wish to stay two years or could not afford to do so, while others wanted to take only one or two courses as "special students." Not till 1913–14 did the registration of second-year students exceed a dozen in any year; but from then onward those who "followed through" all the way to a degree became more numerous. During the first three years the "specials" comprised half the student body, but thereafter they declined in numbers and importance.

The search for suitable teaching methods was prominent in Gay's plans even before the School opened. The "case method" developed by the Harvard Law School had won widespread fame, but there could be no immediate imitation of it by the Business School. Material organized and arranged in case-book form, principles, and teachers were alike unavailable. Yet a more modest plan was worth trying. Why not ask the businessmen visitors, or the faculty members when they became competent, to present the class with some specific problem and the conditions surrounding it. Let the students wrestle with it and submit in writing their suggestions for handling it. Their efforts would form the basis for a critical examination of the whole matter at a subsequent class session. If to the problem approach was added the project approach, in which a student was sent to some factory to study conditions and prepare a report, there would be less complaint that the businessmen of tomorrow were being spoon-fed on abstractions or impractical theories.

The development of the problem method was slow and often painful. Some of the visitors were poor hands at analysis or presentation,[6] and some of the academics too hard-set in old ways. The printed material needed by the problem-solvers was scanty or hard to find. Some subjects were not susceptible to satisfactory study in that way. The visitors could not be expected to read all the students' reports. Gay therefore endeavored to get young men on to the staff and assigned them the task of developing the new method. Melvin Copeland, who in 1909 began what proved to be more than four decades of service at the School, tells how in the early weeks of his first semester Gay asked how he was getting on with his course on marketing. When he replied that he had found enough material to keep him talking, Gay retorted: "Have you found enough to keep the boys talking?" Copeland accepted the challenge and, as he remarked in 1946, "I've never lectured since then."

Another convert to the new method was found when, in 1910, Arch W. Shaw of Chicago,[7] whose magazine *System* was crusading for better business practices, came, saw, and was so conquered by the spirit of the School that he wished to study and teach there. Gay sent him to audit a course in the Law School, to study the case method there, then to work out the problem approach for a new course on Business Policy. Shaw gradually built up his work around living cases rather than written ones, and his *Approach to Business Problems* (1916), like Copeland's *Problems in Marketing* (1920), became standard required reading in business schools all over the country.

[6] Some were very good, as for instance a corporation president who turned the class into a directors' meeting engaged in preparing the annual report; or a Wall Street banker who brought along the unfinished business on his desk and discussed its problems with the class.

[7] Shaw had been interested in business higher education for many years past and in the Harvard School since its inception.

Cunningham overflowed with railroad problems and projects, Accounting was eminently suitable for the new approach, while Taylor's industrial engineers saw the whole field of industrial organization and factory management as a complex of problems calling for solution by experiment and research.

These engineers kept in full the promise given by their chief. Taylor and his associates became well-known figures in the Harvard classroom, as well as in the dining room of the faculty Colonial Club, where visiting lecturers were usually taken for a meal and a long discussion after the class meeting. They found the School a good "sounding board" for preaching their creed — until an Interstate Commerce Commission suit in 1910 and a congressional special committee in 1912 gave them a chance to expound it to the nation, put the new terms "scientific management" and "Taylorism" into the headlines, and made books on the subject almost best sellers.

The "principles" they enunciated in those books had in some measure been formulated through the submission of their accumulated medley of facts, observations, and results of experiments to the friendly but critical scrutiny of their Cambridge colleagues. Gay was especially interested in the engineers' method of attack, and enthusiastic concerning its wider economic and social significance. In this approach through patient research to the solution of managerial problems, to the saving of time and materials, to the enhancement of productivity, and to higher rewards for capital and labor alike he saw a method of studying production which "if generally applied would mean almost a second industrial revolution." From the technical standpoint it seemed to promise "the most important advance in industry since the introduction of the factory system and power machinery." He agreed with Taylor that there must be a complete mental revolution on the part of workmen toward their work, their fellows, and their employers, and an equally complete revolution on the part of management, from the foreman up to the board of directors.

He therefore welcomed requests from the appraiser of the New

York customs service for young men whose training would fit them for applying the new principles to an office which had long been notorious for incompetence and political patronage. He sent students to study the operation of scientific management at the Watertown Arsenal. In 1914 he wrote the Boston Chamber of Commerce, urging it to protest when the American Federation of Labor began another round of its battle to have an "anti-Taylor system" proviso written into congressional appropriations for government factories. The chamber took his letter as the text of its protest, appointed him chairman of a committee to study the matter, and used his report as basis for the representations made to Massachusetts members of Congress. Senator Lodge was soon able to send the reassuring news that the offending clauses had been stricken from the bill in committee; but the attack continued, and in 1916 Gay's committee was still resisting it.

While the teacher of "making things" was being well fed with research material, the teacher of marketing was starved. No branch of business, whether wholesale or retail, had as yet made a serious attempt to gather, classify, and analyze the facts concerning its commercial operations. At Shaw's suggestion the School therefore decided it must try to remedy the deficiency by establishing a Bureau of Business Research. Since the field was vast but the laborers and funds were few, a start was made at a point where interest had already been shown by businessmen. In June 1909, some shoe manufacturers and distributors urged that a study be undertaken of the spread between factory cost and retail price. This spread, wrote one of them, was so wide that "it is distribution that is being sold and not a manufactured product. The product itself and the cost of producing it bears a small percentage to the total amount of labor, thought, and sacrifice that have gone into the transaction by the time the consumer gets the article." By 1911 shoe men who had lectured at the School had aroused enough interest among their fellows to justify the holding of a conference, at which it was decided that the Bureau's first project should be an investigation of costs and bookkeeping methods in shoe-retailing.

The choice proved to be a good one, for the methods then in use ranged from unnecessarily elaborate accounting practices down to rule-of-thumb treatment of such items as depreciation, rent, discounts, dealer's salary, and estimates of profit. In some stores a spindle-file of invoices was almost the only available record. When these conditions were revealed it became evident that no further progress could be made in the study until a uniform system of accounts had been evolved and put into use. The Bureau, accountants, and shoe men coöperated in devising such a system, and in 1912 this first standardized cost-analyzing plan in the country was presented to the trade in the Bureau's first bulletin. Plans for similar studies of the grocery trade, of magazine distribution, and other aspects of retailing were considered, but could not be undertaken for lack of funds. The Bureau's pioneer job had been financed out of the School's meager income, or, as Copeland put it, from the School's deficit; and there were no university funds available for research work until 1920.

The early history of the School had something of the flavor of a cause, a crusade, or a movement beyond the frontier of educational settlement, with Gay as leader, inspirer, and challenger. He never told his colleagues what to do, for he would not have known what instructions to give. Instead he sent them off to explore, with a double piece of advice: to remember that there were no experts in this new field and that the printing of a statement did not make it authentic. His own faith, resourcefulness, and expenditure of energy impelled them to give the best that was in them, so that each man made his own full contribution to policies and programs that were a team product rather than the achievement of any one person.

There was need for every possible bit of team work if the School were to surmount its many obstacles. In the first place, it had no home of its own. The dean's office consisted of three small rooms in one building, the library reading room was in the basement of another, and the classes were held in whatever space could be spared by other departments. In the second place, there was almost universal skepticism among Harvard onlookers about the ability of any university to "teach business" and grave doubt about the wisdom of risking contamination by commercialism. The School instructors grew weary of being accosted by their colleagues with the question, "When are you going to start night classes? Some of us would like to learn how to make money." They grew a little angry when the comments were far less playful. In general the newcomer was treated courteously, or at least tolerantly, but approbation was slow in spreading. In the third place, the venture had no assurance of permanence. What would happen after the five experimental years depended not only on the statistical record of enrollment and other such criteria, but also on the recommendations which the Visiting Committee of the School felt disposed to make to the governing authorities, as well as on the individual efforts the committeemen made on the School's behalf.

The function of the Visiting Committee appointed by the Overseers was to keep a friendly but critical eye on the School and give it a helping hand. When the first year's work began Gay was asked to suggest names for members of the Committee. He submitted a list representing different branches of business — railroads, steel, insurance, manufacturing, commerce, banking, and government — and drawn from a wide geographical area including Chicago, St. Paul, St. Louis, Pittsburgh, Atlanta, and Washington as well as Philadelphia, New York, and Boston. The Committee actually chosen was almost as diverse as this, and, more important, it included men who took their duties seriously from the start.

Among these were Dr. Eliot, whose retirement from the presidency in 1909 allowed him to devote much care to his youngest academic child; Frederick A. Delano of Chicago, president of the Wabash Railroad, who served as the first chairman; Howard Elliott, head of the Northern Pacific, who succeeded Delano in the chair when he moved from St. Paul to New England to manage a railroad there; and T. W. Lamont (Harvard '92), who had moved from a journalist's desk to become one of the leading younger bankers in Wall Street. When Gay in 1908 pleaded his lack of acquaintance with

American businessmen as a reason for declining the deanship, Eliot told him there was a New York banker who would guide him unerringly to the right places to meet the right men. Lamont was all Eliot had said of him. He helped to line up the visiting lecturers and arranged meetings at which the dean could talk about his work. On one such occasion in early 1909 Gay spent the night at the Lamont home, and in later years, when a banker's life was beset by worries, Mrs. Lamont sometimes asked her husband, "Aren't you sorry you did not accept Dean Gay's offer of a professorship that night he spent with us in Englewood?"

The Visiting Committee met at least once a year. Some of its members visited classes as observers or as lecturers. In 1915 those who lived near Boston formed themselves into a subcommittee which inspected the School and produced a report that mingled praise with suggestions for improvement in about equal measure. The latter stressed the need for instruction in business courtesy, business manners, business conduct, how to telephone, how to dictate, and so forth — in short, business presence; for better grounding in fundamentals, with more practice and less theory; for greater efficiency through the effort of instructors to conduct their courses with the promptness, regularity, and dignity of a well-organized business office; and for increased attention to the clock in beginning or ending class sessions.

The dean did not escape attention in the report. He was told that he should not allow too much work to be placed on his shoulders and was urged to relinquish all teaching or active part in any course, especially the one on Business Policy, in which he enjoyed discussing broad business and social problems. Being thus assured of more spare time, he was then advised to establish regular office hours for interviewing students, so that each man could come into contact with him several times a year. "This meeting of the Dean and the students will increase the business presence that we find lacking in the students at the present time."

The life of the School, as well as its labor, was the Committee's concern. By early 1911 the time had come to examine the work already done, estimate future needs, and reach a sound conclusion concerning the desirability of continuing operations after 1913. A subcommittee headed by Dr. Eliot investigated the work in person and was satisfied that what it saw was good. It also asked eighty former students to state frankly the benefits, if any, they had derived from the instruction, together with any comments or criticisms they cared to offer. It asked the employer of each man to report on the quality of his work and estimate whether the instruction he received in the School gave him distinct advantages in learning the business. The replies strengthened the verdict based on observation: the School ought to be continued and put "on a broader and more permanent financial basis." "Permanent financial basis" was another way of saying "endowment." At least $600,000 must be raised for running the School on its present scale. Much more would be necessary if there were to be funds for growth.

The endowment drive began almost at once, but progress was disappointing. One member of the Committee justly observed that while no one felt the School should cease operations he did not believe it had accumulated sufficient experience, achievement, or prestige to provide solicitors with convincing arguments when they talked to potential benefactors. Gay himself was not yet experienced in extracting money from individuals. Even some of his indirect approaches met with rebuff, as, for instance, when he persuaded a railroad president to suggest to a very rich railroad widow that she endow a chair in railroading in memory of her late husband. The reply was that the lady's "leaning was toward Yale, at least for the present, and under the circumstances of course Harvard is precluded." Another potential victim, who had contributed to the original guarantee fund, protested that at the moment he had given as much time and money to Harvard as he felt justified in doing, "considering other calls of a charitable nature which are made on me."

Gay was therefore obliged to rely heavily on Lamont, Howard Elliott, and one or two others for effective campaigning. Their labors were slow in bearing fruit. In November 1911, Lamont announced that "everybody is feeling poor and discouraged" by a temporary recession. A month later he reported: "I have got two or three large men in mind, but they are very slow at this sort of thing. In fact, having spent all their time in acquiring money rather than giving it away, it is going to take more than two weeks to break them in to the other habit." Only after several failures did he succeed in getting $125,000 from Edmund Cogswell Converse, a New York bank president, for endowing a professorship of banking and finance.

With this first large achievement to report, Lamont wrote: "It is time we heard from other precincts." They, unfortunately, were making no headway, and no more endowment was forthcoming until 1914, when Lamont and Elliott obtained $125,000 from "admirers of J. J. Hill, anxious to have his memory perpetuated in a manner that will for all time stand for the position he had held in American transportation."

The anxiety of Hill's admirers was of quite a different kind from that felt by Gay as 1913 approached. The labor had shaken his health. Friction had developed between President Lowell and himself over "a few points of internal policy" and over the President's dislike of a special endowment campaign for the Business School at a time when he wished to embark on a general drive for funds. Lowell sent for Gay some time in 1912, suggested that he resign his deanship at once, and announced that a successor, already picked by him, had been informally approved by the Corporation. Gay refused to resign unless all the facts concerning the differences were first laid before the Corporation, took the initiative in doing so to an influential member of that body, and heard no more of the matter.

The slow meager progress of the endowment campaign therefore darkened the outlook. In 1913 the School came out from under the wing of the Faculty of Arts and Sciences, where it had sheltered for five years, and was established on an independent basis. Status was, however, less important than stature or resources. The resources were now shrunken, as some of the original contributors did not continue their support. The income from endowment, fees, and kindred receipts met less than half the expenses, so it was essential that new donors be found to help in bridging the gap.

Relief came gradually with the endowment of the railroad chair, a marked increase in enrollment, and some welcome gifts. By 1916–17 there were over 230 students in the School and the days of deficits seemed at an end. Then America's entry into the war cut the enrollment down by nearly two-thirds and the income fell once more. Thus the School ended its first ten years still operating on a shoestring. As an experiment in education it had been a success, built on foundations that have endured. It lived in straitened circumstances in crowded quarters until the fees from bumper crops of students were garnered after peace returned and until George F. Baker's five million dollars housed it in a mansion.

When in 1910 the Tuesday Evening Club spent a session poking fun at its own tendency to become a coterie of officials, Gay was charged with being

> That chiefest of administrative sinners
> Spends all his time at grand Lucullan dinners —
> A poor pretence by which he tries to dance
> Attendance on those Captains of Finance
> Who play at teaching as they would backgammon
> In hopes to gloss their partnership with Mammon.

To this indictment the poet put the following defense into Gay's mouth:

> Lucullan feasts, indeed, thou envious Dean!
> Not such within the Colonial Club I've seen.
> No blessings would I call them, but a curse
> To block digestion and vacate the purse.
>
> . . . . .
>
> [You] should not envy me for my alliance
> With modern men whose practice is my science.
> With them I'm nearly always talking shop
> And thus my hours of labor never stop.

Part of this "talking shop" consisted of "selling" the School to the business world. Gay had to seek for customers wherever he could find them. As Eliot told him, "The School is so novel that it must be described in many different places and kept in the minds of the public and of leading business men." Hence he found himself committed to countless talks before Harvard groups in the East and Midwest, as well as to industrial, trade, or professional associations—gas engineers, street railway managers, credit men, the Pan-American Scientific Congress, and so forth down a long crowded line.

To these audiences, as also to journalists who came to interview him, he expounded his gospel with its twin themes—the value of education for business and the value of research to business. By so doing he became something of a public figure in New England and even farther afield. Some individuals or associations were less interested in what he said about business education than they were in him as the kind of man who might aid them in a cause which they had at heart.

Some of these causes were new, others were old ones revived, but all were part of a world-wide upsurge of social unrest during the years before World War I. Rising prices were lifting the cost of living more rapidly than wages or salaries were going up, and thereby stirring discontent among industrial workers. Organized labor grew in strength, and while the older unions relied on traditional methods to achieve traditional ends, new unions, such as the I.W.W., were more radical in aim and aggressive in method. Demands for improved labor laws, for better enforcement, and for minimum wage acts were loud. There was a growing interest in the social insurance schemes that were spreading from Germany to Britain and other countries. And some alert businessmen were pondering over the relationship between all these trends and their own enterprises.

Gay could not expect, nor did he desire, to remain unaffected by this rising tide of concern for social betterment. He does not seem to have gone swimming in it of his own accord, but it was not difficult to persuade him to enter the water, and once in, he swam vigorously. In 1910 his interest was aroused in the need for reforming the factory laws of Massachusetts. That state had been the American pioneer in passing such legislation, but there were wide gaps in the acts and serious defects in the inspection machinery. For many years the Women's Educational and Industrial Union had been endeavoring to improve the working conditions of women and children, and in 1910 a Citizens' Committee succeeded in getting a commission appointed to investigate factory inspection.

Of that commission Gay was a member, and he threw himself without stint into his duties. He had always been interested in factory legislation, and his lecture on conditions in early-nineteenth-century English mills was one of the memorable high spots of Economics 2. He studied the Massachusetts laws carefully and sent one of his students to work in a factory to see how far they were complied with and how effectively the inspectors did their work. On the basis of the information gleaned from these and other sources he prepared a memorandum that could serve "as a possible first step in remodelling the machinery of industrial inspection in this state." After discussing the document with an influential senator, he recast his recommendations in such a way as to get better inspection without employing more men or incurring more expense. "It would be good," he wrote, "if we could get more inspectors, but this would raise the cost, and I am reluctant to introduce anything into the bill that might hinder its passage. It asks for virtually no new powers and no additional expenses, or as little as is consistent with the introduction of the new machinery." The senator's opinion of the amended proposals was such that Gay went away gratified "to find that a conservatively radical recommendation may be made" to the legislature.

He was soon to discover that it was not as easy as all that. There was much more hard work to be done, and need for joint action with other friends of reform. The Women's Educational and Industrial Union was one ally; the Boston Chamber of Commerce committee on industrial relations was another, partly because its chairman was Henry S. Dennison. As the young works manager of his uncle's firm at Framingham, Dennison was helping an old business to shed its skin. He was interested in the scientific approach to management and also in new attitudes toward the firm's personnel. He had helped to introduce aspects of what some people were calling "welfare work"—clinic, restaurant, library, etc.— and to shorten working hours. He was now drafting a plan for converting the ordinary stockholders into recipients of a fixed annual return and for transferring the rest of the profit, through stock investment, into the hands of the middle and upper brackets of the firm's employees. He was a stalwart supporter of improved factory inspection, and induced his Chamber of Commerce committee to sponsor a bill to that end.

To strengthen the offensive a Massachusetts branch of the American Association for Labor Legislation was formed in early 1911. As its first president Gay spent two busy years, for the Association concerned itself with state bills affecting workmen's compensation, child labor, the minimum wage (on which Massachusetts passed the first American law in 1912), inspection, employment offices, machinery for the administration of labor laws, the peaceful settlement of disputes, and other topics, as well as some federal issues then being urged on Congress. Since the state legislature met each year, there was always the fear that a bill passed in one session might be amended harmfully in the next. On the other hand, there was the hope that by bringing pressure to bear on candidates at election time rejected bills might be passed when next submitted.

Such proved to be the case. The first factory inspection bill, sometimes called "The Gay Bill," was rejected by the legislature in 1911; but a similar measure was passed in 1912, partly because the Governor adopted it as his child, and partly because the notorious Lawrence strike and the impending federal election heightened interest in labor questions. All this meant much work, studying conditions, preparing reports, attending committee meetings, conferring with representatives of labor and the Chamber of Commerce, interviewing the Governor, persuading legislators to support or desist from opposing, and resisting the wiles of businessmen who were opposed to the new proposals.

The rewards were encouraging, for the new law made factory inspection much more effective. In Gay's files are letters from workingmen who had read the report of some speech he delivered denouncing the inefficiencies of factory inspection. "I wish to express my sincere thanks to you," ran one of them, "and I know that the men of my craft will deeply appreciate your remarks. We all feel that when men of such prominence that you hold in the state and nation will take up the question which we have been striving for for years, that we are bound to meet with success in the end." In all, it was an edifying experience to work with labor leaders, manufacturers, social workers, bankers, physicians, Cabots and Lowells, and to get a glimpse of how political machinery worked. That experience was to prove useful when later he played a more important role on a larger stage.

Scarcely had the labor law crusade ended when Dennison aroused Gay's interest in a new field of investigation. A British governmental study of profit-sharing and labor copartnership in the United Kingdom (1913) had been followed by a similar survey of other countries (1914). When the latter fell into Dennison's hands he passed it on to Gay and a few other interested men in the Boston area, with the result that a small group met in conference in August 1915, to consider the fundamentals of coöperation between employers and employees. Though Gay was just winding up his summer school courses and wrestling with his Business School budget, he agreed to act as reporter or moderator and found the discussions "decidedly worth while."

The conference commissioned Professor Ralph E. Heilman of Urbana to visit American plants that were developing unusual labor policies, learn what their managers or owners thought about profit-sharing, and prepare a report for discussion and possible publication. Consequently there were draft manuscripts to be read and still more conferences to be attended, until war gave most of the conferees other problems to consider. The report was published in 1918 with the title *Profit-Sharing: Its Principles and Practice.* The authors were listed as W. W. Burritt, H. P. Kendall, Ralph E. Heilman, H. S. Dennison, and E. F. Gay.

Finally, men beyond New England were turning increasingly to Gay for help or coöperation. In 1910 he was invited to become one of the committee which set the topics and judged the manuscripts submitted for the Hart, Schaffner, and Marx Prizes. Mr. Joseph Schaffner inaugurated the competition in 1904 in the hope that it might "draw the attention of American youth to the study of economic and commercial subjects" and attract well-educated men to a business career. He had been especially incensed by the noisy reiterated contention of at least one prominent Chicago businessman that a college education was a waste of time for future businessmen. As news of the aims of the Harvard Business School spread to Chicago, Gay seemed an obvious choice for a place on the prize committee. He continued to occupy that place until the prizes were discontinued in the late 1920's, and his acquaintance with the Schaffner family ripened into a warm lifelong friendship.

Meanwhile Jerome Greene, who had served as trouble-shooter in the months when the School was being founded, had left Harvard in 1910 to become the general manager of the Rockefeller Institute for Medical Research in New York. In 1913 the Rockefeller Foundation was established, vastly greater than the Institute in resources and scope, and Greene as secretary became its first executive. He was interested in the promotion of research in the social sciences, possibly by an institute for economic research analogous to the older medical center. Greene therefore sought the advice of Taussig and Gay. Assume, he said, a governing group free to decide, without regard to expense, what is desirable; a well-paid director with as many associates as he wants, ranging from young "fellows" to senior men; a well-stocked library and all other requisites. "Does the opportunity thus outlined strike you as one that would appeal to a man of first-rate ability, and would he be able to draw other high-grade men in?"

Taussig's response was lukewarm, even cool. He felt that the project should not begin on this grandiose scale. Further, he asserted that so much good research was already being done in the universities that the money would be more wisely spent giving aid there than in erecting a competing institute outside. Gay agreed on the need for starting any venture in a small, inconspicuous way, but thought Taussig overvalued the quality and quantity of university research, most of which was individual or limited in scope. He therefore believed there was real need for the institute and that first-rate scholars could be attracted to it by satisfactory conditions, equipment, remuneration, and permanence of tenure.

When these views were reinforced by the opinion of other men, Greene in March 1914, with the approval of his trustees, called a small group to New York to serve as an exploratory committee. Gay served as chairman. There was prolonged discussion about the "most important subjects of investigation to be undertaken," but instant rejection of a suggestion by some outsiders that the institute embark on a campaign "to teach the masses the fundamental ethical and economic principles underlying true prosperity."

By late June, Gay had prepared a memorandum which served as the basis for the majority committee report. It embodied ideas concerning research needs and aims which he was to restate many times during the next three decades. While conceding the need for popular enlightenment on economics, it insisted that the institute ought not to attempt, at least directly, any educational work. Rather it should strive to establish its reputation as a scientific, impartial, unprejudiced investigator. It "should not only gain the confidence of the scientific world, but also at the outset avoid as far as possible the popular prejudice which may attend economic research generously supported by a great capitalist."

If this high esteem was to be won,

the only wise course to pursue [was] to undertake an investigation of such scope as to be beyond the power of our existing university research facilities and of such solidity as to establish firmly the competency and character of the Institute. That field should be chosen which would yield basic facts underlying the largest number of problems of interest to economists and now occupying the public attention.

The investigation that best fitted these criteria in mid-1914 was the collection of data on prices, wages, rents, gold production, and allied topics.

For this substantial study Gay had his man. The trail of Wesley C. Mitchell's rising reputation ran through Chicago, Harvard, and California. It had just mounted much higher with his appointment to Columbia University and the publication of his epoch-making volume on *Business Cycles* (1913). In Gay's opinion he was the obvious man to direct the project. The rest of the Committee disagreed, feeling that the task of planning the investigation would tax the strength of three men for an entire year. This view prevailed and was submitted to the Foundation. The covering letter was dated August 4, 1914, the day Britain joined France and Russia against the Central Powers. Hence the reply was such as might have been expected: "In view of the general preoccupation with the War [the Foundation has decided] to take no further steps toward the establishment of an Institute of Economic Research." The lights that went out all over Europe went out over that promising project.

The lights that went out over America in April 1917 had a similar effect on another attractive research project. In April 1916, Malcolm C. Rorty, who occupied an important position in the American Telephone and Telegraph Company, descended out of the blue on Gay. The burden of his mission was his belief that "a considerably greater degree of political and industrial stability than now exists could be brought about if certain of the fundamental facts of industry and business were determined with accuracy or within reasonable limits of error." High among these fundamental but unknown facts he placed the volume and distribution of American income. If, therefore, he made himself responsible for raising the necessary funds, would Gay be willing to organize and direct an investigation of national income either through the School's Bureau of Business Research or in some other way?

Gay's response was that the kind of inquiry Rorty had in mind was too large for the School; that perhaps the most suitable instrumentality would be a quasi-public body; that this body might well be created if a voluntary committee first carried out the pioneer study with such competence as to win public favor; and that the findings of research thus privately conducted might become so valuable that the government would adopt the investigation as its foster child. Finally, Gay offered to help in any way he could, then said: "Go talk it over with Wesley Mitchell!"

Rorty won Mitchell's promise to formulate the research plans on condition that Gay and other men of scientific standing were willing to associate themselves with the project, that Rorty raise the money, and that management of the venture rest entirely in the hands of a committee containing, in addition to scholars, "conservative and radical elements in such manner as to secure the widest possible acceptance of its findings." Rorty accepted these terms and agreed to be "wheel-horse" and money-raiser, leaving the two economists to organize an initial committee.

They gradually did so. N. I. Stone, statistician and tariff expert, was added. Professor J. R. Commons of Wisconsin was suspicious of the sources from which the funds were expected to flow, but consented to serve if the group enjoyed complete independence. Professors T. S. Adams and Allyn Young were invited to join, representatives of labor and management were chosen, and when Commons demanded that a farmer representing "the North Dakota movement" be included he was requested to find one. By early 1917 the "Committee on National Income" was thus taking shape. Unfortunately it had no income, for Rorty failed in his spasmodic efforts to find any, and when war came he went into the army.

Consequently the National Bureau of Economic Research, which might have been born in 1917, did not emerge until 1920.

While some men looked to Gay for aid in research, others looked on him as suitable timber for high administrative office in the field of education. In 1909 he was asked whether he would be disposed to accept the new position of Commissioner of Education for Massachusetts. "It is not in my line" was his reply. During the next few years university governing bodies had his name on their list when they went out to seek a new president. After one luncheon to which he was invited in New York, he wrote his wife: "It obviously was to draw me out and inspect me as a possible president. I did not take pains not to shock them and I imagine my views on education were much too radical to please some trustees. I may never hear from them again — so much the better." Another personal inspection ended in an explosion of expletives when a university regent inquired about Gay's religious and political beliefs. A third one broke off when Gay voiced his opinion that the president of that particular university "has to cope with too many inert factors."

He therefore continued to do part of the work he had eagerly undertaken in 1902 and the task he had reluctantly shouldered in 1908. Of the latter, Dr. Eliot penitently wrote in 1912, "Your administrative job is a hard one and for you it is going to last longer than you or I anticipated." Lowell's suggestion in 1912 that he resign at once relieved Gay of any feeling he was under an obligation to continue carrying the load; and when Eliot heard of the incident he agreed that conditions had so changed that he could not consider Gay as bound any longer to execute the trust. Another position, especially such a one as the directorship of the projected economic Institute, would have been a welcome change. It would have freed him from the double duty of serving as dean and teaching economic history. It would also have relieved him from the need to work overtime at Radcliffe and in summer school in the struggle to make ends meet during those years of rising prices and growing children.

In spite of these tempting considerations he stayed at his post. He made it known that though he was willing to participate in the Rockefeller discussions he was not to be regarded as available if the project reached the point of needing a director. When Lamont in 1914 learned of the project, but not of the self-denying decree, he wrote urging Gay to give two more years to the School before thinking of leaving it. The burden of his plea was that Gay's departure might prevent a promising venture from maturing into "an assured fact"; and he said bluntly that to the large circle of Harvard men who were working hard to help the School Gay's withdrawal at this time would look like "putting [his] hand to the plow and then turning back."

Gay's reply to this "great compliment and undeserved reproach" described the rencontre with Lowell, the "double burden" of teaching and administration, the financial strain, and the material as well as intellectural attractions of the Rockefeller possibilities.

> Despite all this, I have no intention of leaving the plow standing in the furrow, but shall take it to the end of the field. I owe this to the enterprise we have undertaken, to the staff I have gathered here, to the friends of the work — you above all — and to my own conscience. . . Till the School is safely anchored I cannot leave the ship.

During the next three years the ship seemed to draw nearer to a safe anchorage. Then war transferred its captain to a larger vessel, more difficult to steer in turbulent uncharted seas. When that assignment ended he did not return to the craft he had built.

# III

## WARTIME IN WASHINGTON

### 1917–1919

On August 5, 1914, Gay wrote his wife: "This terrible war obsesses me and I find myself thinking of it when I ought to be concentrating on other things — such as the proofs of [a student's] book now rolling in . . . Germany's invasion of Belgium seems a bad stroke of business, since it alienates public opinion. Altogether it is a stupendous affair." He hoped that while the outcome of the conflict would not be too disastrous to either side, the exhaustion caused by loss of life and wealth would provide so severe a lesson "that some steps toward international peace [might] be made more possible."

In spite of his debt to German scholarship, Gay's sympathies were with Britain, France, and Russia, and he watched with growing apprehension the successes scored by the Central Powers during the early campaigns. His attempt to be neutral, never very earnest, grew feebler under the combined evidence of German military strength and of the torpedo blows at American vessels. In the presidential election of 1916 he was one of the Harvard group — Haskins, Coolidge, Carver, and Bullock were others — who spoke out in support of Charles Evans Hughes on the ground that Wilson was weak and temporizing in foreign affairs, incompetent and partisan in his choice of advisers, and incapable of the intelligent coöperation between government and business that would be indispensable for coping with postwar economic problems. Within four months of issuing this blast he was helping to draft resolutions for the Boston Chamber of Commerce and a memorial for the Harvard faculty, beseeching the selfsame Wilson to "maintain national principles and international rights," to realize that it had "become the duty of the United States to throw the full weight of its power into the scales," and to employ that power "both by the use of its own forces and by effective coöperation with other nations pursuing the same object — the decisive defeat of Germany."

Gay's immersion in war work was gradual. There were chores to be done near home, such as special lectures on economic aspects of the war, participation in a Chamber of Commerce discussion on price control, the chairmanship of a board that arbitrated a dispute between Boston dock workers and their employers, and some industrial surveys for the Massachusetts Committee on Public Safety. There was also an "expert" estimate of the amount of grain consumed in making beer and spirits, prepared by four Harvard economists, two physiologists, and Irving Fisher for the Boston prohibitionists.

Like these local contributions to the war effort, the first Washington assignment was only spare-time work. On April 4, two days after President Wilson's speech asking for a declaration of war, Gay was appointed a member of the Commercial Economy Board. This Board had been created in March by the Council of National Defense as part of the first attempt to mobilize and direct the country's economic resources. Its chairman, Arch W. Shaw, turned to his Business School friends in search of colleagues. He drafted Melvin T. Copeland as secretary and nominated Gay and Dennison as members. The rest of the Board consisted of W. D. Simmons (one of the country's leading hardware distributors) and George Rublee, a New York lawyer whose knowledge of Washington ways was already profound.

The Board's task was "to investigate and advise in regard to the effective and economical distribution of commodities among the civilian population." There was hope that the economies it recommended would release labor for the army and reduce the civilian demand for materials needed by war industries. At its meetings it considered what could be done to eliminate waste in commercial practices; then how to persuade manufacturers and traders to abandon the uneconomical. Some examples came quickly to mind. Could the baking industry put a stop to the retailer's right to return unsold stale bread? Could delivery services be reduced? Was it possible to persuade shoe manufacturers, the clothing trade, hardware factories, makers of agricultural implements, and others to reduce the number of styles, patterns, models, or grades, to go slow on changing designs from year to year, use less war-essential or imported materials, attach fewer trimmings, pack more cheaply, send goods out on approval more sparingly, and grant credit more reluctantly?

The best way to find answers to the questions was by writing or calling in person on the trade association officials and inviting them to meet in conference. Where no association existed an attempt was made to form a temporary committee. Shaw and Copeland interviewed, invited, and conferred continuously. Gay gave his spare time to special cases. He gathered his shoe trade friends into fruitful sessions on "shoe style conservation." He induced the woolen cloth-makers' association to recommend that its members limit the number of patterns and use more cotton or shoddy. Since the garment trade lacked associations, he urged its leaders to set up committees with which the Board could work. When, however, they were asked to reduce the number of styles and the amount of woolen cloth used, they replied that the problem was complicated by competition from Paris. Where was justice if New York slowed down and made skirts shorter while Paris went its way uncontrolled and uncoöperating?

This question had to be passed on to M. Jusserand, the French ambassador, and since he was a historian Gay was chosen to approach him. The diplomatic mill ground slowly, but in August the ambassador informed the Board that the Syndical Chamber of Parisian Couture had decided to use only 4½ meters of woolen cloth next season against 5½ meters in the last one and 8 meters the year before; that silks would replace woolens; that the *syndicats* of ladies' tailors and of department stores would act in like manner; and that "all of them were happy to have this occasion for showing the unanimous spirit animating all peoples when the common cause is in question." Armed with this assurance the Board could plead more powerfully with the garment makers, and the upshot was that Gay's friends jestingly held him responsible for the increased immodesty of feminine apparel.

The Board had a still more cogent argument. The United States was negotiating with the British government for great quantities of Australian wool needed in making uniforms. As the British had cut their own civilian wool consumption by two-thirds, it was essential that the American negotiators "be able to give positive assurance" of a thorough and intelligent effort to achieve a similar reduction. The Commercial Economy Board was urged to "take early and aggressive action to meet this situation" and Gay was assigned the task of seeing it was done.

The Board's power to take "aggressive action" was, however, confined to persuasion. It could not compel conformity, at least directly. There might be an indirect way, if the War Industries Board were induced to refuse priorities for raw material or fuel to nonconformers; but the use of this weapon was not yet politically feasible. The appeal had to be made to patriotism translated into terms of voluntary coöperation; and patriotism without the backing of a strong trade association, of a really representative trade or industry committee, or of the influential leaders in a business, was not always enough. That was why some industries or trades were hard to handle, since associations were as yet far from general, and those which did exist might not include the leading firms. That was why stale bread took up so much time at Board meetings and so much space in the files.

The bakers had no national association and in many places no local one. It was therefore necessary to write to many thousands of wholesale bakers urging them not to take bread back from retailers; to publish the plea again and again; to prod the industry into creating an emergency council; and to persuade consumers to cooperate by getting into the habit of eating unfresh bread. Though these efforts achieved much of their purpose in most parts of the country, severe competition between "several hundreds" of small bakers in New York and Chicago and the open hostility of the leading bakers and grocers in Detroit virtually wrecked the campaign for "bread reform" in those cities. In the fall of 1917 the whole matter was taken over by Herbert Hoover's Food Administration, and the Board turned to less frustrating problems.

Like every other war agency the Board had to grope its way through trial, lack of information, and overoptimism toward better understanding and performance. In July it was still so understaffed that Copeland threatened to resign unless he was given sufficient help to save him from a physical and nervous collapse. Gay tendered his resignation because he could not spare time for the fortnightly trips to Washington and the trade conferences; also because no one had told him that his travel expenses would be paid by the government, and he had regretfully to report that his limited income did not permit him to travel back and forth any longer. He was promptly ordered to submit a statement of what he had spent; hunted in vain for his receipted hotel bills; learned he could not be reimbursed for taxes paid on rail tickets; received a check which fell far short of his outlay; and repeated his request to be allowed to resign, promising to give advice whenever it was needed.

There was a more serious reason for his desire to resign. He regarded the various advisory boards and committees as purely transitional in character. They had formed "a useful stopgap, but there should be substituted for [them] as soon as practicable individuals to whom responsibilities and authority are given. Such men as Hoover and Goethals[1] form the beginning of a new system." He would be glad to work for any agency of that new system, but felt reluctant to continue countenancing amateurish advisory improvisations. When, however, his resignation was declined, he continued to commute between Cambridge and the capital, and in November became vice-chairman of the Board. Despite his occasional pessimism over shortcomings of organization he sometimes found a journey to Washington encouraging. "After all," he wrote his daughter in July, "a great many competent people are working there as hard as they know how, and they are getting big things done or in the way of being done."

In the last week of 1917 Gay ceased to be a commuter and joined the company of "competent people" on a full-time basis. On December 13 a wire came from George Rublee, who was a member of the Shipping Board as well as of the Commercial Economy group. It asked him to come prepared to stay a few days longer in Washington than he had planned and ended with the statement: "Think shipping matter can be arranged as suggested." Gay complied, and when he returned home for Christmas he had agreed to hurry back to the capital for work that might keep him there indefinitely. To help him in the first phase of that work he took along his son Edward, now a Harvard senior.

The first page of his Washington desk diary records: "Sat up all night of December 31, 1917 and worked all day January 1, 1918, with Ted on report for Mr. Hurley." This report dealt with what had almost overnight become the most crucial of all America's war problems. It would be too much to say that the others were on their way to solution; but at least their complexities had been realized

[1] The Food Administration, with Mr. Hoover in charge, came into being on August 10, 1917, as a result of the passage of the Lever Act. The Emergency Fleet Corporation, with Major General George W. Goethals as its general manager, was chartered ten days after America's entry into the war. Gay felt that most of the work which had been begun by the Commercial Economy Board ought to be carried out by the Department of Commerce "under proper management."

and advisory committees were giving place to agencies — such as the War Industries and War Trade Boards — which eventually secured the necessary authority to act if they had not been given it at the start. All these hopes of better results ahead were, however, doomed unless the shipping bottleneck could be broken, and there was no sign that it had even been cracked.

Until late 1917 the shipping problem had been a grim struggle to get food, munitions, and industrial materials to western Europe in defiance of the intensified submarine campaign. That campaign played such grievous havoc with the Allied merchant fleets that at times during the early summer it seemed possible Britain might be beaten to her knees before the year's end. Gradually the adoption of the convoy system, the addition of American destroyers to the counterattack, and the use of depth bombs made the U-boats' operations more hazardous and reduced the losses of Allied tonnage somewhat; but the improvement was scarcely sufficient to let the supply of new ships launched get ahead of the quantity that was being sunk. The outlook for 1918 was that the surviving vessels would be hard-pressed to carry the goods needed by the Allies.

On top of that difficult task was now superimposed another one equally urgent and burdensome — the moving of a large American army and its supplies to France. When the United States entered the war the assumption on both sides of the Atlantic was that her chief contribution would be money and munitions. The French and British Missions which visited the United States in the spring voiced their recognition that the country could not be expected to raise, train, and transport an army of sufficient size to have any effect on the European theater of operations. True, the sending of a division or two "to show the flag in France" would be a helpful gesture and strengthen French morale; and if events went favorably on the western front, as seemed possible during the summer, it would be good to have American forces on hand to help give the final kick to the staggering enemy.

American policy — and possibilities — coincided with Allied expectations. To draft, encamp, clothe, equip, and train a large army was one job — long and costly; to commit it to overseas campaigning was another, not to be undertaken lightly or done in a hurry. When Pershing was sent to France in May to prepare the way for the first American contingent, Secretary of War Newton Baker told him that an expeditionary force of 12,000 men, mostly regulars, would be assembled and shipped after him, to be equipped with French rifles and coöperate as "a mere division of the French army." Once these troops were settled down to training over there, Pershing could report on the wisdom of sending others. The general staff felt that a second division should go across soon in order to get the advantage of the training received by the first and supply replacements; but as these two divisions would for a while satisfy "the sentimental desire of the French people to see American soldiers on the front," further steps would depend in part on Pershing's recommendations.

His first recommendation, made in early July, was that Washington's plans should contemplate having a million men in France by May 1918. Though only two-thirds of this number had so far been drafted — and not one of them was yet in uniform or in camp — there was a prospect that at least a million soldiers would be available by mid-1918. But, the War Department informed Pershing, the best tentative plan it could formulate, using all ships now in sight, would transfer only about 600,000 men to France by that time. Many of the ships in use would surely be sunk, and the agencies responsible for bringing more vessels into service could not do much quickly.

One of these agencies, the Emergency Fleet Corporation chartered in April 1917, with a capital of $50,000,000, was committed to grandiose plans for launching three thousand ships from nearly a hundred new slipways. It began in August to convert the swamp at Hog Island near Philadelphia into a mammoth shipyard; but the first keel was not laid down till mid-February 1918, and the first vessel built there was not ready for sea until three weeks after the

Armistice. Smaller or old yards did better, but all fell far short of expectation or needs.

The Shipping Board, established in 1916, was perhaps doing a little better than the Corporation, since its concern was chiefly with existing tonnage. It was getting the hundred interned and sabotaged German vessels repaired and back to work. In August 1917, it commandeered all hulls under construction and took control of all seagoing ships flying the American flag. But it left their operation in the hands of their owners, made little attempt to direct their comings and goings, and had no authority over the merchant fleets that the army and navy were acquiring. Meanwhile the War Trade Board was not established until October 1917, and it was more eager to see that exports did not reach the enemy than concerned with controlling imports. Consequently vessels were still in large measure free to go wherever there were good cargoes to be carried or picked up and fabulously profitable freights to be earned, especially on the routes to the markets that had been lost or deserted since 1914 by the British and Germans.

If the war had gone as well in all theaters as, in general, it did on the western front during 1917 the slow-paced building up of an army in Europe might have been justified. But in October the German-Austrian surprise attack shattered the Italians at Caporetto. In November the Bolshevik Revolution destroyed all hope that Russia would continue to fight on the eastern front, and thereby made it easy to forecast that Germany would launch a powerful offensive in the west during 1918. Inter-Allied conferences in Paris and London faced an outlook which General Tasker Bliss, the American Assistant Chief of Staff, described as "undoubtedly critical and grave."

From these conferences two inescapable conclusions emerged. The United States must help on a very large scale during the 1918 campaigns, or there might be none in 1919. She must dispatch twenty-four divisions to Europe during the first half of 1918 and it would take about two million tons of additional shipping to transport these

600,000 men. Therefore some inter-Allied shipping organization must be devised, which would work out a common program for enabling the Allies "by the maximum utilization of their resources to restrict their importations, with a view to liberating the greatest amount of shipping possible for the transportation of American troops."

The recommendations based on these conclusions reached Washington about mid-December. They called for what were virtually changes of policy: in switching from a gradual build-up of the overseas army to a rapid expansion; in coöperating with the Allies on shipping matters, especially with Great Britain since she would have to make up America's deficiencies by doing a large part of the transatlantic carriage for her; and in taking drastic steps to divert more American tonnage to war service. How drastic such steps needed to be was evident from the fact that the January plans provided for the shipment of only 45,000 men and for February the figure was expected to be no larger. At that rate only a dozen divisions would have been sent to Europe by midyear.

Two lines of action seemed essential. The first was to improve the efficiency of ships already in service, by improving the port facilities in America and, still more important, in France, as well as the capacity of the French railroads to handle men and supplies after they got ashore. It had taken some troopships nine weeks to "turnabout" in French ports and some freighters had lain idle for as much as three months. If, in addition, ships were filled with cargo before they were permitted to sail from America, there would, according to expert estimates, be an increase of 30 to 50 per cent in the efficiency of the vessels now in use.

The second line of action was to increase the available tonnage by an arbitrary reduction in the quantity of nonessential goods imported, and perhaps a ban on the entry of some of them. This would involve a shift from the former exhortations to consume less of foreign products to enforced abstinence. There had been very little resort so far to compulsion, save in the conscription of men, and some occupants of high office feared morale would slump if people were deprived of goods. The difficult part of this step was that no one knew what imports were really essential and what could be dispensed with. Pershing was insisting that the use of American shipping for commercial purposes "must be curtailed as much as possible," but no one could say, with any assurance based on knowledge, how much curtailing was possible.

Three kinds of information — none of them available — were therefore necessary preludes to any further development of policy. The probable tonnage requirements of the army program must be ascertained. The kind, quantity, and volume, in terms of ship space, of nonessential imports must be estimated. The character, cargoes, routes, and performances of existing ships must be studied. It was to collect this information that Gay was engaged as a "special expert" by the Shipping Board. Whether he was originally expected to make recommendations based on his findings is not clear, but he certainly regarded this as part of his duty. It is also evident that the Board had not originally intended to do anything heroic. Edward N. Hurley, its chairman, said Gay was to "take charge of priorities work in connection with imports and exports." Experience with priorities had not hitherto been encouraging, for high ones were obtainable by almost anyone who could say he had an army or navy contract.

Whatever the Board's intent, Gay's first report left no doubt that strong measures were necessary. He had threshed it out between December 26 and New Year's Day, calling in person or by phone or wire on anyone who could supply information or make an intelligent guess, and requesting from the War Department the latest word about Pershing's plans as well as the confidential figures on submarine ravages. Though a rush job, it yielded a fairly accurate picture of the serious tonnage deficiency that the military program would create, a rough estimate of the tonnage that might be made available if import restrictions were imposed, and at least an assumption that such restrictions were inevitable.

Hurley sent the report through the appropriate channels. Within a week Gay was called in to discuss it with General Bliss, who was temporarily back home, and learned that he was "in" for helping to make "very high decisions indeed." Next day the State Department called him, then he was invited to present a summary to a cabinet meeting. There is no written record of his experience at this meeting; but the account he gave later to a close friend tells how he began his statement with a casual reference to the "change of policy," meaning thereby the switch from the small-scale slow build-up of the American forces abroad to the rapid transfer of the utmost possible amount of manpower. Some member of the cabinet interrupted to ask "What change of policy?" Flabbergasted, Gay was searching for a reply when Baker said quietly, "Go ahead, Mr. Gay. I'll explain the matter later." Gay did so, and in the ensuing discussion of practical considerations he gradually became aware that of all those present, the President and Baker alone were aware that there had been any "change of policy."

The next few weeks were spent making preparations, in the hope that the necessary decisions for controlling shipping and imports would be made. He hustled round assembling a staff; visited New York to interview shipping men, whose information he found "instructive" but whose views on the Shipping Board were "rather critical and occasionally acrid"; set statistical machinery in motion; wrote reports far into the night; and in spare moments sat at his desk "praying that the powers that be will make what seems to me the only right decision in this very grave crisis."

They did, and on January 19 he learned that the principle of restricting imports to "bare necessities," which he had been working to establish, had been accepted by Hurley, approved by the President, and communicated to Bliss (now back in Europe) in order to assure him that his worries about ships and divisions were virtually at an end. The erection of the organization to carry out this policy took some time — so much in fact that Gay found "the drift above Niagara appalling"; but by mid-February the double job was completed, with new machinery to direct the use of tonnage and procedures planned for restricting imports to such goods as inquiry showed to be essential.

The former consisted of a Ship Control Committee, located in New York City and given power to operate the fleet controlled by the Shipping Board. Since its chairman, P. A. S. Franklin, was president of the International Mercantile Marine Company, a holding corporation which controlled half a dozen Atlantic lines, the task had evidently been placed in competent hands. The Army indicated that it thought so by entrusting the operation of its ships to the new committee. The British agreed to coöperate and their representative was one of the three men who were to do the job. Thus the control of shipping resources became unified. At the same time the Shipping Board decided to participate in forming an Allied Maritime Transport Council which would operate in London, studying the general needs of the Allies and giving advice that would help the British, French, Italian, and American ship controllers to coördinate their separate policies. The vice-chairman of the Board (R. B. Stevens) and Rublee were sent to represent America on the Council, accompanied by Jerome Greene as executive secretary of the "American Shipping Mission," and a staff of some twenty economists, statisticians, clerks, and stenographers.

The policy of import restriction was made public when on February 14 the President proclaimed that henceforth goods could not be admitted unless the recipient had a license to bring them in. The program was entrusted to the Shipping Board and the War Trade Board, working in coöperation. The former was to establish a Division of Planning and Statistics, with Gay as director, to gather information about ships and imports. The shipping data, with appropriate recommendations, would be submitted to the Shipping Board, of which Gay had been made a member; the studies of imports went to the War Trade Board, whose task was to issue the lists of restricted or banned imports and grant or refuse licenses. Gay was chosen to be one of the two representatives of the Shipping

Board on the War Trade Board, so that he could explain in person the findings and recommendations of his Division. Thus, as he described the whole arrangement, the problem of administering the import restrictions program "has been solved by 'coördinating' the thing under my skull."

This arrangement, and consequently Gay's formal appointment, were not made until mid-February; but he had been busy for six weeks, learning, acting, and planning. Methods had been evolved for scheduling the character and movement of ships and for receiving the manifest of every vessel entering or leaving port. Plans had been shaped for the prompt flow of statistics from the Treasury, Department of Commerce, customs service, and other agencies, so that figures would reach the Division within ten days, instead of trickling in two or three months (or more) after the end of the period to which they referred.

More important still, Gay had already gathered together the nucleus of what he called his "cabinet." He needed experts on imported commodities, their uses, sources of supply, and trade routes; experts familiar with ships, their tonnage, types, and uses; and experts in compiling, analyzing, and presenting statistics. When he could not find them he looked for someone whose training and outlook made him capable of studying situations and becoming an expert quickly. He naturally turned first to the men he had come to know through the Business School, and in addition scoured the faculty lists of other universities. A. E. Swanson, dean of the Business School at Northwestern, became the expert on rubber; Walter S. Tower, the economic geographer at Chicago, knew enough to qualify as head of the commodity studies group; C. K. Leith of Wisconsin brought his wide knowledge of minerals; and other men were statisticians of high repute. While the Division's primary task was to gather information about ships and commodities, it was frequently requested to undertake other investigations whenever a new problem demanded attention. Still more "special experts" had then to be enlisted, and by midsummer the roster was a select list of men who were to become well known in the world of social scientists during the next two decades.

The Division was not, however, entirely an academic camp. From the start H. S. Dennison was assistant-director and served in many capacities — as expert on oil, trouble-shooter, personal caretaker of his chief, and as the man whose ability to strike a lighter note relieved the tension in times of stress. Donald Scott came from the Century Publishing Company to work on shipping matters, and was made liaison officer between the Division and the Ship Control Committee in New York City. Thomas Slocum, a New York businessman and member of the Harvard Business School's visiting committee, shouldered the thankless task of hearing and handling the complaints of traders and manufacturers whose supplies were likely to be reduced or cut off when the restrictions went into effect. At least half a dozen others left their businesses to give a helping hand.

The Division grew rapidly. By May the total staff had risen to 170, and by the Armistice it was over 300. Yet the most important job — the preparation of the lists of prohibited or restricted imports — was done during the first two months by a pioneer band of about thirty. One member of the team described how "all hands" worked "a good deal beyond the limit of any preconceived notion of capacity. Eighteen hours is not an unusual day, and on Sundays we manage to walk Mr. Gay around for about three hours in the open air; otherwise we work full shot, and at that we seem to get farther and farther behind." It was not so much that the staff was small and the need for results urgent; the great difficulty sprang from the lack of facts and from the plethora of factors that had to be considered.

Of the latter, at least ten had to be kept in mind — the nature and uses of the commodity, the sources of supply, possible substitutes, stocks on hand, the tonnage required to bring it, the ports to which it came, as well as any political, economic, and financial considerations that affected the United States' relations with other countries. Of the facts there was at many points a veritable famine. As the import statistics usually did not give the port of entry, the country of origin, the volume or the weight of an imported commodity, it was hard to say how much ship tonnage space was needed to import the material, or whether a ban on its entry would hurt a friendly foreign power. Moreover, there were few figures to tell what happened to the material after it entered the country. Few trade associations had statistical departments of their own and no industry could say what its total needs were or give a worth-while estimate of its annual output. The latest census report on occupations was eight years old and the most recently published census of manufactures was for 1909.

Among the many stories dealing with the hunt for information we choose one. The commodity under consideration was sausage casings, of which a substantial quantity was imported — chiefly from across the Pacific — since American livestock could not supply enough tubes of the small diameter needed to satisfy the nation's hunger for "little pig" sausages. On the other hand, casings of larger cross section were exported in considerable quantity to Australia and other countries which, under the influence of their British heritage, liked sausages about an inch thick. The statistics recorded the weight of the imports, but how did one translate the figure into terms of space occupied in a ship's hold? At a very early hour on Sunday morning some member of the Division found a way. He rang up a sausage-maker in suburban Washington and requested him to go at once to his place of production, measure the dimensions of any container that was full of skins, then ring up the Division to report the size of the container as well as the weight of its contents. Thus one more relevant fact was added to the researchers' stock of information.

Other methods were almost as fantastic. So also were some of the blunders from which the professors were saved by the intervention of traders and manufacturers. It was the "practical men" who explained that human hair was used to make filters needed in producing linseed oil, as well as for wigs, hair nets, or toupees; that tapioca was an ingredient of varnish and glue and TNT as well as of puddings; and that corset "laces" were strings, not strips of embroidery.

By early March the team had produced its first list of commodities that could be shut out without injuring the country's welfare. The document passed unharmed through inspection by the other war agencies, but encountered so many objections in the State Department that Gay had a hard time getting the custodians of foreign relations "to realize that we were at war." The list was released to the press on March 22, but the grim news that the Germans had started their mighty offensive the day before drove it off the front page and made the public more willing to accept the restrictions. The importation of some 80 commodities, chiefly metals, foodstuffs, and luxuries, was banned. About 350,000 tons of shipping would thereby be released, making space available for the carriage of 1,500,000 tons of cargo during the next six months. Coming on top of the commandeering of 90 Dutch vessels (of about 400,000 tons) sheltering in American harbors, these figures were a welcome reply to the demand of General March, the new chief of staff, that the monthly movement of troops across the ocean be doubled or trebled.

As the War Trade Board was handed the first list of goods it must exclude, the second (scheduling 46 commodities) started its round of the departments. The third, which reduced rather than forbade the entry of more than 80 materials, was ready for circulation on April 19. The investigation and the decisions concerning about 200 kinds of commodities had been completed within two months of Gay's appointment.

During all this time the pace had been fast, except when it was furious. A cabled request from the Shipping Mission for information concerning the probable extent of the tonnage savings, or a new request from the commander-in-chief for precise (and higher) figures of possible shipping space, would throw the Division of Planning and Statistics into a frenzied effort to provide an answer almost overnight by working all night. When Walter Tower said he could prepare a certain report within six weeks, Gay's reply was, "Today is Thursday, and I want to cable the figures to London by Saturday." He had traveled far since the decade when years were gladly devoted to the quest of "thoroughness" and "ripeness." Now his instructions were

"Get all the facts that can possibly be gathered within the time limit, then use a hunch for the rest." If only 5 per cent of the information could be garnered within the time set, a decision based thereon would be better than one resting on no facts at all.

The compilation of a list did not end the Division's work. Each schedule had to be submitted to other departments or agencies whose consent must be won before the embargo could take effect. Since some of them were making their own demands for ships or imports they were not always easily won over, and when they had given their approval there was still the State Department to be dealt with. After reluctantly accepting the first list, "State" discovered difficulties connected with most-favored-nation clauses in treaties, and held up for ten days the dispatch of the necessary instructions to consuls. The second list made it ponder for two weeks about possible trouble with Brazil.

Gay and Dennison assumed responsibility for handling the departments and found themselves involved in many a fierce tussle. In going his rounds Gay soon discovered that he was earning a "bellicose reputation" as "a good deal of a bull in a china shop," a "very determined person," a "two-handed man," a "pirate." His thick thatch of black hair, heavy eyebrows, big broad mustache, and behavior moved one amateur angler to comment, "He looks like a black bass and behaves like one." He could be persuasive or pugnacious according to need. With Herbert Hoover at the Food Administration his first encounter was a pitched battle. With Bernard Baruch of the War Industries Board he found himself involved in "playing a typical game of Washington poker — a game which I thought I had won last week, but which I must now commence all over again from the beginning."

Gradually the ban on imports began to yield results. Gay estimated that by mid-1918 it had released more than 1,000,000 tons of shipping for transfer to approved routes and essential cargoes. To this figure must be added the tonnage brought under Shipping Board control by seizing the Dutch vessels and chartering Japanese or Scandinavian ships. At the end of August the Board had 8,600,000 tons under its jurisdiction.

To aid in putting those vessels to the best possible use was the second task of the Division of Planning and Statistics. The Division was created "for the purpose of giving the necessary data to determine the trade routes to which the vessels under the control of the Board must be assigned and the standards by which they must be operated in order to give their maximum service." The accumulation of the "necessary data" was a gigantic task, since every detail seemed indispensable. A complete inventory of every controlled ship and of every ship touching an American port was necessary if the Board was to know the types of vessel available for various purposes. A daily account of the movement of each ship and of its cargo was requisite for a composite picture of the tonnage moving in each of the nearly thirty trade areas into which the world map had been divided. From the gallery of charts and diagrams based on these data, it was possible to see the tonnage assigned to different commodities, to know whether the flow of imports was ahead or behind schedule, to detect waste of time through over-long "turnabout" in port, and consequently to move a ship from one route to another, steer it to some less crowded port, and decide whether it could be transferred from commercial to military work.

A summary of the information thus gathered and graphically interpreted was passed on every ten days to the other war agencies. Its chief purpose was, however, to guide the Shipping Board's Division of Operations and the Ship Control Committee. As that Committee was located in New York City, Donald Scott served as the channel between it and the statisticians and chart-makers in Washington. In addition, Franklin, its chairman, came to Washington every Wednesday to lunch with Hurley, Gay, and Charles Schwab (the steelmaster now in charge of shipbuilding), and to confer with the Board. It was the business of his Committee to allocate vessels to routes and cargoes in the light of the new restraint on imports and of the army's growing needs.

By midyear the heads of the Division of Planning and Statistics began to wonder whether New York was wholeheartedly reallocating tonnage or coöperating with the American Mission in London. The German hammer blows on the western front had welded the Allied armies together under a supreme commander. Though similar unity of control might not be politically feasible for shipping, something like it was urgently needed to cope with three problems created by the enemy display of strength. In the first place, the German capture of the Pas de Calais coal fields made it essential that France and Italy be helped at once by larger shipments of coal from Britain and America. In the second place, more American troops must be rushed more quickly to Europe. In the third place, it now seemed grimly certain the war would continue into 1919, and those who were handling ships had to consider how the tonnage likely to be available could most effectively carry its varied heavy burdens for another year. Clearly much closer coördination was required, the purely advisory powers of the Allied Maritime Transport Council should be strengthened, its advice must be listened to more attentively, and each nation would have to harmonize its policy with the demands of allied grand maritime strategy.

To the members of the American Mission these things were self-evident. They were eager to do their part at every point; to be as frank as their colleagues from other nations in supplying information concerning what America needed, what she was doing, and what she intended to do; and to urge on the government back home the adoption of policies that seemed best for the common cause. It was not easy at first for the economists on the staff (James A. Field and Joseph S. Davis) to contribute much information about American trade and shipping except what they could dig out of the *Encyclopaedia Britannica*, the files of the *Commercial and Financial Chronicle*, the latest (but not very recent) reports in the American Consulate, and books in the British Museum. When the flow of figures from

Gay's Division set in the situation was relieved a little, but Davis continued to send almost pathetic pleas for more up-to-date information, no matter how confidential or incomplete it might be. "We need it," he wrote

to serve as a basis for our own contribution to discussion and action in the Council and its committees; to furnish to representatives of the Allied governments the information they require for scrutiny of our policy and practices as we are given the opportunity to scrutinize theirs, and for intelligent deliberation upon the common problems; and to enable us to cultivate the good will of the coöperating governments by responding in kind to courtesies of their offices in opening freely to us their material and methods of work, and by thus giving tangible evidence of our eagerness to coöperate. . . We are still in the debtor class in respect to documents exchanged.

While the statisticians begged for figures, their superiors urged the administrators to consider the Council's recommendations favorably. The response revealed the gap that so often emerges between men of different nations working together in a common cause and the governments or the peoples they represent. An American who spent 1918 with the Mission in London described the situation as follows:

One of the worst faults of our administration in Washington has been its utter provinciality and aloofness from the thought and feeling on this side. Our traditional nationalism and suspicion of European countries has given to many of our public men in the highest places a sort of "You-can't-put-anything-over-on-me" attitude toward England which resembles nothing so much as the attitude of a "rube" who takes every stranger in the city as a bunco steerer.

This attitude was revealed when a recommendation came from the Council in April 1918, that some of the Dutch vessels now in American hands be used to carry coal to France and Italy. There were many reasons, in addition to the urgent need for fuel, why this should be done. Yet Gay was obliged to write Rublee:

I am sorry that it was not possible to push strongly on our side your request. . . It met with strong opposition on the part both of Mr. Hurley and Mr. Franklin, and the request was not supported by the highest military authorities. . . Mr. Franklin, I say to you in confidence, is frankly sceptical of inter-allied control and has a strong tendency to hold as much control on the side of the United States as possible, and in this he is backed by Mr. Hurley.

Rublee was therefore warned that "some discouragements and difficulties from this end are only to be expected and will probably continue." He was urged to seek the support of Pershing and Bliss for any future recommendations. Meanwhile efforts ought to be made from London and in Washington to clear up in the minds of the shipping chieftains the need and practicable possibilities of inter-Allied coöperation. A hint from the President would "greatly influence Hurley" if Wilson could be induced to give it.

By June the Mission was so worried over the lack of information and of support that Rublee came home to insist that the Shipping Board adopt a less domestic outlook. After hearing what he had to say, Gay sent Horace Secrist, who had built much of the Division's shipping statistical machinery, across to London to learn what the Mission needed to know, how the Shipping Board could be of greater service, and in return how the Mission might help the Board. Secrist was instructed to assure the Americans in London that they could have all the information they wanted and were free to hand it on in an open, frank manner at Council meetings, withholding "nothing which would be helpful in the solution of problems." In return he would be justified in asking the representatives of the other powers for "all information which would be serviceable in the handling of our own shipping problems."

During two months in London Secrist was able to improve greatly the flow of information in both directions, but especially westward. He arranged for American access to the intelligence files of the British Admiralty, to records of the Ministry of Shipping and of Lloyd's, and as this material was passed on to Washington the Division of Planning and Statistics accumulated sufficient data for a world-wide survey of the shipping problem. In return the Americans in London were enabled to contribute more to the Council's work, and to help in devising a plan for ship control that would have been of the utmost importance if the war had continued into 1919.

This does not mean that American shipping operations and policy were now being conducted in a goldfish bowl. Some features were far from clear. For example, by June the students of the Division's figures and charts noticed that the import restrictions were not being reflected in a decline of tonnage on some routes. There was instead "a disquieting lack of approximation." The suspicion dawned that "redundant" shipping was not being withdrawn for war purposes, and a watch was set to see whether this was so. In July a large excess of tonnage over trade needs was found operating between the United States and the east coast of South America. Empty ships had been sent to Buenos Aires and the Ship Control office then informed soap manufacturers that space was available for bringing tallow — a commodity on the restricted list — from Argentina. The War Trade Board rejected the applications for tallow licenses that immediately descended on it. Similar conditions prevailed on the west coast of South America, while in the Caribbean many refrigerated banana boats, some large and modern, were plying their trade almost as if there were no war.

Gay asked Scott, returning from a Washington assignment to his post in New York, to inquire about the Argentine situation. Scott was told the whole thing was due to a mistake: after a quota of steamships had been allotted to that route a similar allocation of sailing ships was made. Gay mentioned to Franklin, on the latter's next Wednesday trip to Washington, the serious embarrassment the "mistake" had caused. Franklin replied that it was no mistake, and that he intended to look after the interests of Americans in the Latin American market.

From that time onward Gay knew he had a fight on his hands — one for which he needed better weapons. Whenever he pointed to the apparent surplus tonnage in a certain area and asked why some vessels could not be diverted, the Ship Control men overwhelmed him with technical answers: the boats were not fit for transatlantic service, the surplus was only seasonal, triangular routing made his statisticians' figures misleading, or his experts had used "theoretical" rather than actual measurements of "turnabout." After one such humiliating session he told his next divisional conference that the experience had convinced him of the need for "much more exact information hereafter in justification of any program for disturbing the existing machinery." When Tower informed him that the "turnabout" figures were not theoretical but based on actual performances, his conviction grew stronger. Technical arguments must be rebutted in kind by someone conversant with the character of every ship, its capacity, and its movements.

To prepare for the battle, the ammunition was collected more energetically by the Division's shipping specialists, and an invaluable ally was found in Major Franz Schneider. Schneider was serving in the office of the Chief of Staff. He therefore knew the urgent need for more ships, for in July Pershing had protested that the tonnage promised him was insufficient to supply the needs of the thirty divisions that would be in France by September, was talking about at least eighty divisions by mid-1919, and angrily asking what had happened to three-quarters of the newly built American ships as well as to more than half of the Dutch, Swedish, Japanese, and other vessels. Schneider's chief, General March, was a glutton for ships, and when Hoover on one occasion protested against his desire to annex some vessels promised by the President for Belgian relief cargoes March retorted, "If we don't get men to France there will be no Belgian relief problem."

Most important of all, Schneider was engaged in statistical work. One of his main duties was to present and explain several charts to a weekly Tonnage Conference attended by the top men — secretaries, generals, admirals, and chairmen of all the boards — as well as by Franklin. The minutes of these conferences show that Schneider's turn usually came after someone had surveyed the current strategical situation, and that his report was always "interrupted by discussion," in which everybody contributed information, voiced complaints, cross-examined Schneider, and turned to Franklin for further news or explanation.

The Tonnage Conference was the scene of the final struggle to get the ships released, and Schneider was the obvious man to wage it there. For months past he had been consulting the shipping data accumulated by Gay's men. By early September he knew the character and movements of almost every vessel plying commercial routes but capable of war work; and by that month the need for action was urgent. The American Mission was complaining that New York would not supply any precise figures of tonnage released or soon to be released, and that without them it could not negotiate with the British for the use of a further 200,000 tons of their vessels. The Mission was also greatly disturbed over the effect of Franklin's recent public statement that the British were still running ships exclusively for normal trade purposes in the western Atlantic while America had cut her trade to the bone. This charge had really angered the British, and it was feared they might retort aloud that the shoe was on the other foot.

Moreover, in late August Gay had obtained from the War Trade and War Industries Boards a pledge to cut imports more fiercely in order to reduce the required tonnage by a fifth. The State Department's cable reporting this pledge to the American ambassador in London asked him to assure "British officials and commercial leaders," as well as the Mission, that it would be honored in full, no matter what the effect on American civilian supplies; it authorized him to tell them that the War Trade Board would be happy to learn of any circumstances "indicating failure to adhere to the foregoing policy"; and it hoped the news would strengthen the hands of those Britons who were opposing an attempt by some of their fellow countrymen to get more tonnage assigned for commercial traffic.

The pledge may have mollified the British; it certainly increased the pressure on the Ship Control Committee. That pressure was applied in the Tonnage Conference sessions. There week after week throughout September and October Schneider's charts provoked the high officials to inquire of the Committee's chairman why so many American merchant ships were still operating in the western Atlantic and Pacific. The usual answer was that their size, speed, internal arrangement, or some other disability made them unsuitable for war work. At this point Schneider would produce his facts to cast doubt on the explanation. On one occasion he pointed out that ships described as useless because they were voracious coal consumers were really efficient oil burners. Then the excuse shifted to the lack of adequate port facilities in France. When that statement had been rebutted or reduced in importance, a third plea might be advanced: additional vessels were not needed because there were no army supplies awaiting shipment. Investigation usually disproved this assertion, as for example in September, when it was found there were 700,000 tons of material awaiting shipment and about 700,000 more tons due in October, apart from a great quantity of trucks, railroad equipment, horses, mules, and fodder, the lack of which had seriously impeded the American army's progress when the German retreat began.

At some Tonnage Conferences the Ship Control Committee's spokesman advanced the plea that ships be left alone in order to move the large cargoes piled up in American ports awaiting carriage to Latin America. He contended that it seemed a pity to cut American merchants out of their new-found markets; that the supply of ships ought to be increased rather than reduced; that the British were jealous "on account of our opportunities to secure this trade and now have a considerable number of boats engaged in this manner." The first part of this statement provoked General March to retort that capturing Latin American trade must not be allowed to interfere with the military program. On the last part McCormick, chairman of the War Trade Board, commented that if British behavior was improper it could easily be corrected by being reported to the Allied Maritime Council, and that in any case the sins of others were "all the more reason why we keep our skirts clean."

Under these weekly installments of criticism the Ship Control Committee yielded some ground. The battle reached its climax on October 30, when at a stormy four-hour session the customary arguments were shattered by fire from every quarter, and their exponent collapsed. The Ship Control Committee was ordered to take all suitable vessels off trade routes at once. The army insisted on resuming control of the ships that had been or would be earmarked for it, but agreed to let the Committee operate them subject to advice from Gay and the War Trade Board — not from the Shipping Board. The allocation of what was left of civilian shipping also was transferred to new hands.

"It has been an unpleasant piece of work," Gay wrote his wife, "but the job is done." The results were quickly made evident. The trickle of transferred ships rose rapidly to a flood, and most of the 1,200,000 tons taken out of civilian service between September 1 and November 6 were reallocated during the last few of those days. General March called on Gay in person to thank him on behalf of the army for the battle he had fought. Secretary of War Baker sent for him for the same purpose.

Gay had not been long in Washington before it became clear that he and his associates would not be permitted to confine their attention to ships and commodities. He was called in to help the Shipping Board whenever a pinch began to be felt. In March Hurley requested him to organize "a real labor administration" for the Emergency Fleet Corporation's shipyards. Then he was asked to put the forecasts of shipyard output on a basis of fact instead of on the boastful wishing that had served as foundation. Other requests concerned a survey of American ports with a view to their improvement; measures for alleviating New England's coal shortage; the merits of different kinds of ships; the influence of import restrictions on price levels; the effect of the Panama Canal on routes and rates; and personal support of Hurley in an inquisition by the congressional appropriations committee.

By early June the reputation of the Division was so high and widespread that other war agencies besought Gay to come over and help them. McCormick asked him to take charge of the War Trade Board's Bureau of Research and Bureau of Statistics and Tabulations. In the same week Baruch invited him to take control and convert the statistical section of the War Industries Board into a Division of Planning and Statistics. He accepted both invitations in the belief that by bringing shipping, trade, and industrial figures under one controller a more efficient job could be done on all three. "It is quite an undertaking," he confessed, "but it is necessary to be done and I shall do my best to make the combination work. I may fail—but then I can come home."

The accumulation of duties did not end with that formidable combination. In late May the President requested Baruch to create a special agency for the express purpose of preparing for his attention such a "conspectus of all the present war activities of the Government" as would make possible a "periodical checking up of actual operation and results." Baruch suggested that the task of building and directing this new agency be handed over to Gay. The President concurred, and in early June the organizing of the "Central Bureau of Planning and Statistics" was dropped into Gay's lap. To complete the list, we may add the establishment a little later of a Statistical Committee in the Department of Labor, with Gay as chairman.

Little wonder that his son began a letter with the question: "How many new statistical departments have you taken over?" Even when the Armistice had started a mass exodus from Washington, the staffs under his direct control numbered more than a thousand people in late November. By early July of 1918 his daily program was beginning to develop a rotary motion around four offices: first a spell at the Shipping Board, where he retained his dual position as Director of the Division of Planning and Statistics and member of the Board; then to the War Trade Board, where he helped Swanson, the new director of research, and attended meetings as a member of the Board; then lunch with Hurley and Franklin if it was Wednesday, with the War Trade Board once a week, or with some expert from another department at that inevitable eating and talking place, the Cosmos Club. The afternoon was spent at the War Industries Board, where H. R. Hatfield, the professor of accounting from Berkeley, had been made director of the new Division of Planning and Statistics; then at the rooms of the new Central Bureau; and finally back at the Shipping Board. Dinner was usually devoted to some "shop talk" duet, trio, or chorus, the evening and the requisite part of the night to miscellaneous work in office or committee room, or to plowing through the contents of a bulging brief case at home.

Of the new tasks those connected with the War Industries Board and "Central" took up most time. The War Industries Board had by mid-1918 to face three grim tasks: far-reaching conservation of resources, ruthless reduction of civilian production, and a hard-boiled predisposition to refuse priorities.

Conservation was pressed hard by taking over the pioneer work the Commercial Economy Board had started in 1917. Shaw, Gay, and Copeland brought their experience into the Conservation Division which replaced the old Board. To it was added the indefatigable drive of Brigadier General Hugh S. Johnson, whose reputation for getting things done was already almost legendary; also the services of experts on industrial processes or materials. By demonstration and exhortation the Division achieved a great reduction in the number of styles, patterns, sizes, colors, or finishes of products, induced manufacturers to use substitute materials for those wanted by the war plants, and persuaded the armed forces to take some steps toward standardizing their specifications of goods.

Serious efforts to reduce civilian supplies had been side-stepped by the War Industries Board during its early career. Now, with import restrictions in effect and the whole control machinery being tightened up, the President ordered the Board to see what savings could be made by reducing or eliminating nonessential production. Judge Edwin Parker, chairman of the "Industrial Adjustment Committee" which undertook the inquiry, called on Gay for help at the preliminary meetings, and asked him to write a memorandum on the general rules that should be applied. Armed with this document and verbal advice from its author, the judge went into action so ruthlessly that his group became known as the Snickersnee Committee. Industry after industry was summoned before it, and each in turn saw its requests for material halved or quartered by a single stroke.

The third task of the War Industries Board, and one requiring a competent statistical service, was that of steering, chiefly by issuing priorities to the right people, the flow of sufficient goods to meet the manifold needs of the various war agencies. To do this the Board must know what those needs were, but the knowledge had been unprocurable since the start, especially from the army. That service had at least seven branches submitting separate and often incommensurable estimates of requirements. Some of the figures were fantastically high: one for mules' halters would have been generous even if every beast were hydra-headed, while one for boots could be justified only if American soldiers were centipedes.

If the War Industries Board, its statistical division, and its commodity experts were to do their job well the coöperation of the army must be won, by peaceful persuasion if possible, otherwise by force. Gay was assigned to the job. General Goethals, now in charge of Army purchases, storage, and traffic, supported him by ordering that officers who had been detailed to coöperate with the fifty different sections of the Board should be at their desks in the section rooms during working hours. News of this decree was hailed with delight; yet in very few cases was the command obeyed. Gay and Hatfield therefore carried the fight to a higher level, and eventually secured from the Secretary of War an order placing the army records at the disposal of the War Industries Board's statisticians. The era of unsatisfactory liaison seemed ended; but so also, within two weeks, was the war. It had taken almost as long to convert the army as to conquer the Germans.

Another struggle that had scarcely ended when the Armistice rendered the outcome unimportant was the effort to produce a "conspectus" of war activities of the government. The Central Bureau of Planning and Statistics was established in mid-June to do the work. It was to be an independent agency, responsible only to the President, but reporting to him through Baruch. As its director, Gay was empowered to gather together a group of men who would receive weekly and monthly progress reports from the governmental agencies, and embody the data in concise surveys that would show what was being accomplished. Some surveys would cover only one week or one department; but the main product would be the monthly consolidated conspectus intended to give the President a bird's-eye picture of the whole course of events and afford current reliable information to guide him in reaching decisions on policy.

Gay and Dennison flung themselves into this new task with their usual vigor. By the end of July the first report was on its way to the White House, summarizing the War Department's account of the preceding week's work and calling attention to the significant successes or failures in the army program. It was followed by monthly reports on the navy, the railroads, and changes in the fuel situation. An estimate was made of the tonnage likely to be available for army cargoes in 1919. But the first consolidated conspectus was not ready until early November.

In collecting the material for its reports, the Bureau quickly discovered many defects in the sources of supply. For example, the navy's statistical organization was found to be almost as poor and divided as was that of the army. Secretary Daniels and Assistant-Secretary F. D. Roosevelt admitted that an improved unified system would be helpful. "Central" promptly submitted a plan which found favor and led to action.

Duplication of effort was also frequently unearthed. One war agency eager for facts was usually unaware that another might already have collected them. From this uncoördinated curiosity sprang in part the flood of questionnaires that swept out from Washington or regional offices over the manufacturing and commercial establishments of the country. There were too many of them; often they were badly worded; they asked questions involving a heavy outlay of time and labor if honest answers were to be given; and frequently they sought information that had already been sent, but called for it in such a form that the work had to be done all over again.

The Central Bureau began operations just as a nation-wide revolt was brewing against filling in blanks. It immediately established a Statistical Clearing House to tell any inquirer what information had already been collected and where it could be found. It hired an expert on questionnaires to criticize and improve proposed inquiries and offered his services to other departments. The statisticians and planners in Gay's other offices joined with Central in this campaign for restrained inquisitiveness, but the fight had not been quite won when the Armistice came.

The Central Bureau did not produce statistics. It worked with the men from other agencies and on the material they supplied. Hence it never grew to be a giant. Of the more than a thousand persons under Gay's direction, only about sixty were in Central. Of these, almost two-thirds possessed high professional or technical qualifications. All knew one another and felt a sense of lively loyalty to their bureau and its chief. In their weekly meetings they eagerly discussed what might be done, then mercilessly criticized each draft report submitted for scrutiny. Even more fervently than any of Gay's other organizations did they believe in the motto, "It can't be done, but here it is." Less readily than the other groups did they disintegrate when the news came that fighting had stopped.

That news, though not unexpected after the negotiations of the preceding five weeks, came almost as a personal blow to Gay. For ten months he had, in Hatfield's words, worked

> unceasingly, shouldering any responsibility, shunning no man's criticism, courting no one's approval. Others of us felt discouraged at times. I know that I resigned twice myself, and Swanson of War Trade did so every few weeks. But Gay was always composed, reliant, apparently free from the weakness either of exultation or depression. But when the Armistice came he too fell into the Slough of Despond.

His many labors were just coming to as many successful heads: the overdue harvest of ships for the army was being gathered in; the statistical organizations at War Trade and War Industries were swinging into full productive pace; Central had finished its first consolidated report; and the army had promised to tell all. "The era of unsatisfactory work seemed ended, the opportunity for which Gay and those associated with him had longed and worked and prayed seemed already realized; and then came that wretched armistice." "Of course I was deeply relieved," Gay wrote his wife. "The terrible strain is almost over. But I confess to a personal sense of baulked 'instinct of workmanship.' "

The sense of frustration was short-lived. On November 9 Gay and Dennison found time to carry out a long-deferred plan: they went to have their shoes shined, then walked home to read the *Saturday Evening Post.* On the morning of November 11 McCormick led his War Trade Board staff in a parade to the White House as part of the capital's jubilation. From that march Gay hurried back to his office, where he was absorbed till late at night, as well as many following nights, on a "completely new set of problems, those of reconstruction," bending his energies in a reverse direction. On the 16th he wrote: "There is need for every man I can command, and every bit of planning both for those under me and those over me. But men are leaving right and left, and the necessary organization at the top is not creative." A week later he hoped to be back home by February; but it was the end of June before he got there, and in the meantime there were weeks when he was as busy "buffeting the whirlpool" as he had ever been during the hardest days of the war.

Three duties kept him. The War Industries Board was promptly dismantled and his work there ended at once; but he remained a member of the Shipping and War Trade Boards and was also in charge of the Central Bureau. The boards were deafened by the clamor for an instant return to normalcy. "They are a hungry pack," he observed in early December after hearing a mass delegation demand immediate abolition of controls on foreign trade and shipping.

There was, however, too much unfinished business to permit the granting of these requests. The Shipping Board faced the vast problem of getting the army back home and of continuing for some time the flow of food or fuel to Europe. Further, it was well aware of the fear in some European minds that America would steer the mounting output of her shipyards into an energetic pursuit of foreign trade rather than continue coöperation with her fellow victors. "We play carelessly with high explosives," wrote Tower from his vantage point in the London Mission office, "if our proposed employment of extra tonnage is not promptly declared, in terms that cannot be misread, to be a joint one for the common good."

What Gay called "the messy shipping situation," both in its immediate aspects and in terms of a long-run policy for the American merchant marine, therefore kept the members of the Shipping Board busy and perplexed. One particularly perplexing assignment fell into Gay's lap when the Board was requested to help transfer from Vladivostok to Europe the army of Czechoslovak soldiers who had made their way across Siberia. The plight of the 4000 men, mostly sick or wounded and lacking hospital accommodation, got on Gay's nerves. He vowed he would not rest till he got some transportation "for these poor wretches, freezing in a box-car." He went "from pillar to post — War Department to Shipping Board and back again, State Department, War Trade Board, Red Cross, and then back or around the circle," appealing to the British for aid, learning that some link in the chain had snapped, but finally completing the arrangement. The project started in March, and by mid-August he had the satisfaction of learning that the men had been repatriated either directly through Trieste or across the Pacific, America, and France. Of the men who thus circumnavigated the globe he commented: "Xenophon's march was nothing to that."

At the War Trade Board the process of orderly decontrol was equally full of complex, vexatious problems, and when the acting chairman was laid low by illness Gay had to take charge for a month. He fought a losing battle with the Food Administration and the

Department of Agriculture over the return to free export of pork. He worked long over a draft of regulations to prevent an influx of German dyestuffs and potash until Congress could decide whether American infant producers were to be exposed to competition. Economic relations with Russia provoked a headache for which there was no cure. The War Trade Board was eager to liquidate its Russian Bureau, which had originally dealt with the Tsar's ministers. It could find no way of discussing American claims with the Bolshevik rulers, and meanwhile was being compelled by decisions higher up to provide considerable sums for the anti-Bolshevik cause. After vainly trying to see where this was leading, the Board left Gay to draft a cablegram urging the President in Paris to ban the sinking of any more dollars in Siberian railroads or any other venture. "We seem to have caught a Russian bear that we cannot let go," he concluded, and prophesied that litigation over Russian claims and counterclaims would continue into the third and fourth generations.

While the labor in the shipping and foreign trade fields seemed to yield only a crop of "discouraging weeds," there was one plot in Washington that Gay cultivated with industry, patience, and resourcefulness, ready every Monday morning to "spit on [his] hands again and commence hoeing once more." This was the Central Bureau. The Armistice caught the Bureau changing from low to middle gear, and for a moment it seemed there was nowhere to go. As new roads were never slow in becoming visible on Gay's map, immediate as well as long-run destinations were soon set. One immediate job was to continue helping any departments that were interested in improving their statistical methods. Daniels and Roosevelt were most responsive; State, Post Office, and Interior were willing to accept aid; while the Treasury not only instructed the heads of all its bureaus and divisions to establish contact with "Central" but requested help in revising its organization chart dated 1904. Army alone was hostile, partly because it felt the Bureau's reports had overemphasized deficiencies in the program and failed to point out solid achievements.

Meanwhile weekly interdepartmental conferences of statisticians examined proposals for improving and standardizing techniques and discussed plans for making a business barometer. An attempt was thus made to remedy the defects revealed by the war while the memory of those shortcomings was still fresh.

In early December the Central Bureau was given a first-class task to discharge. When Gay returned to Washington from his Thanksgiving dinner in Cambridge, he found on his desk a memorandum signed by the President. It designated Central as "the official source through which shall be obtained economic data required by the American delegates at the Peace Conference." He was not surprised to receive the assignment or unaware of the fantastic story of American unpreparedness for peacemaking that lay behind it. For more than a year the group of scholars gathered together by Colonel House had been quietly working in New York. "The Inquiry," as it was colorlessly called, had been studying the questions that were expected to come up at the peace conference and collecting data on them — historical, geographical, ethnological, economic, and statistical.

On the first three categories a mountain of material was collected, but to the last two scant attention was paid. Professor Allyn Young, the lone economist, pleaded persistently without avail for aid in making more preparation on the economic side. Nobody, from the President downward, seemed interested either in the economic problems that would arise in the peace discussions or in those which would come as a legacy of the distortion caused by war. When the President was about to sail, the number of Inquiry men ordered to accompany the Peace Commission was cut down by executive order from 80 to 23, and Young's name was among those eliminated. It was subsequently restored, but no other economists were added to help him. The Commission contained no representative of the Treasury, the war boards, or any of the Washington agencies that dealt with international economic questions.

As this queer lopsidedness of representation and interest became known, something akin to alarm spread through the departments.

The Treasury dollar-a-year men drafted a letter, to be sent to Wilson through McAdoo, urging preparation for economic discussions. The reply was that no such action was necessary. Pleas by Baruch and others were similarly rebuffed and no steps were taken to select the chief economic advisers until Wilson was in New York ready to board ship. Only then did his secretary ring up Baruch, McCormick, and Garfield, asking them to be ready to cross the ocean when they were called by cable. Baruch instantly set a group of experts to work collecting data and told them they would go with him if he was summoned to Paris. When the cablegram came it specified that Baruch and McCormick were to come alone; and the same was true of the invitations to Albert Strauss and T. W. Lamont when they were called on to aid in the financial discussions which Wilson had discovered, on arriving in Europe, were to be important items on the agenda.

Concern over Wilson's lack of interest in economic matters stimulated some members of Gay's group to action. The dropping of Allyn Young seemed calamitous and the President must be persuaded to do something to fill the void. A memorandum was therefore hastily drawn up. From the look of the document it was prepared in somebody's lodgings rather than in any office; the typing is amateurish, the paper common, and there is neither letterhead nor date. The four sheets were somehow got through to Wilson before he sailed and he was induced to append what appears to be a very hastily scribbled signature.

This memorandum listed the five divisions or bureaus headed by Gay. It said they were "by far the most able and best equipped organizations for supplying information on economic matters." It referred to the "inadequate" studies of The Inquiry and the limited economic material collected by Army Intelligence. It noted that cables from Paris were already indicating "great confusion in estimates of economic conditions which [were] being made by American representatives gathering there," and that these representatives were feeling ill-prepared to deal with proposals the French and British were making. Hence, admitted the President through the words put into his mouth, "It is believed essential that there be one authoritative and exclusive source for the supplying of information of this character," and the statistical organizations which Gay had built up were, therefore, working together through the Central Bureau, to be that source.

To discharge this major task Gay virtually merged his staffs, set them to work compiling the kind of information the conference was expected to need, and sent a sextet of his most able men to Paris. The job had to be done by a certain date if the product was to catch the boat; so back came the familiar round of unstinted labor, meal-less days, rest-less Sundays, sleep-less nights — and then the discovery that the report need not leave the country for another two weeks. The whole job was therefore done again and improved in another round of vigils. The report — eight volumes — was dashed off by special messenger to Major John Foster Dulles of the War Trade Board, who was to head the Central Bureau team in Paris.

The team of six included, besides Dulles, such veterans of the Gay corps as Tower, Leith, and Leo Wolman. Landing in the midst of a bitter scramble for power and authority between the American groups already in Paris, it immediately discovered that its independent standing, based on the President's memorandum, made it unwelcome. Soon, however, the discord ended and the newcomers were merged in the staff controlled by Allyn Young or in some other group. There was a suggestion that Gay be invited over, but, according to one of his friends, this proposal was always effectively opposed by Dr. Mezes, a former president of the University of Texas, who, as brother-in-law of Colonel House and director of The Inquiry, wielded great authority. His contention, as it filtered through to Central, was that Professors Haskins, Coolidge, and Gay constituted the most dangerous gang in American university life. With Haskins in Paris, and Coolidge only with difficulty kept in exile in Vienna or points beyond, it would be hazardous to let the third brigand come to Europe.

Central's men and material contributed little to the peacemaking. The kind of information they could supply was not needed, for the economic problems actually discussed were such that no improvised fact-finding was of much use. The American Commission's ill-preparedness made at least one of Gay's delegates feel that he and his colleagues were about a year behind their British and French counterparts. Hence the calls on Central quickly died down, and some of the experts returned home.

As the hope of contributing to the peace settlement faded, Gay strove more earnestly to preserve Central as a permanent servant of America at peace. He believed that its periodical reports, comprehensive information service, and widespread contact with departments could be of great value in the years ahead. The Bureau could supply American data to the League of Nations and to Americans attached to the League. At home it could help the national budget system which all observers were convinced must be established to replace the haphazard method of allotting funds. It could scrutinize departmental estimates in the light of its knowledge of operations, requirements, and past performance, recommend to the President what estimates should be approved or reduced, and thus facilitate his task of preparing a single appropriation measure for submission to Congress.

More important still, it could keep the chief executive constantly in touch with his departments, let him know what the government was getting from them for the money it supplied, serving as his eyes and ears and as a yardstick by which achievement could be compared with promise. It would thus function "as a nervous system to the vast and complex organization of the government, furnishing to the controlling brain the information necessary for directing the efficient operation of the various members." For such tasks it would need to be an independent body, preferably attached to the Executive Office.

Gay had a chance to present these ideas to the President in person when Wilson was back home in early March. His reception was "very cordial." The President said he was familiar with the Bureau's conspectus, was in the habit of reading it regularly, wished the good work to continue, and hoped to be able later, when Congress reassembled, to secure the necessary funds. Meanwhile he promised to seek some way of keeping the Bureau alive when its appropriation expired on June 30. In case his search proved fruitless, he urged that all records be kept in such order that work could be resumed when money became available.

Despite the note of hope, Wilson's words were really the Bureau's death sentence. His search was unavailing and when Gay called on the Speaker of the House of Representatives to learn if there was any chance of reprieve, he was told there was none. June therefore brought the end in sight for the Bureau as it did for the other war agencies.[2] Gay helped to close it down in midmonth, attended the final meeting of the War Trade Board on the afternoon of June 30, and took the train for Boston that night. He was one of the last invaders to leave Washington.

"It has been a great year and a half" was his farewell comment. It had been a strenuous year and a half since he first arrived for full-time service and slept in a "rat-hole of a room at the Cosmos Club." Of all that time — about 550 days — only 70 had been spent off duty in week-end trips to Cambridge, one week's vacation, and two bouts of influenza. Mrs. Gay had throughout felt unable to join him, but his son was with him during early 1918, serving as custodian, getting him up in the morning, putting him through setting-up exercises, hurrying him through breakfast and to his office, making him keep his many appointments, turning people tactfully out of his room, and driving the intrusive ones away.

When the son went into army camp, Dennison took over the job as bodyguard. He had brought his wife and children to Washington

[2] In 1921 Congress passed a law establishing the budgetary system and providing for a Budget Bureau in the Treasury. The Bureau helped the President prepare a budget, scrutinized departmental estimates and accounting. In 1939 it was transferred to the President's Executive Office, and its director became solely responsible to the President. Its activities in large measure resemble those which Gay had suggested might be performed by the Central Bureau.

and taken a house in the city (or during the summer out in Chevy Chase). There on week-ends, and later as permanent guest, Gay got a chance to relax by romping with four irrepressible youngsters, joining in the "customary singing," listening to the piano-player or pedaling it himself through a Mozart sonata or an arrangement of a Beethoven symphony. When the *New York Times* had been dutifully read according to schedule, from 1 A.M. to 2 A.M., and the nightly pianola performance ended, he was packed off to bed in a room equipped on hot nights with a large electric fan which made sleep possible. No amount of such friendly solicitude could, however, prevent or repair all the wear and tear of the sedentary work, long hours, and careless diet. Gay emerged from his wartime services much overweight and with a "heart condition."

Perhaps these were small prices to pay for the solid achievements that stood to his credit and for the reputation he won among the men with whom or for whom he worked. Dean Acheson described him as "one of the 'kings' of Washington." His colleagues decided that he was, in Hatfield's words, "a born administrator, indefatigable in work, inspiring to his associates, fearless, outspoken yet diplomatic . . . a real force in Washington." In advocacy, defense, or implementation of policies he thought essential he would fight with all comers, no matter how high their status. But he was equally ready to answer calls in a city where "Get Gay's advice and help!" came to be an instinctive suggestion. When the Treasury requested him to help plan a Thrift and Savings Campaign he wrote his wife: "They are all tending greatly to exaggerate what I can do. I find my reputation seems to be growing far beyond my real capacity. But I can only plug along and do what I can — or rather, since this is becoming my specialty, find someone else to do it if I can."

Others did not accept Gay's estimate of himself and his work. In June 1918, Harvard gave him, in company with the British ambassador and John Masefield, an honorary LL.D. The citation read "Student of economics, who searches its principles in the past, is applying them in the present, and trains men to use them in the future; in each of these arts a master mind." A year later, when he was packing his papers, he put aside a sheaf of farewell letters. One, from a member of the Shipping Board, wound up with the remark: "I think there is hardly a member of your staff who would not roll in the mud at your request, in full confidence that it was going to accomplish some great end." Another, from the Assistant Secretary of the Navy, said: "I hope to see you again before you leave town, but if not, again thank you for the coöperation you have given us regarding the progress of work in the naval establishment, particularly during the war." And a third, written by a charter member of the American Shipping Mission in London, said:

> It is not a bit too much to say that your energy, intelligence, and devotion, applied to what was really the crucial point in American participation in the war, were simply indispensable. I have some idea of the formidable difficulties with which you had to contend, and if there is anyone, from the President down, who did more to win the war, I should like to know who it is.

Perhaps the best measure of a man's work is to be found in the number and kind of jobs he is offered when an old one is completed. Those offers and Gay's response to them make the subject of the next chapter.

# IV

## THE NEW YORK EVENING POST

### 1919–1923

DURING THE CROWDED MONTHS of war work Gay had little time to think about his own future. When a prominent Michigan alumnus asked whether he would be interested in the presidency of his old university, he replied that all his attention would be needed in Cambridge when normal conditions returned. After the Armistice, however, it quickly became apparent that he need not return to his Harvard deanship unless he wished to do so. His name was mentioned by newspapers in connection with presidential vacancies at the universities of Michigan, California, Wisconsin, and Pennsylvania. He was tentatively approached by some business corporations. Shipping Board colleagues urged him to stay with them. Carter Glass, Secretary of the Treasury, invited him to become director of the War Risks Insurance Bureau, an agency with a vast pay roll and records that were in dire confusion.

To these feelers Gay's response was cool or cold, partly because the proffered positions did not attract him, but chiefly because he was considering a far more tempting invitation. On January 14, 1919, Thomas W. Lamont wrote from Wall Street to inquire whether Gay would be in New York in the near future, since, as he said, "I am very anxious to have an uninterrupted word with you." When Gay replied that he could not leave his desk at the moment, Lamont hurried to Washington and the two men spent the evening of January 15 at the house of a friend of both. During a long discussion of peace and postwar problems, Lamont revealed the purpose of his visit by inviting Gay to consider accepting the editorship of the New York *Evening Post,* which he had recently bought. He guaranteed complete independence, both managerial and editorial, and ample funds to make the paper "the leading organ of opinion in the United States."

The offer took Gay completely by surprise; but he managed to ask some pertinent questions, said he would keep the matter "far back in his mind," promised to think most carefully about it, and suggested that Lamont had better think about it still more. Since the banker was leaving immediately for the Peace Conference, further discussion was to be conducted with Dwight Morrow, Lamont's partner in the Morgan firm.

Gay went home as much excited as he was surprised. He wrote his daughter: "You could never guess what [Lamont] offered me. No, it is not a partnership with J. P. Morgans, but something which attracts me much more." He had been led to the top of a high mountain, and from that vantage point the view behind — of classrooms and a dean's office — looked flat and uninviting, while the prospect ahead was both exhilarating and challenging. He had been invited to choose between the two, to make — at fifty-one — a complete change of career. If he went back to Harvard, it would be the old round of running the Business School on a precarious inadequate income, of carrying the double load of teaching and deaning, neglecting his research, and living in "material conditions" which the higher level of prices and taxes would render "too cramped and penurious," even if President Lowell did succeed in his ambitious endowment campaign and was thereby able to raise salaries by 25 per cent.

The new career would offer scope for those executive and organizing capacities which the Washington work had shown he possessed; it would take him into the thick of the world of affairs; and it would end the days of divided vocation. As he wrote to Dr. Eliot after he had made his choice,

There are within me, as you must have observed, two tendencies, one toward scholarship and the other toward administration. The two things do not combine very well; at least I have not been able to combine them to my satisfaction. The appeal of active life has come to be very strong. I know that there is at least one book that I ought to write; it was difficult to do it while remaining at Harvard and it may be impossible in New York. I do not give up the thought altogether, but trust that my previous training will serve a useful purpose in my new work, which I am accepting with a great sense of responsibility.

It is tempting to speculate what Gay's later career might have been if an offer which came in late June had arrived three or four months earlier. When Professor Leith, one of the Central Bureau men sent to Paris, returned home in March 1919, he reported a general agreement among the American delegates that an Economic Commission would be a very important part of the League of Nations; also an almost unanimous agreement that Gay was "the man clearly indicated" as American member of the international fact-finding and planning division of the Commission.

Gay heard nothing more of this matter until George Rublee descended on him in late June, bearing a request from J. A. Salter, the newly chosen head of the League's Economic and Financial Section. As chief officer of the Allied Maritime Transport Council, Salter had come to know Rublee intimately and watched Gay's fight for real inter-Allied coöperation. Salter therefore wrote Rublee:

I am extremely anxious to have associated with me the best possible people I can get — and particularly the best possible person from America. . . From every quarter from which I can get advice I find a unanimous opinion that it would be an enormous advantage if it were possible to induce Gay to come to Geneva. Do you think it would be possible? If so, I wonder whether, as one who knows both him, me, and the general idea of the work, you would mind sounding him.

In this sounding Gay was to be assured that since no organization had yet taken shape he "could have practically whatever he preferred in the economic sphere"; that the Section was free to do "practically anything that proves both desirable and practicable from the international point of view"; and that "if Gay would come he would, I'm sure, have very great scope — certainly I wouldn't (and I'm sure Drummond [Secretary-General of the League] wouldn't) want to crab or cramp his work."

By the time Salter's feeler reached Gay he had virtually decided to take the newspaper job. In informing Rublee of this he wrote: "I feel I can render even more useful service to the cause of international organization in this new capacity on this side of the ocean," then went on to recommend Wesley Mitchell for the post. Events soon proved that he was wise in declining the offer, since it is safe to assume that America's rejection of the League would have forced him to withdraw from Geneva almost as soon as he had settled in there. But other events were later to throw doubt on the wisdom of the choice he had made.

One of the first thoughts that came into Gay's mind when Lamont uncovered his proposal was the recollection that forty years earlier his father had written, "More than either a physician or a lawyer, I think I should like you to be a journalist," because in that profession "the widest and most powerful influence can be used." If the son wished to exert wide and powerful influence it would be hard to think of a better instrument than the *Evening Post.* Founded by Alexander Hamilton in 1801, it carried at its masthead Hamilton's statement of high purpose: "The design of this paper is to diffuse among the people correct information on all interesting subjects, to inculcate just principles in religion, morals, and politics; and to cultivate a taste for sound literature."

Throughout the nineteenth century a series of great editors — including Cullen Bryant, Bigelow, Schurz, and, greatest of all, Godkin — had been doughty defenders of public righteousness, denouncing abuses by capital and labor alike, flaying Tammany and trusts with equal courage, and braving popular displeasure by such policies as damning Cleveland's intervention in the Venezuela dispute or opposing the war with Spain. Consequently the *Post* always had plenty of enemies, but it never lost the respect of those who cared for intelligent treatment of controversies or for some attention to the things of the intellect. Godkin had been a "journalists' journalist"; his paper was one of the most widely "clipped" in the country, and many an editor far away from New York waited to see what the *Post* said before taking a stand on some new issue.

It had always been a "class"—a "middle" or "upper income bracket"—rather than a "popular" journal, and its circulation fluctuated just below 30,000 copies daily. Businessmen were pleased with its excellent financial news. Others liked its sympathetic attention to welfare movements, charitable or settlement work, social experiments, or such schemes for public control as the Interstate Commerce Commission. Many found it the best paper on music, books, drama, or art. It did not cater to the morbid or to sports-lovers; those who desired details of a sordid trial or play-by-play reports of games had to seek them elsewhere.

As a piece of property the *Post* had known better days, some of them very good; but since 1900 only five years had seen dividends paid on the stock—quite small ones. The losses piled up heavily after 1913. Costs rose, competition with six other evening papers became more intense, but neither a reduced price nor a half-hearted attempt to make the paper "popular" did anything to increase circulation or patronage by advertisers. Those who knew the inside of the *Post* attributed the trouble to obsolete equipment, old-fashioned methods, and shattered morale. Outsiders attributed it to the fact that the pacifism of its owner, Oswald Garrison Villard, sounded like pro-Germanism once the United States had entered the war. By 1918 the paper was headed for the rocks and Villard was ready to sell it.

Lamont bought it in mid-1918 for almost a million dollars, of which only one-tenth was paid for the physical assets, the balance for the goodwill. He had two reasons for doing so. The first was his desire to have something to do with a newspaper. Having gone from Harvard into journalism and worked as a reporter on the New York *Tribune* in 1893–94, he bore out the truth of the contention that a man who gets printer's ink on his fingers can never wash it off. To the end of his life he liked to be connected with newspapers, magazines, and periodicals; his friends included novelists, poets, journalists, and publishers. His zest for life and his interest in public affairs could not be fully satisfied by a banking career, even one that touched the highest levels of international finance.

His second reason was the desire to build a monument to his elder brother Hammond, whose untimely death in 1909 at forty-five ended a brilliant career which included six years of journalism in places as far apart as Albany and Seattle, eight of university teaching, six as managing editor of the *Post*, and three as editor of the *Nation*. The younger brother hoped to perpetuate the older one's sense of the journalist's mission in a revitalized newspaper, built on the old foundations and so intelligently, independently, and courageously conducted that it would win (or regain) repute as an American counterpart of the *Manchester Guardian* or London *Economist*. Perhaps the day might come when he would retire from banking and devote his whole attention to public life, with the *Post* as his main interest and mouthpiece.

As that day was probably remote in 1918, he put the control of the paper in the hands of three trustees, of whom Ellery Sedgwick, editor of the *Atlantic Monthly*, was the most experienced in journalistic affairs. Actual management he left, for the duration of the war, in the hands of the old staff. It was clear to him, however, that his paper, floundering and drifting aimlessly, needed a man in the early prime of life, vigorous, with enough experience to take a firm hold of its business and editorial policies. Gay seemed to be the obvious choice. His work at the Business School was intimately known to Lamont; his response (in August 1918) to a request for advice about inaugurating some profit-sharing or management-sharing system for the staff of the *Post* had been a penetrating analysis of motives and methods; and the quality of his Washington performance was common knowledge.

Consultation with Dr. Eliot, Dwight Morrow, and Sedgwick strengthened Lamont's belief that Gay was the man he needed. In a letter which gave Rollo Ogden, manager of the *Post*, a hint that change was in the wind he summed up the assets and liabilities of the prospective candidate as follows:

He has had no training as a newspaper man and he has had no experience as a business man in the ordinary sense of the word. On the other hand he is of such extraordinary capacity, character, and soundness of vision that I should be willing to trust him with practically any job in the country and I feel certain he would walk away with it. He is a splendid organizer. What his politics are I do not know. I hope he is a Republican, but I doubt it. Morrow and all the people at Washington tell me he has done a wonderful job over there. . .

Gay may not be the man at all, although I think he is. I may not succeed in securing his services, but he is the type of man that the *Evening Post* ought to have to build up the paper. He has astonishing energy and staying power, a reach of imagination and ability to arouse loyalty and enthusiasm in those who work with him that accounts largely for his effectiveness. He is courageous enough to fight anybody, but has always enough common sense to know when to accept something less than his full share.

While Gay was being appraised, he himself was taking stock. Through one friend he got Bruce Barton's opinion, which was that the job was "unquestionably *the* great newspaper opportunity of the country." Through another he learned about salaries and the kind of remuneration that ought to be paid for straightening out "the particular paper spoken of." By early May he was ready to submit to Morrow the basic conditions for a fair arrangement. These included: (1) An initial contract for five years, renewable at the end of that time if the paper had become, or was about to become, a success. (2) Complete independence as to editorial policy and business management. (3) The provision, throughout the entire five years, of adequate working capital up to a figure determined by Lamont and accepted by Gay. (4) A salary of at least $20,000, plus a share in any savings or financial gains resulting from Gay's management.

These terms, accompanied by the comments thereon of Morrow and Sedgwick, were sent to Lamont in Paris. The commentators questioned the wisdom of a cast-iron five-year contract, and were a little worried over the insistence on "complete independence" or, as Sedgwick put it, of placing the property for a very considerable period "entirely at Dean Gay's mercy." On the other hand they agreed that management of the paper must be somebody's "complete and entire job," and Sedgwick admitted that he was quite willing to gamble on Gay's judgment and character. "He has been abundantly tried out in diverse directions"; has succeeded in everything; is moderate and sane; his convictions are definite and founded on reason; he works well in harness; and "his political and social temper is pretty near to yours and mine."

Lamont urged Gay to come to Paris in order to settle the matter there and also "to size up the situation while the big-wigs are wigging in Paris and meet the real people." As Gay was unable to get away, further discussion had to be left till Lamont returned. By July he was back, and on the evening of the 18th the two men dined and discussed the terms on his yacht as it steamed up the river to Yonkers. On the 21st Lamont sent the formal invitation to "undertake the active direction and management from January 1, 1920, or as much earlier as you may elect, your personal engagement with me, however, to begin about August 15, 1919."

The invitation set forth terms and intent. Control by the trio of trustees would cease.

> In your handling of the paper I should wish you to feel and to exercise complete independence of judgment and of management. This does not mean that I plan to eliminate my own personality. On the contrary, I should expect you to consult me on major matters and to welcome my frequent attendance upon your councils. But the final determination of policies I should leave in your hands.

Then followed a promise to welcome, when the paper became "a profitable property," some arrangement whereby Gay in particular and his working associates would share in its prosperity. "So far as you and I are concerned I earnestly hope that the relationship, if established, will work out as that of close friends and partners, and I shall do everything I can to that end."

Next came the financial clauses:

Before the property reaches a paying basis it may be necessary for me to make considerable further investment in it. On this point I believe my ideas are fully as generous as your own, and I shall be prepared to back up your ideas to the limit of my ability. If you desire now, before being fully conversant with the conditions, to have me name a sum for development, I am prepared to do so, though I should prefer first to have your full matured ideas.

The salary offered was $25,000, and the first duty was to be a brief trip to Europe to get the feel of conditions and men over there.

Then came a paragraph such as is perhaps unusual in business compacts:

We are both, as you have said, entering into this relationship just a little in the dark, and for that reason I think neither of us should be bound too rigidly. My suggestion is that in the event we should have mistaken each other's ideas and should wish to dissolve the "partnership," each should be free to do so on giving the other twelve months' notice. But in any event and regardless of whether such notice came from you or from me, I should engage that by August 15, 1924, you should receive as compensation an aggregate of not less than $125,000.

Gay's proposal of a five-year contract was thus put aside. In its place was a guarantee that, whatever happened, he would receive the equivalent of five years' salary.

The final paragraph read like a testimonial:

I feel that your qualities of mind and of character destine you for a part in the country's life even more important than the honorable one you have already fulfilled. I hope you will regard the *Evening Post* as offering you this larger opportunity. The decision is a momentous one for us both, and I know that both you and your wife will reach a wise judgment, whatever it may be.

To this offer Gay asked for only one further bit of definition, namely, that the "sum for development" be fixed at $250,000. Lamont promptly complied with the request and expressed his willingness, if this amount should not be sufficient, to make arrangements for providing more working capital. Gay's acceptance was immediate (August 1). By August 5 he was visiting the *Post* building at 20 Vesey Street to meet his new associates and take stock of the situation. He was also inviting colleagues of wartime Washington to join him. Next day he found an apartment on Madison Avenue near Central Park. On the 11th the newspapers announced he was "assuming general direction of the *Evening Post* and becoming president of the Corporation." Two days later he tendered his resignation to Harvard, and by the 23rd was on the Atlantic bound for Europe. His brief case was crammed with letters of introduction to Britons and Frenchmen high in politics, business, and journalism. It was seventeen years, almost to the very week, since he had last crossed the ocean. On that trip the only important documents he carried had been a Berlin diploma and a letter officially announcing his appointment as instructor at Harvard.

So started Gay's third great adventure. It was not a pioneer building job, as had been the Business School and the Washington agencies. Instead it called for the rebuilding of an ancient dilapidated structure. He had accepted the task as the most interesting among a number of opportunities. He was interested in making, or in this case remaking, a newspaper — a clean, honest, independent, and interesting paper. He realized that the *Post* would not leap into great popularity, but could have a gradually increasing circulation of high quality. His sponsor was with him in the desire that the paper be "liberal, progressive, constructive, not fanatical or smugly self-righteous." His friends poured in their congratulations to New York, their regrets for Harvard, and their good wishes for the high endeavor. Here and there a different note was struck. One friend regretted that Gay had "deserted the academic shades to go into uplift work." Another had a "real horror of seeing [him] sacrificed to the undertaking." A third, having tried to dissuade him, felt, as he put it later, that Gay had embarked on "a quixotic journalistic enterprise."

The surprising feature of the negotiations is the lack of any serious attempt to get a firsthand idea of the physical or financial condition of the *Post*. Lamont was too busy to look into the situation, and Gay did not go to the office or plant before he accepted the job. He seems to have bothered little about the state of the finances, and almost the only thing he knew about them was that there had been no profits since 1917. He was aware the enterprise was not in a healthy state, but had not realized how sick it was until he met the men in charge. From them he received a "douche of cold water about the critical situation of the paper in every respect — circulation and advertising and high cost of operation. It was a pretty discouraged group of managers. But after two hours of it," he wrote his wife, "I came away more confident than I have felt at any time that we shall make a success of it."

In that faith he went to Europe to glance at postwar conditions, learn what he could about his new work from men in charge of papers, and establish contact with present or prospective correspondents. Four weeks in England and one in Paris were spent in endless interviewing. The two score letters of introduction given him by Lamont, Dennison, Rublee, and others opened the doors of men whose names read like a very select *Who's Who*. He promptly mailed them, and equally promptly received replies. Wickham Steed, editor of *The Times*, said: "Come round to my office." Lord Northcliffe said: "Come to see me at *The Times* office or run down to my house by the sea at Broadstairs on Sunday next," and supplied a train schedule. Austen Chamberlain, Chancellor of the Exchequer, said, "Call on me at 3:15." Lord Robert Cecil invited him to breakfast at 9:30 but when Gay arrived punctually he found that his host, thinking the hour had been set for 8:30, had long since finished his meal.

As one introduction led to another, Gay's days became a rush from one engagement to the next. He met the leading London editors and got some "useful pointers" from them. But in his interview with Northcliffe he gave rather than got, and a few days later a "Message from the Chief" went out to all the senior officers on the *Daily Mail* staff.[1] Its picture of Gay in action was painted by a master hand. "There is," said Northcliffe,

an able young professor from Harvard in London, studying our newspapers. He called on me one day last week and told me that for the first six years of the *Daily Mail* he was living in London. He had a very vivid recollection of the *Daily Mail* of those days, and reminded me of many things which we then did that I had completely forgotten. He said that our paper had become too ordinary, that you rarely see humor, pathos, or descriptive power in it. It often misses important points in the day's news. That you need writers, and he strongly emphasized the word "writers." That the public cannot expect you to find a George Steevens [the *Daily Mail's* most brilliant special correspondent in the 1890's], but it does expect some relief from the daily monotony of the pages of your paper.

I am sorry to say that he went on to compare the paper unfavorably with several others. . . I argued that what he is witnessing is the improvement in the other papers consequent upon their adopting our methods. . . However I was unable to move him. He goes back to edit one of the most important papers in the United States, with a bad opinion of us. It is not difficult to see why he makes these comments. Take this morning's paper, for example.

And take it Northcliffe did, through many blistering paragraphs full of such comments as "Wasted space," "Lack of contrast," "Who wrote this heading?" and "I hate grumbling . . . but I must call attention to these defects."

When Gay was not talking with journalists he was spending his time with those who could tell him about international and labor problems. Salter welcomed him warmly, took him to meet Drummond and other League men, and pulled strings to get him a westward passage. He met several Foreign Office men, and during his brief trip to Paris saw Colonel House (who was still there), Paul Mantoux (another economic historian who had strayed into public life), and André Tardieu. From them he got the feel of French

[1] Northcliffe founded the *Daily Mail* in 1896 and in 1908 gained control of *The Times.*

affairs and opinion, and discovered that "it seems to be true, to put it very mildly, that we are not very popular over here just now."

Next in importance to international questions Gay placed labor problems, and the paralysis of England at that moment by a railroad strike seemed to justify his judgment. He therefore tried to learn what big business, union leaders, and economists were thinking. Dennison had steered him to industrialists whose views seemed progressive, and he searched some of them out. He saw the leading railroad president, who in turn tried to get him an appointment with "Jimmy" Thomas, secretary of the railroad union; but Thomas was too busy with the strike on his hands to talk to outsiders. Though he did catch one or two labor leaders he had to get the left-wing view chiefly from the intellectuals who sympathized with Labor, such as Sidney and Beatrice Webb, R. H. Tawney, G. D. H. Cole, and Arthur Greenwood. He also met Henry Clay, whom he described to his wife as "a prominent young economist and writer, a really level-headed and sane man, whom I hope we can use on the *Post* work over here."

In rare spare hours he tried to link present and past. One of his first calls was on Hubert Hall, friend and guide in the days of research at the Record Office. Twice he stole away for a few hours at the British Museum, "reading on the Industrial Revolution a few rare books I could not obtain at home. I had hoped for some time there, but my days go very fast." He had cast his lot in with Fleet Street and Lombard Street. In that new life there was no time to spare for Bloomsbury.

By mid-October he was back in America and in early November took up his double duty of directing the editorial and managerial policies of the paper. On his desk awaiting him was a report written at Lamont's request by Simeon Strunsky, who had been with the *Post* for a dozen years and was now chief editorial writer. In it Strunsky dispassionately examined the paper's past, present, and prospects. He assumed that Lamont and Gay had no desire to "go popular" or aim at vast circulation by shedding the *Post's* "historic quality." Rather he expected they wished to build on the old foundations, determining in advance at what point of circulation they would be content to stop, and working toward that goal. He believed a daily sale of 75,000 copies was not impossible, and asked why the paper had failed to reach even half that figure.

This failure he attributed to improper promotion, to the disastrous belief that customers would be attracted by slavish but half-hearted and therefore poor imitations of somebody's "Saturday Magazine Literary Section," "Women's Page," or baseball writer's "weird slang performance." The way to win more steady readers did not lie along that low road. Nor, on the other hand, would it be found if an editor forgot for a moment that "an evening paper is largely a daily magazine of entertainment. Tired people in the subways and trains turn for the first ten minutes to the pictures and jokes and editorial features." If they could be well served by the *Post* for those minutes they would continue to read the rest of the paper.

Strunsky therefore recommended that the popularization either be well done or be abandoned, and that the traditional but now rather stodgy distinctive features of the *Post* be revitalized. Break up the "forbidding succession of column after column in unbroken array" on the Editorial Page, and find a place there for signed articles, essays, sketches, criticism—things of quality, wit, distinction. Strengthen the "Literary Supplement," now looked after in his spare time by a man who wrote editorials, headlines, captions for pictures, "and other fol-de-rol," and left most of the reviewing to his overworked assistant, Amy Loveman. "We should have authoritative reviews and win back the tone of scholarship which we had before popularization began." Get a big name and give more space for art reviews, now notoriously poor. Extend the sports columns and appoint correspondents in the colleges. Improve the foreign service, which Gay had already found to be "decrepit." "At all times the *Times* will beat us," but "our opportunity lies in a steady month in, month out correspondence—even by mail—covering world affairs as they move toward a climax and not only when something exciting breaks loose. Get the foreign colonies in New York to look to us for a steady account of their lands." Push this idea further by developing "foreign correspondence from the United States in the same way as from abroad," with letters from San Francisco, Pittsburgh, and the South dealing with trends and conditions rather than with crises. Finally, let there be plenty of local "human interest news—crime, etc. If there were a Thaw case now I should want it to be covered, though with the necessary amount of discretion."

These recommendations, concluded Strunsky, resolved themselves "into the single factor of a directing head not overburdened with detail. Gay's coming will solve that. Such a man would keep the paper in touch with actualities; at present we are too academic, too much on the outside." If he did that, infused greater vitality into the paper, and gave it more attractive physical make-up, there was no reason why the *Post* should not win and keep 75,000 readers without indulging in any "furious campaign for circulation."

Alongside this frank yet constructive assay was another one, dealing with the physical and financial outlook. Its author, Z. L. Potter, had caught Gay's eye by doing an excellent job on housing problems for the War Department, then won his admiration by carrying through several important pieces of work at the Central Bureau, and was now installed as business manager and vice-president of the *Post* with complete charge of the business and financial affairs of the firm. His report was apparently the first attempt at a critical appraisal of the business side of the venture. It showed not merely that the paper had been losing money lately—which everybody knew—but that the prospect of still larger deficits was inevitable. Wages, salaries, and the cost of paper were all going up. When the present lease expired in 1920, Villard, who owned the building, intended to give the *Post* the choice between buying its home or paying more than double the former rent. The salaries of the new president and of other additions to staff would increase overhead expenses. New presses were needed, at a cost of $100,000, and a similar sum should be spent on other improvements.

From such evidence Potter forecast that the deficit for the first year, if revenue stayed up, was likely to be over $350,000. But revenue was not likely to stay up, much less go higher. The recent increase in earnings had been the outcome of the current advertising boom — itself a reflection of the postwar good times — and was bound to vanish when the boom burst. If this happened soon, the excess of spending over revenue might exceed $500,000 during the second year.

When Lamont read this report he exclaimed to Gay: "The figures of possible deficit are pretty staggering, but I am more hopeful than he is. I hope you are too." If Gay was, it was in defiance of all he was learning about the state of his domain. Everything reflected a very old establishment in which the utmost cheese-paring had been practiced for years. The building was cramped and inconvenient. Accumulated junk filled almost every corner, the stock room had neither lock nor custodian, the roll-top desks were falling to pieces, many of the typewriters were in disrepair and there were not enough of them to go around. The linotypes and stereotype machines were aboriginals. The bookkeeping department moved so slowly that some accounts were not mailed until the 10th of each month, the day when discounts for prompt payment expired. There were no interdepartmental telephones. Even the "morgue" had been allowed to run down. While wages were union rates, salaries were much below the market scale. A small "executive committee," chosen from among the senior men by the three trustees, had no effective control over hiring and firing.

As Gay proceeded with his diagnosis it became clear that he had a very sick paper on his hands. Two kinds of treatment were possible. The first would attempt to nurse the patient quietly and gradually back to health, making improvements bit by bit, infecting the staff with a new spirit of hopefulness, avoiding large commitments of resources wherever feasible, and relying on the inevitability of gradualness to win wider public patronage for a better product as well as to increase productive efficiency.

Perhaps this method would have been of no avail. At any rate it was not given a trial. Instead, Gay decided that a major operation was the *Post*'s only hope of survival. The new management must try to improve the paper radically at once, make far-reaching changes, incur heavy additional operating and capital expenditures — even including a new site and building — on top of the increased costs due to higher prices, rent, and wages, and hope that the results would not be long in revealing themselves through expanded sales, greater advertising revenue, and a diminishing deficit.

This policy may have been inevitable. Perhaps it was assumed to be the natural way of regenerating a paper, and was repeated by Curtis when he acquired the *Post* four years later. It also fit Gay's temperament and impulses. He had always been addicted to ambitious projects of study and research. In the Business School he was obliged to cut his coat according to the amount of cloth available, but in Washington he could work on a grand scale without having to weigh the cost, and had therefore been able to move fast and far. That experience influenced his approach to the problems of the *Post*. By doing things quickly in the big way he would get the desired results. By giving the paper the resources of staff and equipment it would need when it was successful he hoped to make it successful.

For formulating and pursuing this policy he felt he must take sole responsibility and therefore sole control. It had been agreed that trustee control was to go, and he got the executive committee abolished as well, thus securing complete power over day-to-day administrative matters, hiring and firing, and other vital issues. In the exercise of that power he drew on the counsel of an advisory board consisting of nine of his chief associates, and as president of the corporation he was "strictly accountable" to the board of directors, to whom a detailed monthly report was submitted. But the board was in effect Lamont, and with him Gay discussed the paper's problems at a weekly luncheon conference if the two men were in the city. Of the advisory board, three members had been brought in by Gay: Donald Scott, colleague of Shipping Board days, became "assistant to the president" and general right-hand man; Chester Lane, former director of the Harvard University Press, became production manager; and Potter was vice-president and business manager. The other six advisers had *Post* records which in the case of Charles Puckette (managing editor) went back eleven years, of Strunsky twelve years, and of Alexander D. Noyes (financial editor) nearly thirty. The board was thus a fusion of new and old blood; all the members except Gay and Potter had grown up in the publishing world, six of them in newspaper offices.

Throughout the fall of 1919 and the first half of 1920 the work of reorganization and expansion was pushed ahead at a pace which made some of the old hands shake their heads and prophesy financial disaster sooner rather than later. The number of names on the News Department's pay roll jumped from 73 to 117. Some of the new men were engaged to give new services or enlarge old ones. The Industrial Editor and his assistant were to provide "the most dependable and authoritative industrial relations news to be found in any newspaper"; the real estate specialist was to serve those who planned to build a house in the suburbs; the automobile expert would supply reliable information for car-owners and compile a "Motorists' Guide." Specialists were taken on to attract the teaching profession with a weekly page of "Educational News"; to build up a Shipping News Service and take over the Ship News Office at the Battery which the *Herald* was now abandoning; to help the veteran John R. Towse, who had done the *Post*'s dramatic and musical criticism for fifty years; to write on art, provide a column of theater gossip, and "review, in a serious way, the better motion pictures." A librarian was installed, with an assistant. The number of sports writers was more than doubled — from three to seven —

and sports "Extras" were introduced. "I am now convinced," said Gay, "that we have emphasized sports too much . . . Our sports material is . . . not up to *Post* quality"—a verdict open to question, since he never read it.

His own interest was chiefly concerned with improving the political, literary, and international contents of the paper. He expanded the Washington staff from four to seven and soon had what he claimed was "the best rounded Washington news service of any New York evening paper." By December 1919, he had conceived and carried out his plan for ensnaring the free-lance journalist and lecturer, Mark Sullivan, as "national political correspondent." "It was Gay," Sullivan wrote in 1938, "who started me in this work of writing syndicated articles on national affairs." Sullivan received more pay than did the president of the paper, but as his writings were soon widely syndicated the *Post* was relieved of much of the cost of his contributions.

For foreign news Gay supplemented the correspondents he inherited by engaging Charles Selden to cover continental European events and Henry Clay to deal with British affairs. He dispatched Arthur Ruhl and Elias Tobenkin to Russia "to dig out the truth there." Ruhl was to see things from the newspaper correspondent's standpoint, Tobenkin to live among the peasants and view life through their eyes. Neither man saw anything; they were not allowed to enter the country.

Finally, Gay's plans included a drastic improvement of the Editorial Page and the treatment of literature. The old Page was divided between a solid mass of long editorials or reprints from other papers and of advertisements which started at the bottom right corner and threatened to creep both upward and leftward. To get rid of the advertisements was desirable, to lighten the soggy mass of print essential. Perhaps the latter could be accomplished by introducing a column filled with nonsense or with sense in lighter vein or verse.

There was precedent for such a step. Franklin P. Adams—

F.P.A. — was already famous as author and compiler of a column called "The Conning Tower." So also in less degree was one Socrates, whose "Chafing Dish" kept warm the hearts and sense of humor of readers of the *Philadelphia Evening Ledger*. Gay therefore broke a journey back from Washington in December 1919 to spend "several delightful hours" in Philadelphia with Socrates, alias Christopher Morley. The meeting was evidently so pleasant to both that four days later Gay invited Morley to be responsible for a daily column. "The human quality of your work," he wrote, "greatly attracts me as a thing which I particularly wish to see on our Editorial Page." Morley's response was favorable, a bargain was struck, and in February 1920, "The Bowling Green" made its first appearance.

How it got that name is not clear. Morley had submitted a list of suggestions, some admittedly "rather silly," such as The Tuning Fork, The Mulberry Bush, Prunes and Prisms, The Electric Chair, Elbow Room, and Since You Insist. His *Ledger* colleagues said the column ought to be called "Post Toasties." Gay rejected all these, vetoed any play on the word "post," but was sure Morley had "such a genius for titles" that something satisfactory could be found before the first column appeared. "The Bowling Green" proved acceptable and served its purpose for four years.

Close on Morley's heels came William Rose Benét. Benét already had published three books of poetry. At the moment he was working for *The Nation's Business* in Washington, but when Morley informed him of Gay's desire to print more book reviews he sent out a feeler, swearing there were few things he would prefer to do in the line of honest toil above the work of handling a book review section. He followed this with an uninhibited description of himself; was sure the *Post* with his aid could beat even Grant Overton of the *Sun* and Heywood Broun of the *Tribune* at reviewing; confessed that reading was his "chiefest vice," and admitted that he had written everything "from light verse to business articles and editorials. Also advertisements."

By this time Gay and Scott were wrestling seriously with the book problem. Royal Davis, who had looked after it, was transferring his whole attention to editorials, so there was a real vacancy as well as opportunity to plan ambitiously. Henry S. Canby, assistant editor of the *Yale Review*, was invited to come to the *Post* and take charge of the Saturday Book Section. Amy Loveman, who had been Davis' assistant, was to carry on, but Canby would need still another colleague, and Benét was therefore invited to fill that position. He accepted in March, pledged to "root hawg or die." Canby also accepted the challenge to turn out "the best literary supplement—the name is an abomination—that ever was or is." With Canby, Benét, and Amy Loveman working full time, and Morley, Allan Nevins, and other members of the staff or outsiders giving a hand, *The Literary Review*, as it came to be called, quickly became the unchallenged leader in American literary criticism, studded with articles, reviews, and poems by the greatest names on both sides of the Atlantic.

To supplement his greatly expanded staff Gay called frequently on the expert knowledge of his academic friends, paying them a "space rate" which recognized more generously than was usual the fact that the scholar is worthy of his hire. Coolidge and Haskins wrote on current international questions. A series of articles on the tax problem by T. S. Adams attracted so much attention that it was reprinted. Cunningham of the Business School was an ever-ready contributor when railroad issues became acute. Wesley Mitchell, Leo Wolman, E. W. Kemmerer, and others wrote frequently on economic themes, while the annual Economic Survey, published on the last day of each year, looked like a collection of papers read at a meeting of the American Economic Association.

Dr. Eliot could also be relied on to do what he was asked, such as review Bryce's *Modern Democracies;* but he did not always wait to be asked. In June 1920, for example, he sent an article on Prohibition, with a covering letter which said: "If you find any unnecessarily offensive words in it, please strike them out or change them.

I have tried to make the article as inoffensive as possible to opponents of Prohibition." It was printed unaltered in a prominent place, as were several others which were so strong in tone that they were accompanied by a note reading, "If you think it inexpedient to print, wire me."

Business friends were also roped in. Dennison did a series on "Selling," and Dwight Morrow's name appeared occasionally at the head of an article. George O. May, a leading authority on the theory and practice of accounting and Gay's friend since early Business School days, could be counted on to help when tax problems called for elucidation, though eventually he had to insist that if his contribution was to be printed it should appear substantially as he sent it. "I have learned from experience," he wrote, "that your young men in their anxiety to improve my literary style may go astray on my facts."

The *Post* had always followed faithfully its urge "to inculcate just principles in religion, morals, and politics," especially the latter. Under the new administration there was no weakening in its advocacy of what it thought right or its condemnation of what seemed wrong; but there was a greater effort to study situations and issues more thoroughly before passing judgment, urging action, or taking a stand. In the determination of what the judgment, action, or stand should be Gay's word was law. Occasionally he might say that word by writing the editorial himself in order to shoulder direct responsibility for what went into print. When, for example, the question of restricting the number of Jews admitted to Harvard was being violently discussed, Strunsky, himself a Jew, wrote an article favoring limitation; but Gay tore it up and did one condemning restriction.

In general, however, the strategy and tactics of editorial policy were worked out at daily morning meetings of the editorial staff and at weekly staff dinners. At first there had been some thought of inviting Lamont to the meetings, but since he was a busy man he was given instead a standing invitation to the dinners. He occasionally came, and talked about reparations, inter-Allied debts, the Far East, or some other topic on which his business experience gave him inside knowledge. He was not alone in making such contributions, for many other guests spoke there of matters on which they were authorities.

When in town, Gay tried to attend both meetings and dinners, and read each day's editorials before they went to press. He was, however, frequently absent from the office, and did not know what his associates had written until he saw it in print. While he was usually satisfied, even delighted, with what he read, occasionally he deplored the line or tone of an article. If, for instance, he had not been in Detroit studying the layout of a model newspaper plant he certainly would have insisted that the condemnation of Mayor Hylan for recognizing De Valera as "President of the Irish Republic" be more clear-cut and cutting. On another occasion, when a "much too strong" attack had been made on the Governor's message, he exclaimed, "It looks as though I could not be away from the office. I grant that things may be bad enough when I am here, but they are certainly no better when I am away."

This confession was made to the *Post*'s most avid reader and constant critic — its owner. Lamont had agreed that though he paid the piper he would not try to call the tune. He kept his word; but this did not prevent him from saying what he thought of the performance or from urging improvements in the players' technique. During the first half of 1920 he was in the Far East, but on his return he soon made his presence felt. Not daily, yet frequently, one of his first tasks when he reached his Wall Street office was to dictate a letter voicing his opinion of some especially good, poor, or bad item in the preceding evening's issue. The letter went by messenger to the *Post* office. On one occasion he was so disturbed that he sent the letter even though Gay and he were to meet for their weekly luncheon conference two or three hours later.

His criticisms ranged widely over the particular and the general.

One headline was "worthy of Hearst at his worst." The front page cartoon oppressed him "with the fear that this is repelling more readers than it is attracting." A cabled dispatch from Selden was interesting, but "doesn't it strike you that the length is quite unnecessary? It burns up a tremendous lot in cable tolls." One editorial seemed to be "no good for anything except to make Will Hays [then Postmaster General] mad." Another gained nothing by including a gratuitous "little fling at Borah. Lord knows I have no fondness for Borah, but what is the use of slurring him unnecessarily and getting him more and more indignant?" A third one, like many others, was judged very good indeed.

More general criticisms were provoked by the apparent failure of editorial writers to learn all the facts available, and especially to ascertain what the accused person had to say before condemning him. Lamont not merely insisted that "due investigation" was the bounden duty of a reputable journalist. He believed that such inquiry could be conducted more easily by members of the *Post* staff than by those working for other journals, because the paper's reputation, together with his own position in the business community, would open the doors of corporations and large employers to an inquirer from 20 Vesey Street. It ought, therefore, to be possible to learn by access to documents, but preferably by personal interview, the pertinent facts and points of view; and consequently to present a well-informed, considered, and constructive—not to mention exclusive—treatment of such questions as whether a telephone company was justified in asking for higher rates or whether the railroads could afford to raise wages to meet the rising cost of living.

If some such procedure was not adopted, if the staff continued as in the past to keep aloof in its "little cloister," writing critically about things it had not properly investigated and propounding no constructive suggestions, then Lamont felt the outlook was gloomy. "We may get ourselves in the position somewhat of the *New Republic* and lose our influence." He felt that they would do grave injustice to individuals and firms, cast undeserved slurs, alienate the sympathy of people who knew they were wrong or ill informed, and needlessly lose much valuable advertising. "If we keep up that way all the money in the world can never put the paper on its feet."

With most of Lamont's concept of good journalism Gay was "entirely in accord." He did, however, feel that "the tradition of 'wrist-slapping' in our editorials is giving way to this better habit of trying to get the facts." He gently questioned the assumption that corporation doors could be swung open by uttering the magic words *Evening Post,* and gave an instance where an attempt to get the facts and "to put a good man on the job in order to write some special articles" on the telephone company's "real situation" had been dexterously side-stepped. Further, he had

no illusions about attaining ultimate truth. It cannot be done, even with months and years of scholarly investigation, still less in the rush of daily decisions which make up the business of a newspaper—or any other business. The main thing is to get the right habit of mind and the spirit of accurate fairness. I think our staff is getting this habit more and more. I also think you are very patient.

Patient, yes, but also persistent in his protests whenever an editorial contained a blemish that could easily have been avoided by making a 'phone call. When an editorial on Harding's cabinet (February 1921) deliberately withheld judgment as to the administrative ability of Andrew Mellon, the new secretary of the treasury, Lamont's comment was: "Ordinary inquiry from me or from banking and business circles generally would have elicited the fact that Mr. Mellon is one of the most successful administrators of his time . . . This is another of those subjects that if somebody felt free to call me up I should be greatly relieved and saved embarrassment."

In referring to "embarrassment" Lamont was not revealing any secret. No matter how much he protested, he could not convince his business friends (or anyone else) that he was not responsible for what the *Post* said. In vain did he remind them that when he bought the paper he "executed a self-denying ordinance . . . to the effect that [he would] leave it independent." It was equally unavailing to say, "I cannot expect to ask men of independent character and judgment to take charge of the *Post* unless I expect them to show that independence." Friends regarded such statements as unwise; others hinted they were untrue.

The embarrassment first became acute when the *Post* had to take its stand during the election of 1920. Lamont and Gay were at one in their pro-League attitude and their belief that the Senate ought to ratify the Versailles Treaty. Having been through the Peace Conference, Lamont was by September 1919 "greatly disturbed at the attitude of mind that insists on such calamitous fumbling [by the Senate] with the most critical situation that the world has ever seen." His disquiet increased as the fumbling grew more calamitous and the presidential battle took shape. Though a stalwart Republican, his loyalty would be severely strained if his party was lukewarm or hostile on the League issue, and he knew Gay would feel the same way, only much more strongly.

The first strain on loyalty was applied by the vague wording of the Republican platform and Harding's nomination. The *Post* prepared an unflattering article on the candidate, showed it to Lamont, and after deleting one or two such harsh words as "insult" published it. Lamont sent Gay a grim report of its reception downtown. Even progressive Republicans who were disappointed with the nomination thought the editorial a brutal attack on the personal character and mentality of a man who, Lamont was surprised to learn from them, was "apparently a good deal of McKinley sort of man, with warm and devoted friends in many directions."

What the unprogressive Republicans thought was revealed when Gay went to Wall Street to discuss the situation with Lamont. There he met one man who had come to vent his feelings on bankers who consorted with journalists.

I happened in opportunely [Gay wrote his wife]. This time the conservatism was not stodgy but fiery. It seems that the personality of the candidate was of no account. Any skite will do. The important thing is to support the Republican Party, which is alone able to save our imperilled institutions. Property rights are endangered, the United States is on the brink of revolution and chaos. Harding will save us. We had a little debate, smiling on my part. He had come, it seems, declaring he would never read our vile rag again; but he left saying he was glad to meet me and we must talk again. Meanwhile J. P. [Morgan], like a genial master, stood by watching the fight, saying he agreed this time with [the angry one], but was a friend of the *Post*, etc. When I came back to the office I asked Gavit to write an editorial on "Going Fishing," which appears in to-day's *Post*.

The article created widespread uproar. Gay's mail was crammed with letters, some praising the editorial but most of them full of violent abuse. At least one very old friend washed his hands of the renegade "in sorrow and anger." "It's a spicy life," commented the victim, and it became more piquant when Cox, the Democratic candidate, made utterances on the League only a little less unsatisfactory than those of Harding. Gay therefore embarked on a one-man campaign to see if he could force the candidates to reveal their stand more clearly. It began with a breakfast at the Washington home of the Democratic vice-presidential candidate. In addition to noting that Franklin D. Roosevelt's breakfast table was "adorned with the right size of coffee cup, the biggest I have ever seen," Gay was able to record "a frank and interesting talk with [his host] and obtained a favorable reflection of Cox as seen by him." Then he boarded a train on which Cox and Roosevelt were traveling westward, and had "quite a talk" with both of them.

Next morning he left that train, caught one bound for Marion, Ohio, interviewed Harding there, then hurried back to New York.

The trip was a great success [he told his wife], in giving a definite answer to my questions and settling my doubts. But it was also a disappointment. I continued to hope against hope, until I talked to him, that we might be able to support Harding. He is impossible; a good man and kindly, but with no real ability for the job. His confidential statement to me about what he expected to do regarding the Treaty settled the problem for me. [Harding had said that in order to maintain party harmony he must accept the plan of the Irreconcilables.]

Cox is of very different calibre — a man of real ability developed from a common mould, with a lot of growth left in him. He belongs distinctly to the new generation, while Harding is a left-over. . . I have told Lamont that we cannot support Harding, and he agrees that this is the right course for us. But we hold our hand until Cox's notification speech.

As that speech was not due until about August 7 every effort was made to influence Harding before it was too late. Gay worked on Hoover, Wickersham, and other pro-League Republicans, urging them to do their utmost to push their candidate away from the Irreconcilable position. When Cox's speech was delivered, its section on the League was so equivocal that there still seemed to be a chance for Harding if he would move. He need not move very far to get near Cox. But while he could not be budged, Gay and Rublee were able to influence Cox by going to see him and giving him an intensive course of indoctrination.

By mid-August the *Post* had to say where it stood. In an article drafted by Lamont and licked into final shape by Strunsky it announced its support of Cox and Roosevelt, simply because "their espousal of the League embodies the highest American ideals." Gay immediately threw himself and his paper vigorously into the battle. He planned a Writers' League for the League, and made his first (and last) political speeches at one or two Democratic rallies. Then Woodrow Wilson's health and speaking tour collapsed in late September, and a month later Gay was invited to be one of the delegation that called on the stricken President. He went reluctantly, feeling, as did some of the others, that "to come in the middle of a busy week to act as audience or vehicle for the President's message to the country was something of a bore."

But [as he wrote his daughter], the moment we entered the room where the President was seated in his wheel-chair, our feeling changed at once. It was in this room that I had seen him after his first return from

Paris. He then looked a little tired, but his step was vigorous, his eyes alert, and his complexion healthy looking. Now he sat in his chair looking like a dying man. I remember once, years ago, I saw a dying man in a Paris hospital with his whole being concentrated on a crucifix which he held clasped close to his breast. So the President has concentrated all his being on the Covenant — and Article X.

He had his speech typewritten on three sheets of paper lying on a table at his side, and when [Hamilton] Holt had finished reading his little address the President excused himself for not rising and for reading his answer. His voice had lost its old resonance; it was dry and small, quite audible because we were very still, but it seemed that it was with difficulty that he read. Before he had finished the first page he laid it down on the table and I thought he was going to ask Tumulty, who stood behind him, to continue the reading for him. But he picked it up again and went on. Twice later, once when he referred to the lives lost in the war and again when he spoke of the honor of the United States, his voice broke as if he were repressing a sob.

When he finished, Tumulty, faithful soul, was in tears, and none of us were dry-eyed. The reporters were outside, so I suggested that Dr. Brown should draw up a statement for all of us, giving our impressions of the occasion. After it was typewritten the last sentence was added about its being perhaps the final appeal of the President to the country before the decision. Tumulty leaned over to me and said, "Perhaps the final statement ever." I do not know what Dr. Grayson means by putting out statements about the President's good health.

Within a week the country gave its decision in favor of Harding. The verdict, though expected, was disappointing to Gay. One of the few bright spots of the strenuous campaign was the frank complete conversion of the *Post*'s proprietor. On October 26 Lamont wrote a letter and authorized him to print it in the space usually occupied by the main editorial. Occupying two-thirds of a column, it began:

Dear Mr. Gay: In framing the policies of the *Evening Post*, you have had an absolutely free hand. Your decision to support Cox and Roosevelt was your own decision — not mine. But if, as a life-long Republican, I had for a time certain misgivings as to your decision, I may now say that the developments of the campaign have resolved my doubts. I intend to vote for Cox and Roosevelt. My chief reason is, of course, that Cox is for the League of Nations and Harding is against it.

When one of Gay's friends read the declaration he remarked: "It seems to me this letter is worth its weight in radium to you." When the *Post*'s Republican rivals read it they reacted in various ways. The *Herald* was "glad" to learn that the owner and his newspaper were

> at last in harmony. . . This is one of the most remarkable incidents in journalism. There is nothing like it in all journalistic history. Obviously it is a case of the League bug in the blood. How else can it be accounted for — TOM LAMONT, a rich banker, member of the great international banking house of J. P. Morgan and Co., capitulating to the antagonistic management of his own newspaper.

Hearst's *American* was above such genial teasing. Its thesis, reiterated throughout the campaign, was that the League would commit the United States to wars all over the world; war had already given millions of profit to Morgan and Company; more wars would give more millions; consequently Lamont was naturally for Cox, and his avowal might well have added "and so it is with every member of my firm."

The election helped to make 1920 a very crowded year for Gay. As his wife said, the paper alone kept him "working quite at the rate of teaching and deaning," but in addition many other interests in New York, Washington, and Cambridge claimed his time and thought. In the first place, the plans which Malcolm Rorty had discussed with Gay and Mitchell in 1916–17 had been revived and led to the establishment of the National Bureau of Economic Research during the winter of 1919–20. Gay was the Bureau's first president. Almost immediately after came the steps leading to the formation of the Council on Foreign Relations in 1921. Gay was a member of the committee that drafted the Council's constitution, then served as its first secretary-treasurer.

In the second place, he did not sever all ties with Washington when he left the capital. He was a member of an advisory committee, appointed in early 1919, to help the director of the census improve the decennial counting of the people. The chairman was W. S. Rossiter, publisher of the *Atlantic Monthly*, and one of Gay's chief aides in the Central Bureau. He took his duties very seriously, especially after he discovered the gross inefficiency and widespread spoils system prevailing in the census organization; and he made his colleagues carry a full share of the load. The trips to Washington grew more numerous when in 1921 Gay had cause to go not only for census discussions but also to aid Hoover in reorganizing his Department of Commerce and to talk confidentially with Hughes, now Secretary of State, about the latter's plans for doing the best he could in international coöperation within the bounds of the mandate given at the election of 1920.

In the third place, Cambridge had not let Gay escape when he resigned. In 1919 he became a member of the Board of Overseers of Harvard College and was put on various committees, including one that conducted an endowment drive. Meanwhile in New York the Civil Service Reform League and the Libraries Association put him on their governing bodies. He was a member of the committee that organized the American section of the English Speaking Union, and became one of its directors. He rejected an invitation to give a lecture course on economic history at Columbia. "It tempts me to keep my hand in," he confessed, "but I had better decline." Requests for occasional speeches he was rarely able to decline. After listing those he had consented to give in late 1920 he wrote his daughter: "I hope I shall be wise enough and firm enough some day to refuse these pressing invitations to belong to things and to support worthy causes by talking on subjects which I don't know much about."

His diaries for 1920–1923 show that he did not grow sufficiently in either wisdom or firmness. When Arthur Morgan, the engineer, took charge of Antioch College in Ohio, initiated a program which obligated students to divide their time between academic subjects and work in factories or commercial establishments, and transformed its governing board from a coterie of doctors of divinity to a mixture of engineers, businessmen, and editors, Gay and Ellery

Sedgwick represented the press in a group that included Dr. Eliot, Dennison, Frank A. Vanderlip, and technicians from Ford and General Motors. When Franklin D. Roosevelt invited Gay and nine others to meet at his home in March 1921 to discuss the raising of a fund as a tribute to Woodrow Wilson, Gay let himself "be drawn, a little unwillingly, on the temporary committee, partly because of a sincere admiration for much that Wilson did and a belief that his contribution will be more justly appraised by history than by many among his immediate contemporaries." The Woodrow Wilson Foundation was thus born, a fund of a million dollars was sought, and Gay drafted the statement describing the annual awards that were to be given to individuals or organizations in recognition of distinguished service in the cause of good government and democratic endeavor. He remained a director of the Foundation till 1939.

Through these varied activities Gay widened still further the range of his acquaintance with people prominent in the public, business, and intellectual life of the eastern states. His evenings were filled — sometimes solidly throughout the week — with dinner and other engagements. It was a rare treat to have an evening free at home, reading, doing crossword puzzles, playing solitaire, or listening with infinite enjoyment to the Steinway Duo-Art Self-Operating (but ugly) Pianola which had taken the place of the beautiful walnut grand piano of Cambridge days.

As 1920 drew to a close the center of Gay's interest was compelled to shift from reorganizing and building up the *Post* to the grim task of trying to save it. The original policy, "to maintain, with enlivenment, the quality of the product and to raise our advertising rates in the various classifications on the basis of a quality circulation, not quantity," had been pursued with some success. The daily circulation had risen from an average of about 30,000 to 38,000, while the addition of the "Graphic Section" and of the "Literary Review" had lifted Saturday sales to nearly twice that figure. The advertising rates had been raised, and during the business boom between the Armistice and the spring of 1920 the paper harvested at least its full share of the richer crop of publicity dollars from metropolitan retailers as well as from "national" advertisers. By year-end the collapse of the boom had diminished the revenue from these patrons; yet the total receipts from all sources were 25 per cent larger in 1920 than in 1919.

The expenditure, unfortunately, was 80 per cent higher, and the loss on the year's operations soared from less than $100,000 in 1919 to more than $750,000 in 1920. Rising costs were responsible in part for this great jump: wage rates had risen by 40 per cent, the rent had more than doubled, as had the cost of paper, ink, and delivery service. But much of it was due to the rapid growth of the staff and the purchase of large quantities of equipment or materials. In the red light of the deficit, the plans for reorganization and expansion appeared too grandiose, hasty, and rash. Too many men had been hired too quickly, without adequate consideration of whether they were necessaries or luxuries.

It was not merely that they cost so much—"Just see the money pour over the cliff!" said one of them. They got in one another's way; the general utility journalist who knew how to write had to keep out of the field assigned to the expert, who might not be able to tell his story attractively—and if he was an academic might be too long-winded as well. There was not enough space in the columns for all the good copy that was written; yet the daily meal of good food might be so large that a serious reader could not get through all of it in his spare evening hours. Finally, Gay had, as it were, assembled a large faculty for his experiment in adult education; but the modest increase in circulation did not suggest that a large part of the population of New York City was eager to come to evening classes.

Rapid expansion therefore gave place to almost equally rapid retrenchment during the latter part of 1920 and throughout 1921. The new plans called "for a considerable reduction of expenses and a tightening up of the *Post*." Estimates were prepared of the maximum permissible monthly deficit and the inflexible rule was made that this figure must not be exceeded. If revenue fell below the estimate, expenses must be trimmed accordingly.

It was a painful job, done summarily and ruthlessly, so that men wondered whose turn would be next, and morale, which had been greatly improved, slumped again. The veteran London correspondent was dropped, Clay's contributions were cut down in readiness for being cut off, Selden's contract as European correspondent was terminated, and three other foreign journalists soon met the same fate. Bit by bit the number of reporters, clerks, sports writers, department heads, experts, circulation and promotion men, and morgue custodians was reduced. Some of the newly created departments, such as Education, were wiped out. The budget for outside contributors was cut hard. The order for new presses was canceled, plans for a new building on a site acquired uptown on 33rd Street went into the wastepaper basket, then the land was sold. Smaller light bulbs replaced stronger ones, and boys were sent around to see that fans and lights were switched off when not needed.

Meanwhile every conceivable method was used to stimulate circulation or expand advertisements. One line of appeal emphasized that the *Post* catered to the 39,485 people in the city who, according to the new federal income tax report, had incomes of $6000 a year or more. "There is no more certain, direct, or economical way to reach these people — limited in number but of high purchasing power — than through the *New York Evening Post*." This snobbish emphasis on "quality circulation" and insistence that it was worth while to pay higher advertising rates in order to get at the well-to-do reader failed to impress some large advertisers who had wrung cut rates or strategic page locations from the former management. The attempt to raise the linage charges and in one case to eject the firm's advertisements from page three led to the loss of at least two very good customers. All efforts failed to check the decline in advertising revenue as depression closed the purses of patrons. The gap between income and expenses remained as wide as ever, and the total deficit for 1921 — about $750,000 — was almost the same as that for 1920.

To bridge the gap the *Post* drew on Lamont, borrowing the money and handing the lender notes that bore 6 per cent interest. In the beginning it had been hoped that a loan of at most $300,000 would suffice. Actually it was about $800,000 in 1920, and it looked as if the need for 1921 would be no smaller. Little wonder that Gay confessed in January 1921: "The problem we faced a year and a half ago has since almost doubled," and the situation was admitted to be "grave." Little wonder also that Lamont, once more away in Paris, exclaimed when he saw the returns up to April: "My heart is still in my mouth. I have been so hard hit that I think I have dropped my nerve somewhat. I am waiting with interest the further reports and am ardently hoping that we can get through the summer period without disaster."

His hope was not fulfilled and when he returned to America in late June he voiced the fear that he might not be able to hang on to the paper much longer. He was loath to reach a decision, for selling the *Post* would be a hard blow to his hopes and his pride. Yet he was too busy to give any time to the paper's business problems; and meanwhile he was paying out far more than he had ever anticipated would be required, far far more than the $250,000 Gay and he had assumed in 1919 would suffice to put the *Post* on its feet.

The summer returns, revealing a more than seasonal heavy slump in advertising revenue, left him no choice. In early October Gay wrote one of his aides who was absent on sick-leave:

> You might as well go on to California for the winter — or look about for a new job. The executioner's axe has at last fallen on our necks, in the gentlest and most considerate way, but nevertheless quite definitely. Negotiations are already under way for the sale of the property, and it is now only a matter of weeks, or at most two or three months. . . Our high hopes have fallen low!

Selling an unprofitable paper in those depressed days was not easy. The only person willing to offer any substantial sum was

Frank A. Munsey, and when he made it clear that his plan was to merge the *Post* with his own *Evening Sun* Lamont drew back. To let the paper go was hard enough; to hand it over to an executioner was unbearable. As Gay was equally distressed by this prospect, the two men discussed other plans, and Lamont offered to sell the property on generous terms to a new syndicate if Gay cared to organize one. Gay examined the financial situation and prospects, called in a business friend to scrutinize the estimates independently, and when this double check gave hope that "we can pull the paper across and pay our way" he embarked on the task of forming a syndicate with a capital of $1,500,000.

He had only a month in which to do the job, since Munsey insisted on a reply to his offer by January 9, 1922. He approached his friends, sought out those acquaintances he had made in his varied business, public, and educational activities, and solicited the support of anyone else who sympathized with the kind of policies the *Post* espoused. But "in these hard times" his target proved too high, he had to lower it to $750,000, and secured cash or pledges amounting to only $600,000. When he reported this figure to Lamont the latter offered to consider some other plan. Two days sufficed for working one out, Munsey was informed the paper was not to be his, and on January 13, 1922, the leader column of the *Post* announced that Lamont's stock holdings in the paper had been acquired by a group of thirty-four prominent citizens, whose names were published.

The terms can be stated briefly. The vendor had paid nearly $1,000,000 for the stock in 1918; he now parted with it for $125,000 in cash. By the end of 1921 he had advanced nearly $1,700,000 to meet deficits and make purchases of equipment. On these advances the unpaid interest exceeded $100,000. His total claim as creditor therefore amounted to about $1,800,000. A small fraction of it was to be paid in cash by the new company and the rest was converted into 6 per cent mortgage bonds, most of them due to mature in seven or ten years' time.

Lamont thus pulled out of the *Post* with bonds covering most of what he had lent, but wrote off seven-eighths of his original investment. He was now freed alike from the sniping of journalists who refused to believe that he kept the policies of the bank and of the paper separate, and from the weekly visit by the borrower from Vesey Street. The former had embarrassed him more than he cared to admit. The latter had strained his resources at a time when most business and financial ventures were experiencing the difficulties of adjustment from war to peace conditions. The "partnership" with Gay was now ended. It had not lasted five years and there had been no agreement that it should do so. It had not terminated in the manner set forth in the compact of 1919—by one member giving the other a year's notice; and there seems to be no evidence that the financial arrangement agreed on in case it should be dissolved before 1924 was remembered in the hour of separation.

> Now [wrote Gay to his mother], we start on Chapter II. I feel glad that these [subscribers] came forward to save the *Post*, but I feel no personal elation, for I have only taken on still heavier responsibilities. Chapter II is going to see plenty of hard work and anxiety. It will last two or three years and then we hope Chapter III will be a bit more cheerful.

Some of his friends regretted that he had not been content to write a short story and warned him that he was undertaking "altogether too heavy burdens for any man to carry without physical disaster." To one of them he replied:

> Retirement from the job was the one impossible thing under the circumstances at the time the change was made. The only hope of saving the *Post* from extinction was to carry on with the new group which I myself had brought together, and I certainly must go on with it for a time at any rate. If we can only manage to put the *Post* on a sound basis I shall be satisfied enough to call it one of the good things of life.

The "new group" combined enough public spirit, business energy, and material resources to give hope to any man. The list included such names as Norman H. Davis, H. S. Dennison, Cleveland Dodge, Marshall Field, Sam Lewisohn, George O. May, Frank

Polk, Franklin D. Roosevelt, Joseph Halle Schaffner, Martin Vogel, Paul Warburg, George Wickersham, Clarence Woolley, Owen D. Young, and Mrs. Willard Straight. One newspaper remarked that some of the names indicated a purse as well filled as that of the former owner and that many of them were well known "in partisan alliances and also in radical circles." Four of them had subscribed for $50,000 of stock apiece, others for amounts ranging down to $1000. Gay had gone in deeply, borrowing heavily in order to purchase half as many securities as did any of the largest stockholders.

Some of the group may have felt their investment would one day yield a profit; but most of them were chiefly interested in saving a famous paper, and at least a few would have endorsed the statement of one of the heaviest subscribers: "My interest has been in Gay and in the social service he might render." If we count heads, the majority of the names on the list were there as a testimonial to the man who compiled it and as an act of faith in his ideals and courage.

Yet even before the deal was closed everybody knew that insufficient capital had been raised to give the new venture a fair chance of success. A quarter of the $600,000 was in pledges that need not be honored before the end of 1922. From the $450,000 actually in hand, about $300,000 was subtracted to meet the cash terms of purchase, leaving only $150,000 for bridging the gap between expenses and income in 1922. The estimated deficit was $280,000 for that year and $90,000 for 1923, after which the forecasts promised years of mounting surplus. Hence it was clear that, no matter how expenditures were trimmed, more capital would need to be raised quickly. When therefore the stockholders elected Gay president of the corporation his role, having passed through the stages of enthusiastic hiring and of ruthless firing, became what a friend described as "a combination of impecunious Scotch auditor watching the pennies and an expert beggar."

"Chapter II" was divided into three parts, each starting and ending with a financial crisis. The first was devoted to a search for new stockholders during the spring and summer of 1922. After combing New York and Philadelphia without avail, Gay turned to Chicago, Milwaukee, Cleveland, and Detroit. Like a traveling salesman he spent his evenings compiling lists of telephone numbers, his days in ringing people up and calling on them. But the eastern product he was offering did not attract midwesterners and his sales talk could stress only promise rather than performance. In Chicago five men consented to buy stock worth about $20,000 in all; others either promised to "consider" or bluntly said no. The other cities did not yield a single buyer.

From this disheartening trip Gay hurried back to Vesey Street to make still more cuts in staff and "features." The Ship News Office was closed to save $50 a week, a cartoonist was fired to save $150, the art critic was not reëngaged, the promotion manager's place was not filled when he went to another job, the Chicago grain news wires were canceled in order to whittle $30 off the weekly telegram bill, some of the poorer delivery routes were abolished, and salaries were cut 10 per cent. One of Gay's colleagues, away on holiday, wrote him: "I opened your letter this morning with some trepidation — and then was relieved to learn that conditions at the office were normal; that is, that expenses were to be cut once more."

These economies were scarcely enough to offset the decline in revenue. By July it seemed certain that the deficit for the year would exceed $400,000 and that all the available cash and bank credit would be gone by the end of August. The second part of the chapter therefore began with an attempt to replenish the till by tapping the pockets of the stockholders. Some of these people were by now attributing the paper's troubles to the policies Gay was pursuing and were unwilling to provide more cash unless they gained power to say how the paper was to be run. After rumbling underground for a time this discontent broke through to the surface at a stockholders' meeting in mid-August and led to the appointment of a committee of three, consisting of the chief critic, a supporter of Gay, and Owen D. Young as chairman, to study the whole situation.

The committee recommended that an executive committee, chosen from the board of directors, be set up to collaborate with the management and exercise full regulatory power over the business end of the enterprise. Gay disliked the plan because it impaired the "independence" he had enjoyed from the start and failed to draw any really clear line between business and editorial policies. His critics disliked the plan because it seemed to draw too clear a line and to leave too much territory on the editorial side of the divide. When, however, Owen D. Young consented to serve as chairman of an executive committee on which both factions would be represented, the recommendation was accepted, as was the proposal that each stockholder be asked to increase his subscription by one-fifth, that a renewed hunt be made for new investors, and that further banks loans be sought.

The new plan provided sufficient money to carry the paper on for a few more months in the hope that the crucial corner would soon be rounded. The stockholders bought a further $100,000 of securities. New buyers were almost as hard to find as ever, and by mid-November Gay's roster of persons "Seen and Refused" contained 122 names; but sufficient purchasers were found to provide an additional $50,000. More economies in operation were combined with attempts to bring new blood into the paper. Gay tried to persuade William Allen White of Emporia, Kansas, to come and take charge of editorial and news policies, or at least of the Editorial Page. That it was a seductive invitation is evident from White's reply:

> Your letter . . . gave me a thrill that few men get once in a lifetime. Caesar got it when he refused the crown for the first time; Joseph had it at the climax of his interview with Mrs. Potiphar; Carlyle got it when they offered to make him a lord. I have no doubt they all appreciated the compliment, all wished they could enjoy it. For one reason or another, probably not as creditable as history tells us, they reluctantly turned aside from the guilty joy that would come with acceptance. And I must turn aside too — I can't do it. My roots are too deep out here, and no amount of money would tempt me . . .

I probably will regret the decision, but must obey my impulse. For it is a very deep impulse and has governed my whole life — this feeling that I must stay out west, where I can make my mistakes inexpensively. If I can help the *Post* in any other way I will gladly do so. It is the one real hope of American journalism, and I most earnestly beg of you not to let it go by the board.

Meanwhile the executive committee, in the words of its chairman, "industriously labored to save the *Post* and to make it succeed." It gave much time to the paper's business problems, solicited advertisements, and fought rent battles, newsprint battles, bank battles. It decided to hire a Publisher and General Manager, and found one in John H. Fahey, a Worcester newspaper owner and publisher who had won the reputation of a miracle-worker by the job he had recently done in reorganizing and revitalizing the United States Chamber of Commerce. He was engaged to take managerial charge of the *Post* in May 1923, thus leaving Gay free to concentrate on editorial affairs.

By that time the till was almost empty once more and the paper had passed through another financial crisis into the third phase. While the revenue had continued to be far below the estimates, the expenses were only a little "below bogie," and the deficit for the first quarter of 1923 was $68,000. The executive committee saw "ground for hope" that the venture would be self-sustaining by the end of 1924, but recognized that until the hope was more firmly grounded there was no possibility of selling more stock to old or new buyers. It therefore proposed that funds be borrowed by the sale of 6 per cent gold notes, maturing in five years and convertible at any time into stock. The members of the committee said they were willing to purchase a large fraction of these notes on condition that the remainder could be sold and also that the stockholders hand over their securities to a voting trust composed of the present members of the executive committee. Since the paper was to be kept alive by borrowing, those who lent the greater part of the money were to be in effective charge.

The plan was accepted and by the summer of 1923 about $180,000 of notes had been sold — half of them to the executive committee members, the rest to outsiders who had become interested in the paper. More than half the stockholders bought none; they were unable or unwilling to contribute further to save the *Post*. Even if they had done so, there still would not have been enough money. The deficit for the second quarter was as large as in the first; that of the third quarter — a season when circulation and advertisements always fell low — was twice as large, making a total of over $250,000 for the nine months.

The "psychological reaction" to this figure was violent. In September the anti-Gay group pressed through the executive committee a request for his resignation at year's end. Some of his supporters countered the stroke by asking the committee to stay its hand until they had made an attempt to raise sufficient money to ensure the paper's survival under his direction. They were given the "right of way" to see what they could do, but the hunt for funds reached only halfway to its objective. The executive committee therefore faced the alternatives of financing its own program with a new editorial manager or of handing the paper back to Lamont as bondholder. Since there was no hope of the former, the latter was inevitable.

When in early December Young and Gay reported this choice to Lamont he instructed them to sell the paper to Cyrus H. K. Curtis of the *Philadelphia Ledger* and *Saturday Evening Post*. By December 21 the sale had been approved by the stockholders. Curtis assumed the entire bonded obligation to Lamont and handed the *Post* a check for $125,000. This cash was used to repay 70 per cent of the $180,000 borrowed by the sale of gold notes. The noteholders thus lost $55,000 of what they had lent. The stockholders lost all the $720,000 they had invested. If to these losses are added those incurred earlier by Lamont, the total amount sunk in the effort to save the *Post* was about $1,600,000.

To the new proprietor Gay wrote wishing "all possible success in developing what is more than a mere newspaper property. It is publicly regarded as an institution which involves special responsibilities. I have always felt it to be a precious heritage . . . which I pass on to you with hope for its continued growth, influence, leadership, and prosperity."

A few days later he sent two reports giving his appraisal of the paper's staff and problems. One by one he described the men of his team. There was Simeon Strunsky, "the best editorial writer in New York"; Allan Nevins, "one of the most useful men on the staff," whose history of the paper had been published that year and whose "range of reading and encyclopaedic knowledge" made him indispensable; and Christopher Morley, "open minded, honest, inquiring spirit with a philosophy more genial and humane as well as more richly humorous than that of any other columnist." There was the *Literary Review* trio — Canby, Loveman, and Benét — who had given the *Review* an international reputation and a steady independent circulation of more than 10,000 copies a week; Cass Canfield, whose skill in handling publishers had captured for the *Post* more book advertising than any other paper save the *Times*; Towse, the dean of New York's dramatic critics; Finch, one of the two leading musical critics in the city; and the financial specialists — Franz Schneider, O. W. Scroggs, and Paul Garrett — who had kept the *Post*'s daily and annual financial reports the best in the country. Finally, there were the management men — Lane, Puckette, and others — who had stood up under the strain of adversity and austerity.

They had been a good group to work with. As Canby wrote later, the staff was "as rich in eccentrics as a university, and stuffed with personalities." Yet they had shaken down into a team, with a captain who won their loyalty by his concept of what the *Post* ought to be, his courageous stand on such great but unpopular causes as the League of Nations and internationalism, the economic expertness which enabled him to offer a more penetrating interpretation of current events than did any other editor, his energy, hopefulness, and willingness to work even harder than he expected them to do. Their admiration of these qualities could not smother their disquiet over the impulsive grandiose reorganization and expansion of 1919–20 or allay their dismay at the summary ruthless way in which discharges were made during 1921. When, however, the grim struggle for survival set in during 1922 their criticism of Gay's methods and mistakes was submerged by a deep appreciation of the brave battle he was waging. As Canby later recalled, "Everybody, from the editor . . . down to the office boys, was made to feel that the *Post* was an institution more important than private welfare, and that we must save it — and for a time we did."

Now in the hour of disaster they told him what they felt. By word of mouth across his desk, by letter or round robin, and at a crowded farewell dinner, his colleagues voiced their admiration, gratitude, and regret. They urged him to recognize that his defeat had been an honorable one and to find some cheer in contemplating the vast contrast between the demoralized derelict he had boarded in 1919 and the proud though penniless vessel he was leaving. One of them, a prosaic executive who was there when Gay came and remained a little while after he left, subscribed his testimony with the word "affectionately."

Even as the farewells were being said, the new masters swarmed through the building, making plans for installing new presses, new linotypes, new this, that, and the other. Gay listened to them, then wrote: "It makes me rather dizzy after our long régime of economies. . . And it is a touch of irony, after our long efforts, to have from Lane yesterday a report that probably December will show our income equalling our expenses." [2] Then he spent the last day in his office writing to the score of stockholders for whom he felt a special concern because he personally had induced them to share in the hapless venture. He thanked them for their support; regretted that

[2] December, with its heavy Christmas advertising income, was scarcely a reliable barometer.

the effort had ended in failure and in individual loss at a moment when the paper was definitely on the upgrade and had nearly reached its goal;[3] and added, by way of consolation, "But at least you helped to preserve this old institution from extinction."

The replies reminded him that it was he who had succeeded in saving the paper, admired the spirit in which he had struggled against terrific and insurmountable difficulties, and wondered what he planned to do next. One of them assured him he had no cause for concern about his stockholders' losses and went on, "I knew exactly what the hazards were at all times and made my investment on that basis, and all the others have had at least as much business experience as I have. You have made the finest and pluckiest race any one could, but the grade was an impossible one."

One of the most equable responses came from the vice-president of the Fidelity and Deposit Company of Maryland, but with a Broadway address and dated January 4, 1924. It read:

My dear Dean Gay:

Many thanks for your awfully nice note. It is too bad that we could not have all kept going together, but it is a real satisfaction that we have saved the good old *Post* from extinction or from being Munseyized. However I am rather horrified by the appearance and editorials of the paper during the last two days. Its make-up and handling of the news is too darned much like Philadelphia. As to the editorials, they are either vapid or wholly reactionary. I cannot help feeling that if all the New York papers except those of Hearst take the point of view of ultraconservatism and of those whose understanding of America is in inverse ratio to their wealth, we shall the more quickly come to unthinking radicalism.

Very sincerely yours,
Franklin D. Roosevelt.

On New Year's Eve Gay handed over his keys to 20 Vesey Street. They had been in his pocket for more than four years. During that time the dream of restoring the paper's reputation for outstanding independence and authority had in part come true. But there is no

[3] To the end of his life he was convinced that "it could be done if the stockholders had been patient enough to see it through."

law of nature or of journalism to decree that independence and authority will win wide circulation or reap adequate material rewards. Something more was needed than a good financial section, an interesting editorial page, and an excellent literary review if the *Post* was to get anywhere near Strunsky's suggested optimum circulation of 75,000 in competition with six other evening journals. Perhaps the demand for the paper and for advertising space might have been greater if the sports reports had been livelier and if the news, especially that on the front page, had shown less concern with what Potter called "things and great big world intricate problems" and more interest in "the human drama," in "the fascinating revelations of human nature that come out in the news of every day."

Such bids for the popular vote were, however, ruled out. To Potter's plea for them Gay had replied "I shall win out on our present line — or not at all."[4] Since the kind of paper he insisted on producing failed to attract more than about 40,000 buyers, the rapid expansion of staff and expenditure at a time when all costs were mounting fast placed a burden on the paper's shoulders that could not be shaken off even by all the later rigorous economies. Once the transfer was made from an "angel" with an open purse to a venture on a short corporate shoestring, the inevitable result was a series of hand-to-mouth postponements of disaster. Perhaps the double moral of the story is that journalism is territory which amateur owners, managers, and editors enter at their peril; also that, as the *New York Times* remarked in its obituary notice of the corporation, a newspaper cannot be "commanded by a mass meeting" — especially in a period of deficit financing.

On January 2, 1924, Philadelphia came to New York to see what it could do with the paper. The new *Post* looked much like the *Ledger*. Gone were Strunsky's editorials, for he had moved on to the *Times*, there to be a distinguished contributor for the next two decades. "The Bowling Green" on which Morley had played so jovially for nearly

[4] The two men parted company in 1921 because of this conflict of opinion over the relative merits of "quality circulation" and its "quantity" alternative.

four years had been cut up into small plots planted with unjovial paragraphs about Washington politics. True, there were more pages, many more columns of news, and congratulatory messages from President Calvin Coolidge and Premier Raymond Poincaré. But the price was up from three cents to five. As *Time* said of the "Curtis-morphosis," "It remains to be seen whether the New York public will welcome for five cents a paper distinguished chiefly for its news. If not, the burden of the mistake will be borne by Mr. Curtis' pocketbook." Events were to prove that it was. Neither Mr. Curtis nor those who followed in his steps found the *Post* to be a gold mine.

Meanwhile Gay was staying indoors, catching up on rest and sleep, and trying to move off "the knee of the gods" the answer to the question "What next?" Into the *Post* he had poured without stint of his energy, and the strain had told on him. His face had lost some of the full strong confidence of Washington days, and the twinkle was not nearly so evident in his eyes. Into the *Post* had gone more than energy. He had borrowed heavily to buy stock, his share of the loss was $30,000, and it took him nearly twenty years to repay the debt.

As he looked back in judgment on his latest venture he decided, "This effort must remain, like my work in Washington, an unfinished torso. It will be called a failure, but I cannot believe it to be that."[5] Now, at fifty-six, he was unemployed, with no idea of what he was to do next. He was not allowed to remain long in that uncertain state.

[5] His disbelief was fully justified by the subsequent career of the members of his team. Nevins went to the *Sun*, the *World*, Cornell, then Columbia. Lane and Puckette soon joined the business staff of the *Times*. The *Literary Review* group operated for a time in what Canby called "a kind of sealed chamber," but when Curtis wished to change the character of the *Review* Canby decided to start an independent journal and the *Saturday Review of Literature* made its bow in August 1924. Mark Sullivan had transferred his base from the *Post* to the *Tribune* in 1923. Hamilton Fish Armstrong, selected by Gay in 1919 to specialize in international news, became managing editor of *Foreign Affairs* when it was founded in 1922 and editor in 1928. Paul Garrett, picked to be financial columnist in 1920, remained with the *Post* till 1931, when he became public relations director for General Motors. Leaving the Bowling Green, Morley henceforth divided his time between the *Saturday Review of Literature* and independent work, as essayist, poet, novelist, and playwright. Thus the team made its continuing contribution to journalism and letters.

## V

# HARVARD AND THE SQUIRREL CAGE

## 1924–1936

As GAY'S FRIENDS watched his struggle to save the *Post,* some of them felt he was waging a hopeless battle — or a worthless one — and tried to gather him back into the academic fold. In July 1922, for example, Allyn Young asked to be informed if at any time there was "a glimmer of a chance" he might be induced to return to Harvard. Three months later Mr. Hoover urged him to examine sympathetically an impending offer of the presidency of the University of California. This, he insisted, was no ordinary state university job; it gave scope for a vigorous reorganization of the whole educational system of the state; and in doing such constructive work Gay would make "an infinitely greater contribution to the community" than in the position he now held.

The reply to these and similar approaches was always the same. Gay told Young he had seen the rocky capes ahead when he undertook to steer the *Post*; navigation engrossed his whole mind, and he was not giving a moment's thought to what he might do if he should fail. To Hoover his answer was, "I feel myself morally bound to stick by the ship here, at any rate until she is off the rocks and safely on her course again."

When the ship foundered, his "only consolation — a poor one" — was that he had stood by her and given no thought to escape. Now it was time to start thinking, and by the day he handed over his keys he was becoming inclined, unless "the right kind of business opening" appeared, to "go back into academic work, but not academic administration." No suitable business opening appeared, but it did look as if a position with the *New York Times* might do so. An invitation to lunch with Mr. Ochs, proprietor of that paper, was followed by a tour of his splendid new plant and a heart-to-heart talk which Gay described as follows: "He told me again he would like to have me come with them, but I said I thought he would be perplexed to fit me into his great organization in any way which would be acceptable to him and to me. To that he said he would like to see me again and indicated there were many kinds of things to do on the *Times*." The two men did meet again later, but by that time Gay's plans were settled. "I feel relieved," he wrote, "to close that door definitely and to leave the newspaper world for good. It has been a saddening but enriching experience — in some ways — even if it leaves us poorer than ever."

Within a week of leaving the *Post* several personal and official feelers had reached Gay, strengthening his inclination toward "being a simple professor and trying to do some writing," or, as he put it to his mother, "to go back to the teaching and writing of economic history — my first love and now long interrupted." Archibald C. Coolidge of Harvard was the first to make a move. As soon as he heard that the paper was sold he put the personal question, "Are you willing to come back as a professor here?" He assured Gay that the history department, the economics department, in fact Harvard as a whole needed him badly and that his return would cause widespread rejoicing. Gay's reply was that it would take a very exceptional business call to appeal more than the pull of his old love, and if Harvard really wanted him he felt it had a prior claim.

Other claimants put up a brave fight. Dr. J. R. Angell, Gay's classmate at Ann Arbor and now president of Yale, tried hard to ensnare him. Michigan and California wired offering chairs in economic history at salaries far above normal. George Wickersham wanted to get him as provost at Pennsylvania and Leith was eager to set the wheels turning at Wisconsin, where the presidential chair was vacant. All these approaches were held at arm's length until the prospects at Harvard became clear. There the situation was delicate for many obvious reasons, but in February, after informal talks and exchange of letters with Lowell and Taussig, the former said officially that there was a chair awaiting Gay if he decided to return to academic life.

By that time a complication had developed. The National Bureau of Economic Research had decided it would like Gay to join the staff on a part-time basis as codirector with Wesley Mitchell. Gay was willing to do this, partly because he regarded the Bureau's work as valuable and also because the remuneration would be a very welcome supplement to his professorial salary. He had no desire to live in New York; but if he resided and taught elsewhere he would have to divide his time between teaching in one place and directing the Bureau in New York. Angell pointed out the excellent location of New Haven (and Yale) for such a way of life, but Harvard countered by consenting to his carrying two jobs. He thereupon accepted Lowell's invitation to become professor of economic history.

Though the appointment was not formally approved by the Overseers until mid-April, the news had gone all over the faculty grapevine before two days of March had passed. Its reception was enthusiastically favorable. "We are all very glad," said Carver for the economics department, and the individual members spoke for themselves: "You don't need to be told again how delighted I am that you are coming back to us and how warm a welcome you will have from all your colleagues" (Taussig); "When you went away you left a big hole in the department and we haven't been able to plug it up" (Bullock); and so on. Coolidge rejoiced and Haskins said, "*Nunc dimittis*! It is the best news for Harvard in many years." It was quite clear that old colleagues were making ready to kill the fatted calf for the returning prodigal.

That return was, however, still six months away. In the meantime there was need for work to do and income to be earned. The need was met immediately and almost simultaneously when in early

March Gay took up his duties at the National Bureau and also was appointed "expert consultant" to the Department of Commerce. He held the former position until 1933, and his work there will be examined later. Though the latter was a temporary job, he could throw himself into it with zest, for it offered a belated opportunity to effect some of those improvements in government statistical and information services which he had urged after the Armistice.

His hopes for getting on with this "unfinished business" had been lifted high when Herbert Hoover was chosen Secretary of Commerce in early 1921. Till that time the only postwar work he had done in Washington was as member of Rossiter's advisory committee on the census. The committee had saved the census of 1920 from ignominious failure by revealing the incompetence of the political hacks who were in control, compelling the director — an unqualified spoilsman — to entrust the work to a capable experienced assistant, and improving the census machinery. But all its proposals for expanding the scope of the census had been rejected by Secretary of Commerce Redfield on the ground that Congress was in a mood to reduce rather than increase appropriations.

With Hoover in charge there was a chance of better things. Gay and he had collided head on at their first encounter in 1918, but thereafter soon came to know and respect each other. As soon as Hoover's appointment was announced, Gay began to ply him with suggestions for improving his department. He was responsive but laid down a condition: "If I have to undertake this terrible stunt, I want to secure the working of your intellect from this moment forward." He outlined his desire to turn what had been an insignificant branch of the administration into a living growing department, capable of providing information useful to American businessmen and also "of scientific world value." He asked Gay to lay out plans for reorganization and expansion, to suggest names of men competent to serve on an advisory board, and wound up: "As you are pushing me into this job, I am not going to have any reserves in going after you for advice."

When Hoover went to his office for the first time he found on his desk a confidential memorandum from Rossiter's committee, describing the conditions they had unearthed, the reforms brought about, and the deficiencies still needing correction. He invited the committee to call on him and asked its members to serve as an advisory committee on statistics to his department. For at least a year he drove them hard. He requested them to investigate the statistical organization and methods of the New York customs service. He welcomed their suggestions for studies of domestic commerce, periodical reports on business conditions, and other topics. He went to one of their meetings and asked them to find him an economic adviser immediately. As they were unable to do this they had to resolve that, since he was reorganizing so much at such a rapid pace, one or more of them should be on call for duty throughout the summer.

When Hoover's plans required additional appropriations, Gay and other members came forward to plead the cause before congressional committees, and did succeed in securing funds for a census on distribution. When the President convened a conference to examine the serious unemployment situation in 1921, Hoover persuaded him to recognize the committee, strengthened by the addition of more members, as the official economic adviser on the "many questions of an economic and social order that are likely to arise." When new policies called for new men, Gay was frequently asked to suggest suitable people. On his recommendation Julius Klein, a former graduate student and teaching assistant, was appointed to the post of Director of the Bureau of Domestic and Foreign Commerce; Walter Tower was chosen to be commercial attaché in London when Hoover began to expand the hitherto small overseas commercial service; and some of the members of the unemployment conference were on that body because Gay said they would satisfy Hoover's need for "men of the economic type who have a vision of the forces at work in this present slump and of social conditions generally."

When news of the *Post* débacle came out, Hoover and Klein immediately decided it would be good to have Gay on hand for a few months. He was invited to the capital to see Hoover, and found that the Tea Pot Dome investigation and other congressional activities had made the Secretary "a little more dour and grim . . . than usual." The two men talked about beds of roses; Gay said they were not to be found in journalism or politics, Hoover wished he were a professor, then they turned to discuss plans. Within three weeks Gay was on the pay roll[1] and spent four months, mostly in Washington, working on three problems assigned him.

The first was a critical appraisal of the department's index numbers and a search for ways of making them more accurate. The second was the improvement of the monthly summary of business conditions. The third, and more interesting, was the formulation of a practicable program and appropriate organization for the new Division of Domestic Commerce. It was almost like old times to be determining broad objectives, drawing organization charts, seeking interdepartmental coöperation, hunting for the right man to fill some new niche, and getting the wheels turning. Gay enjoyed the satisfaction of having his proposals on all three projects adopted, saw the new creations "running on the right track and in the right directions," and agreed to continue on the books as consultant, returning to Washington from time to time for a tour of inspection. Then the family left New York at the end of June for a few weeks' vacation on the shore of a New Hampshire lake, in preparation for settling into an apartment in Brookline and Gay's resumption of work at Harvard.

The next twelve years quickly took on a pattern that persisted till it was broken in 1936 by the second resignation from Harvard. Apart from one year's sabbatical leave during 1933, the perennial round in what Gay often called "the squirrel cage" went on without respite. An equally fitting name would have been "the eternal triangle," with Cambridge, New York, and Washington at the points, but with

[1] The department had no funds for employing an "expert consultant"; Gay had therefore to be paid out of an appropriation made for the study of the current crisis in the supply of rubber.

digressions that sometimes turned the figure into a rectangle or pentagon.

There were bound to be difficulties and some sense of anticlimax in the return to Harvard. The place was bustling with growth, change, and much planning of new scholarly enterprises. The Business School, which had fallen to a wartime low enrollment of a hundred in 1917–18, now had seven hundred students, and the day when it would move into a stately mansion was not far off. As Gay looked on these things he was at one moment disposed to think that where he had failed another had succeeded, and the next moment to resent the apparent belittling of his foundation-laying by some who lauded the superstructure. In the seven years of his absence many colleagues who belonged to his generation had slipped out of middle age into the status of Grand Old Men, with their eccentricities and temperaments so accentuated that the observer was tempted to seek in a dictionary for the masculine counterpart of *prima donna*. And Gay's colleagues quickly noted that the same sort of thing had happened to him.

Younger teachers were more numerous and a whole new generation of students filled classrooms. Some of them may have heard his talk in early 1923 on "Business as a profession," and recalled his assertion that teaching and the ministry were better careers than business. Others may have remembered his Phi Beta Kappa oration on "The Rhythm of History" in June of the same year, partly because he presented it in the form of a dialogue between a lecturer and an audience of persistent hecklers and partly because Christopher Morley, the other speaker, had read a baker's dozen of his own sonnets. But to most students and not a few of the faculty the returner was a stranger — or at best a reputation. It was not easy to come back and to refit oneself to the life of an academic community.

Much time and labor were needed to regain the lecturing habit and still more to catch up on the unread literature of the last decade. Though the field to be covered was now limited to the Industrial Revolution and after, the preparation of two or three lectures a week for Economics 2 proved little easier than it had been twenty years before. It took Gay three years to get the course into satisfactory arrangement and content, and seven years to discover that overpreparation could be a handicap. The discovery came when the "two hours of further preparation" he had planned to give to "the difficult problem of serfdom in France" were taken up by the visits of two colleagues. Hence, he wrote, "I went to lecture only half-prepared; but I presented the subject in a new way and was surprised at the intense interest shown by the class — usually so bored by agrarian history." It is a pity his colleagues had not interrupted him a quarter of a century earlier.

Gay's sense of obligation to his graduate students and his demands on them were as heavy as before. The latter earned him a new nickname drawn from the vocabulary of World War I: he was christened "The Prussian." To a newcomer there was nothing negative or easygoing about his personality or reception. As one of them recalled, "I was, in fact, scared to death of him during my early association with him." The assignments of work were large, the emphasis on foreign languages was great, and the criticism could be brutally severe. The student who went to a conference feeling elated by what he had to report might emerge badly deflated; but on the other hand the man who came to confess himself unhappy over the inadequate results of his efforts was likely to go away conscious that he had not worked entirely in vain and only needed to follow the new pointers he had received in order to turn failure into success. To any student judged worthy of aid the help was as generous as ever in the suggestion of topics for investigation, the guidance to source materials, the detailed scrutiny of manuscript, and the assistance, both editorial and financial, in seeing a finished work through the press.

Day after day, for example, during the crowded summer school session of 1926, Gay spent two or three hours in conference, mostly going over a thesis with one student. Though the work was tedious it was deemed worth doing because the man was "sagacious, canny, careful yet enterprising, with a good head on his shoulders, and I believe he will give a good account of himself." When the same man returned eight years later with another manuscript Gay gave it equally exhaustive general and minute criticism. When one of his oldest students, now a professor of many years' standing, needed a subsidy for the publication of a costly monograph, Gay handed over to the printer the whole of the compensation he had received for serving as acting dean of the Faculty of Arts and Sciences.[2] Those who signed up to work under him entered a club that conferred potential life membership. His files reveal how they continued to draw on his counsel at crucial moments of their careers to the end of his days.

Outside the classroom and office Gay was pulled into many Harvard activities. In 1927 the Business School added a professor of business history to its faculty, took the lead in founding the Business History Society, and established a *Journal of Economic and Business History*. The *Journal* was intended, *inter alia*, to build a bridge across the Charles River, linking the interests of the Business School, now housed across that stream, with those of the economic historians on the Cambridge bank. With that intent Gay was appointed editor, while N. S. B. Gras, the new professor of business history, became managing editor. Though not sure there was a real distinction between economic history and business history, Gay took his duties seriously, even to reading all the galley proofs. The *Journal* quickly established its reputation as one of the best in the field, but the bridge could not stand the strain imposed on it. In 1931 Gay resigned the editorship and the magazine succumbed a year later, victim of monetary malnutrition during the Great Depression.

Other assignments were such as came to many men during a decade which saw American universities expand greatly in size as well as in the diversity of their interests. Gay could not hope to escape appointment to committees, especially to those which had to cope with troublesome topics, to plan some large new development in

[2] The check would have paid half a year's interest on the debt incurred to buy stock in the *Post*.

teaching or research, to reconstruct a department, or to raise funds. Meanwhile President Lowell called on him for counsel in countless ways. The two men might often be seen walking in the environs of Cambridge and, according to legend, passers-by would hear Lowell say, "What I would like to do for Harvard is. . ." When the Dean of the Faculty of Arts and Sciences died suddenly in September 1931, Gay was drafted to be acting dean and carried the load until a successor took office five months later.

This work as teacher, active citizen, and elder statesman could well have absorbed most of Gay's time, yet leave him with some free days or weeks for writing. Instead, by his own choice, it had to be dovetailed into a timetable which earmarked all spare hours during semesters and virtually the whole of short or long vacations for external interests. Of these interests the two most sustained and absorbing were centered on the National Bureau of Economic Research and the Council on Foreign Relations.

As we have already seen, those two institutions had much in common. They were created by alliances between scholars and men of affairs. Their function was to initiate research and disseminate information on subjects hitherto relatively neglected which the war had shown to be in urgent need of attention, but which the universities were not investigating for lack of funds, facilities, men, interest, perhaps even courage or vision. In a period of great social stress and international upheaval, when the air was filled with the improvisations of reformers or the panaceas of revolutionaries, they expounded no cause or creed — save the faith that scientific inquiry would bring a better understanding of society's problems and make possible an intelligent search for their solution. They could concentrate their investigation on large but carefully chosen topics. In their organization and procedures they enjoyed an elasticity, adaptability, and coöperation between the scholar and the outer world that university life lacked. Finally, the task of finding financial support for their growth, or even their continued existence, was a constant challenge to the ingenuity and salesmanship of those in charge. For a quarter of a century, from their birth until the end of his life, Gay found great satisfaction in the work he did with and for them. A brief survey of that work is more than part of his story; it is a chapter in a new era in American scholarship.

On the evening before Wesley Mitchell's departure from his war work in Washington, Gay and he had a long talk about the deficiencies that still barred the claim of economics to be regarded as a science. Gay reported the discussion as follows:

> Mitchell asked me if I thought economics could ever be made a true science, and I told him that I sincerely believed it possible, but it would take some fifteen or twenty generations more of hard and painstaking work and the accumulation of a long series of statistical studies for five hundred years or more before the base line is long enough to make statistical deductions from social measurements.

Mitchell was enough of a historian to appreciate the long view. His own "hard and painstaking work" on prices, the business cycle, and other aspects of the money economy was based on such statistical raw material as he could unearth. His scientific deductions had come from the patient study of social measurements, processes, and interconnections; and, as Professor Arthur F. Burns has put it, he had already "demonstrated that broad economic generalizations based on empirical observations were possible." He was doing with much success what Gustav Schmoller and his school had tried to do in Germany.

The two men were therefore agreed that the advancement of economics to the stature of a true science depended more on inductive quantitative studies than on deductive analysis. In that faith they welcomed Malcolm Rorty's return from military service and his revival of the plan for research by the Committee on National Income organized in 1917. By the end of 1919 he had raised some money, the Committee was converted into a board of directors, and the bylaws of what had been christened the National Bureau of Economic Research were approved. At the first formal meeting, in February 1920, Gay was elected president, Mitchell director of research, and the venture started on its ambitious career

to encourage, in the broadest and most liberal manner, investigation, research, and discovery, and the application of knowledge to the wellbeing of mankind; and in particular to conduct, or assist in the making of, exact and impartial investigations in the field of economic, social, and industrial science.

The Bureau's organization embodied the idea, hatched much earlier, of collaboration between scholars and men representing all walks of business, economic classes, social and political viewpoints. Its board of directors contained economists, statisticians, bankers, accountants, engineers, representatives of labor and of farmers, and left-wing authors. These men were expected to read and criticize the draft studies prepared by the research staff, so that the final results could appeal for popular acceptance on the ground that they were not the product of any class or social creed. As Mitchell said in his first annual report, "The plan of bringing together into one board men who represented so many and such divergent views of public policy, and of asking these men to unite in assuming responsibility for the publication of such findings as the Board's staff might reach, was a very bold plan." The directors not merely did their homework conscientiously, making countless valuable suggestions; they also accepted readily the researchers' findings on the first subject studied — the size and distribution of the country's national income.

In May 1921, Rorty invited the Board to a dinner to celebrate the completion of the first piece of work and the grant by the Carnegie Foundation of funds that assured the Bureau's existence for another year. The first volume, *Income in the United States*, saw the light in December, the second in 1922. The demand was unexpectedly large. As Mitchell said, "The number of people who care enough about the details of our estimates to pay $5 for a cross between a census report and a treatise on statistical method shows that there is a much wider interest in what we are doing than we had supposed."

By the end of 1921 the Bureau had chosen and begun to break ground in its second field — the study of business cycles. But already outsiders were calling for aid and seeking to divert the handful of research workers to other tasks. The President's conference on unemployment had appointed a standing committee, with Hoover as chairman, and requested it to produce practical proposals for preventing the recurrence or mitigating the severity of future periods of unemployment. Hoover asked Gay if the National Bureau would help his committee by preparing a report on business cycles and unemployment, and have it ready within six months. After consulting his colleagues, Gay replied that the Bureau would do the job, provided (a) its report was first read and approved by the directors as usual, (b) its work was confined to fact-finding, without expectation of a neat list of recommendations, (c) it was free to publish the report if it desired, and (d) the government defrayed part of the cost. Hoover agreed to these terms, but had no funds available and therefore had to ask the Carnegie Corporation to foot the bill.

It did so, and 1922 was "Unemployment Year" at the Bureau. By engaging fifteen temporary assistants to help the six regular researchers, by overworking these men as well as the directors, the final report was rushed to Hoover just before the dead line. It took his committee almost as long to decide what recommendations should be made to the President as it had taken the Bureau to collect the facts. "We were quick, they were terribly slow," lamented Mitchell. Perhaps the job had been worth doing. It had led to the accumulation of much useful data, to valuable contacts with government and business organizations, and to the discovery of great areas of ignorance on such matters as the number of unemployed persons in the country. But it had revealed the danger that the Bureau might become swamped with requests from federal, state, or other agencies for *ad hoc* investigations; that the time allotted for them would be too brief for more than a rush job; that the staff would be sidetracked from the plan of basic work it wished to undertake; and that the directors would be overloaded with "bursts of heavy reading."

The Bureau was therefore in the mood for retreating into its own shell when Gay joined Mitchell as codirector in early 1924. For nine years the two men worked together. The qualities of each complemented those of the other to make an almost perfect combination. Under a general division of labor Gay managed the Bureau while Mitchell managed the research, carried on his own study of business cycles, and brought his great statistical talents to bear on guiding the work of about half a dozen investigators. The division was not watertight, for Gay knew enough about what the researchers were doing to help them block out their work. He discussed their materials and ideas as the studies progressed, read the manuscripts carefully, and in one case spent much time "composing, or rather extracting from [his] innards a preface" for the book. His attitude toward the younger men was like that toward his graduate students. He was at their disposal, to criticize, to encourage, to give them an enthusiasm for their work.

His main task, however, was to serve as promoter, selling a new kind of article to a new kind of buyer. The Bureau, like the Council on Foreign Relations, was a private non-profit body, unattached to any institution, and devoted to an ambitious piece of scholarly public service. Its operating costs could not be met entirely by individual subscriptions and it was not likely to be financed by any university or to receive substantial endowments. But its infancy coincided with the appearance of new foundations and the recognition by some of them, as well as by a few of the older ones, that the social sciences merited a measure of the support hitherto given almost solely to medicine, public health, or the physical sciences. War had made the country more conscious of the importance of economic questions and of the need for refuting Frank A. Vanderlip's contention that the American people were "a nation of economic illiterates." The attack on illiteracy must be many-sided, long, and expensive; it was therefore good news to learn that some foundations were willing to defray campaign costs if the strategy, tactics, and personnel seemed worthy.

As strategist and tactician Gay was among the best in his generation. He possessed rare skill in mapping out a broad project, dividing it into specific parts that could be handled, plotting the kind of organization that would be needed, estimating the likely cost, drawing up a budget, finding men for the work, and presenting the whole plan in a cogent manner to those who held the foundations' purse-strings.

These qualities he exercised to the full for the benefit of the Bureau. By 1925 less than half its income was coming from individual subscriptions, the rest from the Carnegie Corporation, the Laura Spelman Rockefeller Memorial, and the Social Science Research Council (founded in 1923). Neither kind of support could be dispensed with, and Gay spent one night in 1927 drafting a "longish letter" which the treasurer wished "to circulate in order to extract as painlessly and agreeably as possible, contributions to meet the Bureau's $5000 deficit." It was not an easy letter to write, for it had to explain why there had been few publications recently; to describe the delays that came when the results of painstaking work were found to be unsatisfactory and had to be cast aside; to report that the discovery of new sources of information necessitated a complete reworking of a subject; to emphasize the time-consuming, patient perfecting of statistical techniques; and to point out the terribly high cost of publishing books full of figures.

It was easier to explain these matters to a foundation official. Consequently a well-beaten track gradually appeared between the door of the Bureau and those of the foundations. There were times when the journey seemed fruitless, as, for example, in late 1928 when the prospective termination of the Carnegie grant seemed to doom the Bureau to extinction or to absorption by Columbia University. There was great delight when in May 1929 Gay reported that he had worked out and sold plans that would give the Bureau over $100,000 of "new money" each year, assure sufficient funds for the next five years, thereby allowing it to move to better quarters, build a laboratory and a library, and embark on projects which hitherto had been too costly to be more than pipe dreams. It was with deep anxiety that he spent an evening in depressed early 1932, going over the finances with his colleagues, and after they had left worked far into the night preparing "three budgets to meet three possible contingencies in the grant or non-grant of additional funds" from the two chief foundations.

As the Bureau's activities became known more widely, requests for special investigations came in from various directions. Having seen his own plans sidetracked by the unemployment studies of 1922, Mitchell was loath to admit any further distracting projects or to let the Bureau become known as a miscellaneous general service station. Gay, on the other hand, favored such work, provided it could be well done, because it would render a needed public service and in addition might tide the Bureau over a period of financial stringency. He got his way sometimes, usually on condition that he shoulder the responsibility for arranging, managing, and financing whatever assignments were accepted.

Of these there were many. In 1923, when immigration was a burning topic of public controversy, the Social Science Research Council asked the Bureau to explore some economic aspects of migration and offered to provide the necessary funds. This request led to a comprehensive inspection, interpretation, and critique of the available statistics of international migration throughout the world. The collection and tabulation of the figures was entrusted to the International Labour Office at Geneva, since it had the necessary facilities and was interested in recent phases of the subject. The interpretation of the statistics was done by a score of specialists under the direction of Professor Willcox of Cornell. The planning and execution of the project abounded with difficulties and complications which caused Gay a good deal of worry: but when the two volumes were published (1929 and 1931) a new bench mark had been made not only in the study of migration but also in international scholarly coöperation.

Less ambitious inquiries were undertaken, by request, into recent trends in philanthropy; into the policies of corporations toward charitable gifts and especially toward the Community Chest drives which had recently become a common feature of city life; and into the purchase of medical care through fixed periodical payments. The institutions which asked for the investigations were so reputable and the subjects of such importance that Gay worked hard on each project. When, however, a leading chain store offered $100,000 for a study of retail grocery prices, even he felt this was beyond the bounds of the Bureau's public service.

Mr. Hoover's proposal in 1927 that the Bureau undertake a survey of "recent economic changes" was a disturbing suggestion. It was not easy to say no to him, yet the task was obviously far too large and diffuse, and of course far too costly unless sponsors were found. When they were, acceptance of the assignment meant the diversion of nearly all the staff from their planned studies, the introduction of much outside help, and a rushed job. The contributors had scant time for considering the suggestions or criticisms made by the director-readers; but the book, in two large volumes entitled *Recent Economic Changes*, appeared on schedule in the summer of 1929.

Gay's part in that work was the assembling of more than a dozen authors and the writing of a brief introduction where, under the guise of portraying the views of foreign visitors, he expressed his own ideas about the outstanding features of the American economy. In addition he proofread the whole book, making all corrections on the galleys, then on the page proofs, and finally on the revised page proofs. After working night and day through most of May 1929, he wrote his daughter: "It is well for my old eyes that the job is nearly done. I am sorry to be obliged to read these 950 odd pages so many times over, for each time they look more and more stodgy, dull, and meaningless. At the present moment I have a very poor opinion of the book and of practically all its contributors."

Within a few months his opinon was probably poorer, for the book had given no hint that recent economic changes would work out as they actually did in the fall of 1929. In fact, the brief treatment of cyclical fluctuations had rightly shown that these phenomena had been "notably moderate" since 1922. Soon Gay had a research project of his own on his hands — a study at first hand of the effect of business fluctuations on the income of the Bureau. The depression reduced greatly the amount received in individual contributions. Since these were "matched" by one of the foundations, every loss of a dollar from a personal pocket meant the loss of a foundation dollar as well. His task therefore became one of emergency financing, of scraping, paring, hacking at expenditures.

Of this thankless work he grew rather tired; he had done so much of it ten years before; and he was now approaching his mid-sixties. Besides, he felt keenly the criticism voiced in some quarters that the Bureau under his persuasion had wandered too frequently away from its original high purpose into special studies. He was not quite reassured by the contention of his friends that these investigations were good things to do as long as the money was available for them, but that now, when cash was scarce, the more fundamental researches could once more be given the right of way. The phrase "right of way" had an unhappy ring to it, for that was what his supporters had requested in the final struggle to raise money and save the *Post*. When he resigned from the codirectorship on the eve of his departure on sabbatical leave in early 1933, the outlook for the Bureau seemed little less dark than did that of the nation. The best bits of news he heard during his absence were that the country was recovering and that the Bureau had received grants ensuring its existence for three more years.

On every visit to New York Gay spent some time at the office of the Council on Foreign Relations. The Council was the outcome of a merger between an older body with the same name and a new-born Institute of International Affairs. The former began during the war as a dinner club which gave those residents of New York City who were interested in international affairs — and who could afford expensive meals — an opportunity to hear speeches by distinguished foreign visitors. The latter was composed of members of the American peace delegation, who, in discussions among themselves and with their British counterparts, had realized their ignorance of each other's viewpoints and their need for continuous study of international relations.

When the peace negotiations were nearly ended an Anglo-American group met in Paris and decided to form an Institute of International Affairs, composed at the outset of two branches, one in the United Kingdom, the other in the United States. The British returned to London and set up what soon became known as the Royal Institute of International Affairs, with a home at Chatham House and a staff which during the last three decades has published many noteworthy studies. The American group went by another route and merged with the existing Council on Foreign Relations, taking the name of the latter but grafting the Paris plan of study on to the Council's combination of eating and listening.

When the two groups decided to coalesce, a steering committee was set up to work out plans. Gay was invited to serve on it, then to act as secretary-treasurer when the Council was incorporated in 1921. The petition for incorporation set forth the Council's aim:

> To afford a continuous conference on international questions affecting the United States, by bringing together experts in state-craft, finance, industry, education, and science; to create and stimulate international thought among the people of the United States, and to this end to coöperate with the Government of the United States and with international agencies.

The first honorary president was Elihu Root, the first president John W. Davis. Hamilton Fish Armstrong, then a member of the *Post* staff, was appointed executive director, and Gay was secretary-treasurer from 1921 until his departure on sabbatical in early 1933 led him to insist on being allowed to resign. In accepting his resignation John W. Davis truthfully said, "As one of the original members of the Board and as Secretary during the [last] eleven years . . . you have more than any other individual influenced its policy and guided its course."

So long as Gay resided in New York his influence was continuous, and it was during those years that the Council mapped out its main lines of action. But he was ever on call after he left the city. As secretary he looked after the Council's staff, not always an easy task. As treasurer he hunted members and donors, invested surplus funds, and drew up the annual budget. When in October 1929 the Council got a chance to buy a home of its own, he spent a busy day downtown "tapping the international concerns and sending Armstrong out on a quest for subscriptions." The result of their joint efforts was the raising of over $150,000 and the president was therefore able, when thanking Ramsey MacDonald for his speech at a Council dinner a day or two afterwards, to hint that the next time MacDonald spoke it would probably be on the Council's own premises.

From the start Gay felt that the chief task of the Council should be the publication of an authoritative quarterly journal on foreign relations. When he propounded this idea he was promptly appointed chairman of the Publications Committee, and went to work with such vigor that in September 1922 the first number of *Foreign Affairs* appeared. With Archibald C. Coolidge as editor and a distinguished list of American and foreign contributors, it quickly established itself as the country's leading publication in the field and within three years its circulation had mounted to nearly 10,000 copies.

On Coolidge's death in 1928, Gay experienced "dreadful but inevitable anxiety" about its future editorship, and pulled (or tied up) strings so as "in any case not to leave any initiative to the editorial board." His anxiety may have been unnecessary, since Hamilton Fish Armstrong already had five years' experience as managing editor; but Gay did want to be sure of a choice which has justified itself by lasting more than twenty years. Perhaps the best measure of his belief in the importance of *Foreign Affairs* is that he was persuaded to write three articles for it — on "War Loans or Subsidies" (1926), "The Gold Problem" (1931), and "The Great Depression" (1932). He did them reluctantly, with great labor, and without much satisfaction over the product, yet all are masterly performances. To them could be applied what Wesley Mitchell said of the last: "The kind of thing which only a scholar with full knowledge of an immense mass of detailed information concerning economics, statistics, politics, and international relations can produce."

Next in importance to *Foreign Affairs* Gay placed study by small groups, leading to research on international questions. During at least three periods he served as chairman of such a group. The first one met monthly during the winter of 1924–25 to study the problems of the Ruhr and Rhineland, and Gay came from Cambridge to conduct it. Its sixteen members included such friends and present or former colleagues as Dulles, Leffingwell, Mitchell, Rublee, Schneider, Strunsky, and Tower. Similar study circles were led by Coolidge, Isaiah Bowman, Walter Lippmann, and others. The early hope that their discussions would produce publishable reports was scarcely ever fulfilled. It therefore seemed desirable to establish a Research Committee and employ or commission competent men to undertake inquiries that would be worthy of print. Gay was made chairman of this committee, and under its auspices there appeared annual surveys of American foreign relations, an annual political handbook of the world, and occasional research monographs. Through these volumes and *Foreign Affairs* Americans were offered a clearer view of the outer world and of the part they were playing in it.

Wesley Mitchell once called the 1920's "The Social Sciences-Conscious Decade." The description was apt in a double sense. On the one hand, the general public became conscious of the importance of at least some of the social sciences, especially economics and psychology — though there was some doubt what sort of science the latter was; the universities admitted the need for expanding their social science departments; and the foundations recognized that the study of man in society might be as worthy of support as was that of man in hospital. On the other hand, the social scientists became conscious of the need for working together. They could not hope, or even desire, to halt the trend toward specialization, the tendency of the individual scholar to know more and more about a smaller and smaller facet of man's relations with his fellows. It was useless to sigh for the good old times when a man occupied a davenport and taught such a combination as history and political science and economics. Outside the small colleges the davenport had been sawed up into chairs, and these in turn were being so subdivided that many teachers and researchers sat on small stools, surrounded by partitions fencing off urban sociology from rural, land economics from all other kinds, business history from economic and from social, and so forth in a motley of cubicles.

There was merit in this division of labor, but there was also need for an antidote. The specialist must break down some fences, leap over them, or at least look over the top to see what could be learned about the tools, techniques, and findings of others. The *expertise* of men in different "disciplines" — as they were now being called — ought to be brought to bear on a problem that interested them all. Such phrases as "cross discipline problems" or "inter-discipline problems" began to circulate — for a while in "quotes." There was hope of great achievement from interrelated effort; there was growing willingness to coöperate, provided the vested interests and equal status of departmental divisions were respected; and it must be admitted that some nostrils were keenly sensitive to the odors from the foundations' fleshpots. Hence, as H. G. Moulton put it in 1929, "Coöperation in social science research has within the last few years become a veritable slogan."

The breadth of Gay's interests, fostered by his long many-sided training and his varied experience, made him a leading figure in this new development, while his skill in promoting and planning ensured his inclusion wherever there was blueprinting to be done. It began when in late 1923 the American Sociological Society proposed that delegates from the various social science associations meet to consider the production of what finally emerged as the *Encyclopaedia of the Social Sciences*, sponsored by ten learned societies.

Professors Seligman, Clive Day, and Gay were chosen to represent the economists, but as Gay could not attend the first general meeting he had to learn from Day what happened. The latter told a sad tale of his reduction "to abject despair" by the lack of any real ideas concerning the scope of the job, the desire to have everything covered in an unlimited number of huge volumes, and the total disregard of cost. He therefore tried to resign from the committee and urged his fellow-economists to keep aloof unless plans became more modest and precise.

Seligman and Gay were of a different mind and mold. They took the project in hand, brought it down to earth, gave it bounds and design, and hatched a scheme for financing it. Gay was chairman of the committee that selected the executive committee and he worked hard persuading some reluctant nominees to accept the assignment. Seligman shouldered the editorship-in-chief and by Christmas, 1925, the plan for the *Encyclopaedia* was ready to be submitted for approval by the associations. Thereafter the pace became fast, especially when Alvin Johnson and a corps of brilliant young assistants were drafted to carry the real burden of editorial work. The first of the fifteen volumes appeared in early 1930, the last in 1935. Gay withdrew from active service when the executive committee had been chosen, and his subsequent contributions were limited to serving as an advisory editor and writing one article (on the Putting Out System). But Mitchell, watching the development at close quarters, wrote him in 1927, "Accept my congratulations upon the perfect working out of your original scheme for the *Encyclopaedia of the Social Sciences.*"

The *Encyclopaedia* was a valuable product of temporary coöperation between scholars of various disciplines and countries. The Council of Learned Societies (1919) and the Social Science Research Council (1923) were set up in hope of enduring collaboration. With the former Gay had a little to do in 1930–1936, but the latter engaged part of his active interest from 1925 to 1932. It was born of the desire of the political scientists to improve the facilities for research in their field. A committee appointed in 1921, with Professor Charles E. Merriam as chairman, made the kind of recommendations that were expected; but it went further by urging the establishment of a social science research council, containing representatives of the associations of economists, sociologists, historians, and political scientists, and charged with the task of developing research in the social studies.

With the acceptance of this proposal by the political scientists, economists, sociologists, and statisticians the Council came into being, pledged to "promoting and coördinating research by furthering the development of research methods in the social studies." Soon the psychologists, historians, and anthropologists joined in and so there were seven sponsors. The establishment of the Council was happily timed, for it was coincident with the expansion of the Laura Spelman Rockefeller Memorial from a small unit carrying on Mrs. Rockefeller's charitable work to a foundation with nearly $80,000,000 of capital. Under Beardsley Ruml's direction it marked off as its field the study of man in society. The social sciences and the Social Science Research Council were obvious claimants for its support, and they received it — in all to the tune of $25,000,000 during the years 1925–1928.

Proposals for research projects quickly poured in to the Council and forced it in 1925 to establish a special committee on "problems and policy." This committee — soon known as "P. and P." — did what its name suggests. Its task was to "canvass the general policy to be followed and consider specific problems already before the Council." In addition to scrutinizing projects submitted by others it could formulate proposals of its own. It could appoint advisory committees of experts to aid its deliberations and to thresh out ways of handling an investigation.

It met frequently in New York during the winter; but its most strenuous work was done in a series of sessions held at Hanover, the home of Dartmouth College, during late August and early September. There P. and P. discussed projects, conferred with its advisory committees, decided what recommendations should be made, then submitted them to the whole Council for approval or rejection. By way of light relief all present gathered in the evening to listen to men who had new things to say or novel views to present. Going to Hanover thus became a perennial pilgrimage for many of the country's leading social scientists.

Though not a member of the Council, Gay was invited to be one of the first members of P. and P. He served for three years, in the company of such men as Arnold Bennett Hall (Wisconsin, then Oregon), Guy Stanton Ford (Minnesota), Clark Wissler (Yale), Shelby Harrison (Russell Sage Foundation), H. G. Moulton (Brookings Institution), and R. S. Woodworth (Columbia). It was a revealing experience and at Hanover could be an exhausting one—unless one avoided being slated as *rapporteur* of some project to the Council, took one's golf clubs and insisted on using them. Gay was slow in learning how to avoid anything; his attempt, made long ago, to learn to play golf had been quickly abandoned as waste effort; and there were many projects on the agenda in which he had a very lively interest.

He therefore endured full employment during the Hanover meetings. The first, in 1925, did not take too seriously the 268 subjects, questions, and ideas that had been submitted. But it did scrutinize carefully and give its blessing to proposals for research on the family, Mexican immigration, internal migration, race relations, agricultural economics, and the Eighteenth Amendment, and set up advisory committees to explore them. During the winter it added to this list, so that in 1926 P. and P. and its ten advisory committees spent three weeks preparing recommendations for the meeting of the Council in the fourth.

The endless series of sessions, the study of many reports, the "fierce drive" through weekdays and Sundays in order to have the recommendations ready, the switching of one's mind—from crime to the family to pioneer belts to prohibition to industrial relations to Mexican migrants to prohibition to agricultural issues to international relations to corporate relations to prohibition—and the sense of responsibility in weighing the absolute as well as relative merits of such diverse topics, all left Gay and his colleagues on P. and P.

"rather pumped out and limp . . . It is interesting," he wrote, "to watch this bit of human machinery evolving and operating, and it would be especially interesting to sit in as a spectator; but there isn't so much fun in being one of the scene-shifters."

There may not have been much fun, but there was some sense of satisfaction when, on the retirement of Hall and Gay, the Council voiced "its appreciation of the long and arduous services of Mr. Hall and Mr. Gay on the Committee which has so devotedly and admirably carried a large share of the work and responsibilities of the Council." There was more tangible reward in the winning of approval for research projects of which Gay was the father or foster father. Some of these were endorsed while he was on P. and P., others after he had served his time there. The National Bureau and the Council on Foreign Relations alike gained by having some of their plans carefully scrutinized and finally blessed. In addition at least three of Gay's own projects were helped through to achievement.

The first was a study of the extent to which American business was in the hands of corporations and of trends in corporate development. Gay molded into concrete form the suggestion that research be done in this field and insisted that the study be undertaken by a lawyer and an economist working hand in hand. The chief outcome was the volume by A. A. Berle, Jr. and Gardiner Means on *The Modern Corporation and Private Property* (1932).

The second began to take shape in 1926 when Gay felt the need for such uniform methods of computing wage statistics in different countries as would permit at least rough international comparisons. He interested H. S. Dennison in the idea, secured his appointment as chairman of the industrial relations advisory committee, and thus brought him to Hanover. There Dennison presented the plea for international uniformity so persuasively that the Council granted some money for the work.

Gay thereupon prepared to go to Europe in the summer of 1928. There were many reasons for the trip: to enlist collaborators for the new *Journal of Economic and Business History;* to represent the Social Science Research Council at a conference in Paris on population studies; to discuss the improvement of wage statistics with the International Labour Office in Geneva and the statisticians of the different governments; and to have his portrait painted by Sir William Orpen.

The Business School had decided there ought to be a good picture of its first dean in the new building. Dean Donham raised a fund he thought would be sufficient to cover Orpen's fee and pay Gay's expenses for going across to sit. He wrote Orpen asking his price, then left for Egypt. When the answer arrived and the guineas were translated into dollars, it became evident there was not enough money available to pay the artist, much less the traveling expenses. Gay felt the fee was more than ought to be spent and at his request the plan was abandoned. Since this meant that the Social Science Research Council would have to meet the entire cost of his trip, he insisted on calling it off.

The journey was actually taken during the following winter, squeezed into the January weeks of the Harvard "reading period" and midyear examinations. For four days Gay, Dennison, and Leo Wolman conferred in Geneva with British, German, French, Italian, and International Labour Office representatives, exploring the "possibilities of so improving wage statistics as to facilitate international comparisons." Dennison presided, Henry Clay led the British delegation, and the Anglo-American teamwork was "excellent and most useful." The resolutions passed were far more satisfactory than Gay had expected, but the Americans were forced to realize that the very purpose of the meeting was odious to many people. The International Labour Office's earlier attempts to make comparisons of real wages had stirred up opposition from those who said that the figures were misleading or that they led to discontent in low-wage countries. The conference, initiated and dominated by Americans, was regarded as merely a device for proving more accurately how much better off American and British wage-earners were than their continental counterparts. While therefore a second conference met in 1930, the effort came to naught, for in 1931 the International Labour Office was forced to abandon entirely the publication of real wage comparisons.

On his way home Gay stopped in Paris for another international conference. This one was composed of economic historians and its task was to plan a study of the history of wages and prices. Thirty-five years earlier Schmoller had suggested the price revolution of the sixteenth century as a topic worthy of Gay's attention. Since returning to Harvard Gay had found, in Earl J. Hamilton, a student eager to investigate the Spanish contribution to that epoch-making event; but a wider survey, covering Europe and the eastern United States and pushing the figures as far back as the records would permit, offered economic historians their "one possible long statistical measure," their only "dependable causeway over the morasses of earlier economic history." Yet, as far as he knew, the only people working with modern tools on price history were Hamilton on Spain, Anne Bezanson and her co-workers in Philadelphia on colonial America, and Sir William Beveridge, who for some years past had been conducting a private inquiry to supplement or supplant the English figures dug out by Thorold Rogers during the last third of the nineteenth century.

Gay sold his idea to the Hanover meeting in 1928 and was granted sufficient money to defray the cost of the Paris conference. The scholars who attended it from England, France, Germany, Austria, and the United States agreed that if funds could be obtained there should be undertaken, on a coördinated international basis, a comprehensive study of prices and wages in their respective countries and, if possible, in one or two others as well. Gay submitted this decision to the Social Science Research Council, along with a detailed description of scope and methods. In September 1929, the Hanover meeting approved the project, hoped that funds would be forthcoming, and recommended that the organizing international committee include Beveridge (chairman), Henri Hauser of Paris,

Moritz Elsas of Frankfurt, A. F. Pribram of Austria, and Gay. In October Gay applied to the Rockefeller Foundation for an annual grant of $50,000 for five years. The application was successful.

Having laid the timbers and seen another ship safely launched, Gay was content henceforth with only general attention to the price history studies. He crossed to London in May 1930, to confer with the Europeans who were to do part of the work; went on to Geneva for the second conference on wage statistics; and was on board a west-bound liner within eighteen days of having disembarked at Southampton. A Harvard colleague, Arthur H. Cole, administered the funds and participated in the investigation of American prices. Many difficulties bedeviled progress during the thirties and many disappointments awaited the researchers. Outside England there was a lack of price data for the Middle Ages, so the "causeway" could not be built as far back as had been hoped. Even for later centuries the gaps in the evidence were wide; only a few scattered figures could be found relating to transactions in northern Europe's greatest market, the Amsterdam Bourse, during the sixteenth and seventeenth centuries. The German inquiry came to a halt when Hitler's secret police seized all the materials collected by Elsas, dismissed three of his four assistants, and drove him into exile in London — where, fortunately, he had sent duplicate copies of his notes. Yet the volumes began to appear, and it seemed possible that the whole series — almost a score in all — might be brought to completion. War suspended operations in Britain and the end of the work there is not yet in sight; but one of the Dutch volumes was permitted to be published during the German occupation of Holland.

Of Gay's many other activities during the booming twenties there is no space to say much. Washington continued to call for aid with old tasks or to add new ones. When in 1927 a sample census of distribution was taken in eleven cities, he helped plan the inquiry and went to one or two cities to explain its aim. As the sample was intended to justify a nationwide stocktaking of wholesale and retail distribution in the 1930 census, he was asked to spend a morning in early 1928 "on the hill," urging a congressional committee to provide the necessary funds. He did not get much chance to urge, for

Most of the time was taken up by southern representatives who demanded that the southern farmer be given the facts, so that all the profits would not be drained from his pockets into those of the unspeakable middleman. They didn't know what figures are available or what a Census of Distribution was, or what limitations there are to census figures. But there was one really intelligent member of the committee . . . a socialist member from Rochester. He must be lonesome in Congress.

Next year Gay was assigned the kind of government job he enjoyed. The chairman of the newly created Federal Farm Board was Alexander Legge, a wartime colleague, now president of the International Harvester Company. Gay declined Legge's invitation to spend a year in the capital organizing the Board's statistical work, but offered to give part of the summer to helping him set up the Board and recruit its staff. The Board was established just as farm prices were beginning to break, and its task was to use its $500,000,000 in an effort to stabilize markets. For this work it needed, among other things, a world-wide crop-reporting system that would supply reliable information to American farmers about current yields and stocks in other lands and thus let them know what competition they had to meet.

To procure this information Gay recommended the appointment to American embassies of agricultural attachés, comparable in rank and qualifications to the commercial attachés for whose creation he had in earlier years worked so hard. The only trouble with this suggestion was that it uncovered deep-seated ancient antagonisms between the Departments of Commerce and Agriculture. The former feared that the agricultural attachés would compete with and overlap the work done by its men abroad. On such an issue a fight to the death could be expected, and to Gay, striving to mediate the conflict, the cream of the jest was that both the contending chiefs were his former students.

In the subdued light of a hotel dining room he could get them to agree on a formula that promised clear demarcation of function; but in the glare of a conference room their discovery of countless ambiguities and sinister interpretations threatened to wreck the compromise. It took a second, even a third, good meal to produce lasting harmony, and when Gay returned to Washington in October to present his final recommendations the meeting was a veritable love feast. The Secretaries of Commerce and of Agriculture and the chairman of the Farm Board were of one heart and mind; they pledged coöperation with one another as well as with the State Department; and meanwhile helped themselves to oranges from a large dish of fruit in the center of the table. Gay left the capital so elated that he stormed downtown New York next day, emerged with a mass of money for the house the Council on Foreign Relations wished to buy, then went home feeling he had won a double victory.

A perennial item on Gay's calendar was the work of helping to decide which where the best manuscripts submitted for the Hart, Schaffner, and Marx prizes. He had been on the committee of judges since 1910 and never sought to be excused even in his most crowded years. The work was burdensome because the entries — with their "hundreds of typewritten pages, some of them rather obscure carbon copies" — reached him in July or early August, when he was in the thick of summer school. In 1929 J. Laurence Laughlin, chairman of the committee of judges since 1905, resigned. Gay stepped into the position as a stopgap, but stayed there to liquidate the competition during the early thirties. The prizes had achieved little of their original purpose — to "draw the attention of American youth to the study of economic and commercial subjects" and to attract well-educated men to a business career. Conditions had changed greatly in a generation: business schools were now doing the latter, while scholarships, fellowships, and grants-in-aid provided financial aid to promising young (and not so young) scholars. Yet in its day the venture had made many valuable additions to American economic literature. One of its volumes — O. D. Skelton's *Socialism: A Critical Analysis* — was described by Lenin as the best work of its kind on that subject. Another one — Frank H. Knight's *Risk, Uncertainty, and Profit* — was selected in 1933 for inclusion in a British series of "Economic Classics."

One of Gay's heavy spells of duty in these years was fortunately the kind that comes only once in a lifetime. In 1929, as president of the American Economic Association, he was responsible for arranging the program of the annual meeting held just after Christmas. The sudden switch from boom to depression obliged him to change the whole tone of the program, and there was endless trouble in finding appropriate themes, speakers, and leaders of discussion. This helped to prevent him from getting on with the preparation of his presidential address, and in mid-December he had "only a few fragments of ideas" in his head. His address on the subject of "Historical Records" was concerned with the price history project, the value of statistical measurements in history, and the usefulness of business documents in helping the historian to penetrate beneath the economic surface. It was not expected to "raise anyone's temperature above a quiet normal," but only to be "a sober thing" of seven pages in print, an unpretentious report on work in progress and on working methods.

In that year Harvard, having laden Gay with a new assignment, provided him with a secretary. As she endeavored to evolve a filing system for his correspondence she discovered that he was actively participating in the work of twenty-eight organizations or permanent committees. In addition he continued to accept invitations to talk before academic or professional audiences. Twice, in 1925 and 1930, he spent a month as chairman of one of the "round table conferences" at the Williamstown Institute of Politics. Started in 1921, the Institute sought "to advance the study of politics and to promote a better understanding of international problems and relations." To the verdant campus of Williams College it brought distinguished public men or scholars from abroad to deliver courses of evening lectures; it selected about eight well-known experts — mostly American professors, occasionally public servants, and at times foreigners — to be chairmen of round-table conferences which met three mornings a week; then it invited the attendance of those persons who could contribute something to the round-table discussions, wished to hear the lectures, and had four weeks to spare in July and August.

The novelty of the Institute, the prestige of its speakers, and the urgency of postwar problems made the first gathering a serious concourse of experts or of people already sufficiently well informed to participate in the discussion of the problems that were to be examined. By the time Gay went in 1925 the novelty and urgency had worn off, the qualifications for attendance had been lowered, with the result that the enrollment was double that of 1921, largely through an increase in the number of passive listeners who had little to contribute to discussions but wished to hear the distinguished speakers and enjoy a pleasant vacation. Hence there was little of the round table about either Gay's sessions or those of his fellow-chairmen. He prepared countless sheets of statistics, questions, and bibliographies, did all the talking at some meetings and drafted Coolidge, Leith, Armstrong, or other friends to speak at the others. When he or his guest had given a lengthy exposition or analysis — in 1925 of some aspect of "The Economic Recovery of Europe" and in 1930 of "Recent Economic Progress in Europe" — there might be time for a few questions, then the session was at an end. It was strenuous work, but perhaps it did some good.

If the activities described in this chapter had been set forth chronologically instead of topically they might have given a better picture of the intense, ceaseless, and varied work of the years when Harvard was both a career in itself and a base for far-ranging excursions. When in 1932, on the eve of Gay's departure on sabbatical leave, his former students honored him with a banquet and a volume of essays, Wesley

Mitchell expressed the hope that he would break with past practice and not carry abroad three or four brief cases filled with manuscripts, all of which he had promised to read; that the cabins on either side of his would not be occupied by bright young secretaries who would appreciate very much three or four hours of his time daily; that he would not be met by any organizations eager to present him with problems they themselves had been unable to solve; and that instead he would find a haven of refuge in the Record Office, in the British Museum, in manor houses, and in haunts of ancient peace.

By that time Gay himself was feeling the need for a change of scene and labor. The depression had ended the great decade of building and promoting. To keep the buildings intact and inhabited even by a diminished staff was now difficult enough; to launch new research projects was out of the question. Until conditions improved, the kind of work that had filled his days for so many years had come to a dead end. He therefore turned to his own personal project. To write a fresh account of the Industrial Revolution had long been his desire. In 1929 he enthusiastically accepted an invitation to do Volume XI, entitled *The Economic Revolution*, in the twenty-volume series on *The Rise of Modern Europe* which Professor W. L. Langer was editing and Harper was to publish. He lectured on the subject every year, read as much on it as he could, and steered graduate students into the field. But the years were slipping by, he had reached his sixtieth birthday in 1927, yet was not ready to start writing, and would have found it hard to deny the charge that he never turned down any invitation which gave him an excuse for not starting.

His old colleagues chided him at times on this score. After complimenting him on the "marvelous job," the "remarkable performance," he had done on *Recent Economic Changes*, one of them went on to say, "I cannot help adding that I hope you will not be led to tackle the same sort of thing again. You know what we expect from you on economic history over a larger sweep." His younger friends puzzled their heads about ways of providing him with a private secretary to relieve him of writing letters by hand, or, better still, with a competent research assistant. And Gay himself, on his sixtieth birthday, talked of his "distracted and dislocated career."

It was five years before he was able to make an effort to pull that career together by taking a year's leave from February 1933. As already intimated, his old students had planned to present him with a *Festschrift* to commemorate his twenty-five years of teaching at Harvard and thirty years of service to economic history in America. The volume, *Facts and Factors in Economic History*, containing essays by thirty-four contributors, was therefore given him in December 1932, at what became a *bon voyage* party as well as a testimonial dinner.

To the words of happy, grateful, and affectionate reminiscence spoken there, Gay replied by saying what he thought about "this man Gay":

> A scholar who might have been a scholar, an administrator who might have been an administrator, an editor who might have been an editor, if circumstances had conspired in his favor; a variety of tasks that he has not fully accomplished, that is really the situation. I am hoping that before the career of this man Gay is over, I may be able to bring some final measure of order and completeness to a career which started out in one thing but which has been switched off. I am rather hoping that in the next ten years I shall be able to retire to some activities dear to my heart.

Gay and his wife sailed for England in late February 1933, determined to devote their time to a study of the eighteenth-century economic history of that country. It was more than three decades since they had been in London together, yet as they revisited old haunts it seemed only a few years ago and "a certain dreamlike quality" enveloped all the intervening span of time. But there was nothing dreamlike about the task they had come to do, except that it was a daydream to believe they could half-accomplish it in the few months at their disposal.

Even if they had been at the British Museum every minute it was open they could not have got through the printed sources they wanted to examine; and often they were not there. They now had many friends in England, and it would have been churlish to allow work to preclude hospitality. Gay had to go to Manchester to receive in person an honorary degree which had been offered him in 1923, and that meant a few days' absence from London. The Harvard Club at Cambridge insisted that he come and give them the latest news of the Yard. The price history called for consultation with Beveridge, then for a conference with the continental colleagues at Locarno, and that trip filled up a week. An invitation to represent the United States at a meeting in Madrid of the League of Nations Permanent Commission on Arts and Letters took up another ten days. "Altogether May is going to pot," Gay wrote his daughter.

June fared no better. As chairman of the American delegation at a conference of institutions for the scientific study of international relations he had to attend the meetings and make a speech at a banquet. He rejoiced that he had nothing to do with the World Economic Conference which assembled in June, but could not avoid spending some time with the swarm of friends who were in London for that or other meetings. In fact he was eager to learn from them all about the Roosevelt Revolution which had swept the country since he left it busily closing its banks. "When I poke my head out of the eighteenth century," he wrote, "the news of the United States makes me blink."

It was July before the distractions were over and the researchers could get back to unbroken work. By that time it was clear that they could not finish the course through the long line of books and pamphlets. There was more than enough work to keep them busy till the last minute of the sabbatical year; but the fear of wintry weather in England and on the Atlantic made it seem wise to leave for home in the late fall, firm in the resolve to come back in the very near future. "I must get back here as soon as I can," said Gay. "I have my teeth in my work as I have not had since I worked here over thirty years ago and I can think of little else. My life has been so diffuse in the long interval that now I appreciate intensely this opportunity for concentration."

On landing in New York in early November, Gay did not take a taxi from the pier to his old desks; but he was back in the city two days later. Though his resignation from the directorship of the Bureau and the secretaryship of the Council had relieved him of many duties, enough remained to call him to New York at least once a month. Meanwhile new chores at Harvard or elsewhere filled up some of the time he had expected would be spare. With a new president in charge and many new men on the faculty, Harvard was moving along new lines of action, and Gay was frequently asked for advice or aid, whether the project was a field of research or the planning of the program for the Tercentenary celebrations.

Outside Cambridge the learned societies gave him work to do. The American Economic Association made him its representative on the Council of Learned Societies, and appointed him chairman of its nominating committee and of its committee on policy — all in 1934 or 1935. The Agricultural History Society elected him president in 1934. Tulane University offered him an honorary degree and asked for an address as part of its centennial proceedings. Buffalo booked him for a few lectures in 1935, Illinois for some in the spring of 1936. There were single lectures in other places, and always the summer school.

Only one thing did Gay escape. His absence from America at a crucial period — and perhaps his long association with Mr. Hoover — saved him from being drafted by the New Deal.[3] If he had been in the country during the spring and summer of 1933 he might have been called on and certainly would have responded. He believed that the movement toward economic planning, both national and international, was inevitable and necessary. He realized that "the

[3] There is some oral evidence that he was approached by Louis Howe during the presidential campaign of 1932 with an invitation to serve as adviser to Mr. Roosevelt on some aspect of his platform and policy. There is, however, no documentary evidence to support the statement. If the invitation was tendered, it was certainly declined.

evolutionary process, at any rate in social life, is sometimes *per saltum*" — by leaps and jumps. Yet as he watched from London the leaping and jumping in Washington, the performance seemed "so light-heartedly improvised" that he went about heavy-hearted in fear of its failure. When he returned home he continued to be a spectator, worried at times, but more often ready to accept some New Deal policies as contributions to the country's search for security and stability, and therefore conforming to one phase in the rhythmic swing of history.

In the revived round of engagements no time could be spared for looking at the notes garnered in London, much less for adding to them. The research came to a dead stop and so long as Gay remained at Harvard there was little chance of its moving again. In 1935 he was elevated from ordinary professorial rank to the Henry Lee Professorship left vacant by the retirement of Taussig, who had held it since 1901. The honor entitled him to carry on at Harvard until he was seventy-five (1942–43); but it made no difference to the amount of work he did with students, and in any case there was no hope that these remaining years would offer any more leisure for writing than those which had gone before. They would continue to be absorbed by "the overhang of the obligations of a busy life."

An unexpected chance of escape appeared in mid-1935. Immediately after summer school ended, Gay went to California in response to an invitation from the trustees of the Huntington Library and Art Gallery at San Marino, near Pasadena. "Here I am," he wrote his wife, "settled down for two weeks, without any definite idea of what I am to do, but obviously to be kept busy having people talk to me." It soon became evident that he had been invited to look over the great collection of English books and manuscripts, especially those dealing with the Tudor and Stuart centuries; to look into plans for using these materials for a systematic study of the English Renaissance; and to be looked over as a possible addition to the Library's research staff.

As the mutual appraisal proceeded the trustees revealed their desire to secure Gay's services, while he in turn saw opportunities for doing research work in the economic and social history of what he later called his "favorite sixteenth century." No formal offer of a post was made before he left the West, but he thought one would be forthcoming and indicated that it would have to ensure sufficient income and leisure to permit trips to the East and even to England in search of material for his Industrial Revolution study, not to mention an escape from the summer heat of southern California.

When the invitation came it was subjected to probably the most prolonged consideration ever given any major step in his life. To leave Harvard would be hard, even though 1936 was to be the year of exodus for such surviving fellow-veterans as Charles Bullock and Roscoe Pound. To leave the east coast, crowded with the friends, acquaintances, triumphs, and occasional failures of thirty-five years, was vastly harder. Already one journey had let him realize how the miles and the wide expanse of desert or near desert made the West seem terribly remote. Further, the migration would entail a grievous breaking of family ties which were very strong on each side and especially precious to his wife.

Against these things must be set a job free from classes and advisees and administrative duties, in a library well stocked with rare documents, with what looked like an ample salary and six months' leave each year, on full pay, to work wherever he wished. Here, indeed, was an opportunity, as his Harvard colleagues later recalled his deliberations,

> to divest himself of those numerous activities, both in the University and in the world at large, in which his wisdom in counsel, his knowledge and judgment in human affairs, and his capacity for organization and administration had for years involved him. He wanted at last, in the seclusion of the library, to devote himself to the life of pure scholarship and research of which he had always dreamed.

By going to California he could put a continent between himself and his own haunts. He could climb into the most ivory of ivory towers and cut the rope after him.

The opportunity was too tempting to be put aside. On September 9, 1936, accompanied by his wife and daughter, Gay boarded the train for California.

# VI

## IN AND OUT OF THE IVORY TOWER

### 1936–1946

Rarely does a professor retire to such pleasant pastures as those which awaited Gay in California. In appointing him to the research staff of the Huntington Library the trustees gave him a chance to carry on, under well-nigh ideal conditions, the work he most wished to do. In return they gained his collaboration in shaping plans for studies, based on the Library's rich collection of original materials, of the English Renaissance. His research on Tudor inclosures qualified him for investigating the economic and social aspects of the period; the wide range of his interests and scholarship might give a sense of proportion and interrelationship to the political, cultural, and religious studies on which others would be engaged; and his presence would make his advice, criticism, and inspiration available to scholars working at the Library, no matter what their status, subject, or length of sojourn. If in the meantime the annual half-year's leave of absence enabled him to complete his study of the Industrial Revolution, he would crown his career with a double accomplishment — a survey of the modern economy in the making and a substantial contribution to our knowledge of the two preceding centuries.

There seemed to Gay to be plenty of time for doing both. At sixty-nine his energy appeared unabated, longevity was characteristic of his forebears on both sides of the family, and escape from the squirrel cage should make life simpler as well as more leisurely.

Besides, the Huntington Library is a very near approach to heaven on earth — or to what Gay called it, Elysium. It is set in the seclusion of two hundred acres that contain also an art gallery, a park, and a botanical garden. Massive gates, landscaped lawns, trim flowerbeds, exotic shrubs, and statues suggest a smaller version of Versailles or of some English ducal mansion. When eyes grow tired of reading there are restful walks through the Oriental or the Desert Plant Garden. When hunger strikes there is a cafeteria within the grounds where one can eat perhaps the cheapest meal in North America in the congenial company of permanent staff members or of visitors attracted from beyond the mountains, the desert, or even the oceans by the treasures awaiting their inspection. If one feels an urge to forget the world of gasoline and smog and four-lane highways outside the gates, the Art Gallery offers an escape into the architecture, furnishings, and art of Georgian England. And if one becomes oppressed by a sense of being foreign, stranded, and homesick among these expatriate artifacts, there is consolation in the discovery that almost everybody and everything here seems to be immigrant, that virtually nobody, nothing, is indigenous.

When Henry Edwards Huntington, railroad and real estate millionaire, embarked in the twenties on the conversion of his private estate into a public institution and of his private library into a research center, he handed over about a hundred thousand books and a million manuscripts. Many of the former were collector's items, published during the first two centuries of printing. Most of the latter had been bought from tax-impoverished English landlords, from whose muniment rooms the massed miscellany of letters, diaries, deeds, bonds, mortgages, account books, reports of lawsuits, and odds and ends had been transferred to California.

By the time Gay arrived the research center had taken shape; the books had been classified and supplemented by the necessary reference volumes; a small permanent research staff of scholars assembled by Max Farrand, veteran American historian and now director of research, was at work; associates or fellows were being appointed year after year; and a quarterly journal had been launched. Enough progress had been made in processing the manuscripts to clarify the need for a scholar competent to extract from them the raw material of economic and social history.

One collection of documents contained thousands of papers dealing with the activities of the Temple family from Tudor days down into the eighteenth century. The Temples were the kind of landlords whose inclosing zeal Gay had measured, largely from external evidence, forty years before. Perhaps their records would give the inside story, show how they managed their estates, how they fared in the decades of rapidly rising prices during the sixteenth century, then in the period of stable or falling prices and political strife that followed. There might be enough detail to tell the tale about those "two great categories of income" — rent and interest — on which so little was known. At any rate, since virtually no one had as yet studied the English landed class through its own private archives, work on the Temples through many generations would have the double flavor of being personal and pioneering.

Into this task Gay flung himself at once with something of the zest of his years at the Record Office. Sorting, reading, note-taking, he plowed steadily into the material, much of it hard to read and harder to interpret. By 1939 he confessed he had "become very tired of the Temples. Working through the pile of bills, accounts, cancelled bonds, letters and legal papers is rather heavy drudgery." Yet the labor of seeking relevant facts and of fitting them together as in a slowly emerging jig-saw puzzle picture gripped his attention, and in any group of fellow historians an inquiry about the Temples would launch him on an eager account of his latest finds, conclusions, and unanswered questions.

The first fruit of his research appeared in the *Huntington Library Quarterly* of July 1939, under the title "The Rise of an English Country Family: Peter and John Temple, to 1603." The article was a success story, showing in rich color and detail how Peter, "beginning apparently with nothing but his title of gentleman, the younger son of a younger branch of an old but not particularly distinguished Leicestershire family," prosperously practiced sheep-farming, bought or leased more acres, and "laid the foundation, which his son John built upon, for the creation of a 'family,' with entailed lands, social recognition, and political influence."

The second installment appeared a year later. Its title was "The Temples and Their Debts," its theme the difficulties encountered by the third and fourth generations in raising, or even maintaining, the standard of living and way of life to which it had pleased the first and second to call them. The difficulties were caused in part by broad impersonal factors, such as periodical agricultural or general business slumps, the marked slackening in the rate of increase in farm prices, and the conflict between king and parliament. But it was the emphasis on personal factors that gave this article and the third one, which appeared in 1943, their novelty and value. The nature of the source materials obliged one to take the family, not the individual, as the unit for consideration, to consider the entrepreneur as "family man" rather than "economic man," and to think in terms of what Professor Frank Knight once called "familyism" rather than of individualism.

Consequently Gay had to show not merely where the family income came from and how much it was, but also what it was expected to do. The head of a landed family might control the purse, but he in turn was controlled by law or by the custom of his class, and certain things were demanded of him. Since primogeniture decreed that the eldest son receive the estate while entail handed it to him intact, the other children had to be provided for in other ways. Sons must be given a proper training and set up in life with a "settlement" that would at least keep them from poverty. Daughters needed dowries, dowagers had to be cared for. Social and public obligations must be adequately sustained, and meanwhile the estate must be extended wherever possible by further acquisitions of land.

The third and fourth generations of Temples had difficulty in carrying all these burdens, partly because the family was given to high birth rates and unusually low death rates. The third generation was almost ruined by having to provide for four sons and nine daughters. It postponed disaster by borrowing money to such an extent that Peter, head of the fourth, inherited debts equal to possibly ten years' income. He pawned his plate, lived in hiding in London, but could not elude the hundred creditors when they mobilized for an attack, and died in 1653 fighting with his back to the wall.

The third chapter of the story told how Richard, head of the fifth generation, bargained for fourteen years with the creditors and finally persuaded them to settle for less than half of the principal sum; tapped his assets by selling lumber; secured government posts that paid him more than he received from his land; married a widow with a useful dowry; and thus emerged free of debt, with money to spare for rebuilding the family mansion and for stocking it with books and pictures. When he died in 1675 the family was well established among the upper gentry and his achievement led one of his friends to describe him as "the fountain of exemplary contrivances and managements."

There were to have been more articles, dealing with the effect of falling rents, lower prices, and higher taxes on the sixth and seventh generations; but these were never written. The three published chapters, covering in all a hundred pages, are therefore a torso, a minor but stimulating contribution to the work that other scholars, British and American, were doing on Tudor and Stuart rural history when World War II came—and are carrying on today.[1] From their joint labors on family archives in great houses it is becoming possible to repaint the picture of the English landowning class. Gay's case study lets us see the individual and the family in the class. The Temples may not have been "typical," though we cannot decide that point as yet; but they were very human, and we still have to be shown that

[1] English landlords, even the largest of them, have in recent years opened their estate and family records to accredited scholars. Work on these documents has already yielded rich returns.

the "ideal type" — whether capitalist, landowner, laborer, or entrepreneur — is more than a scholar's crude working tool or a controversialist's weapon.

In pursuing this new line of research Gay did not allow the old one to be forgotten. Now that the conflict between scholarship and action had ended in victory for the former, there was danger of a new schism developing through the claims of two periods for his attention. In fact, by 1940 he was chafing a bit because the writing of the next Temple article was occupying time that ought to be spent on the Industrial Revolution.

It quickly became evident that research pilgrimages to Europe were out of the question because of the cost, then the rising international tension, and finally the deterioration in Mrs. Gay's health. There was a passable substitute for the British Museum in the rich collection of old books and pamphlets recently given to Harvard and now housed in quarters of its own — the Kress Room in the library of the Business School. Yet a visit to this and other eastern libraries was impossible unless lecture engagements or some other missions furnished funds to defray the cost of the journey. When the high rent and operating expenses of the California home had been paid and the long-standing *Evening Post* debt had been "serviced," little money was left for travel.

Gay's attempts to complete his research in the east were therefore confined to three occasions when other assignments took him across the continent. The first was quite futile, since the month spent in the old haunts during the spring of 1937 was too crowded to leave time for the reading he had "half hoped" to do. He had lectures to deliver in Buffalo and Philadelphia. In New York old friends and institutions were on his trail all the time. In his words, "I have seen all the usual people and talked, or been talked to, about their troubles. . . The old accustomed whirl of seeing people . . . which I used to take as a matter of course, I find a bit more strenuous after an absence of only these few months." In Cambridge things were no different. There were countless conference lunches or dinners to be eaten. He sat in at a departmental meeting and "listened to discussion at cross purposes — like old times." President Conant sent for him and reviewed the latest batch of Harvard problems and policies. Students waylaid him and insisted on discussing their unfinished theses. There was no time left for visiting the Kress Room.

The outstanding reason for this brief trip to the east coast was an invitation to attend a ceremony at the house of the Council on Foreign Relations. Previously, when the board of directors heard Gay was going to California they not merely refused to accept his resignation as vice-president and director but also decided that a portrait of him must be painted. Gifts poured in and the list of donors, nearly sixty in all, ranging alphabetically from Angell to Young, reflected the wide range of associations Gay had established during three decades with leaders in education, business, finance, industry, journalism, and public life. The portrait was painted during early 1936 but the "little ceremony" of unveiling and presenting it was left until he could come east in 1937.

It took place on May 19, and was far from the "ordeal" he had anticipated. He had gathered together some ideas on his "working hypothesis" about the course of history but was afraid that the speeches preceding his own would be so overwhelming in their expressions of gratitude and praise that he would be jolted off the track. His fears proved unfounded, as the speakers were too well aware that he disliked fulsomeness. His reply could therefore concern itself with a sober review of the rhythm of history; an attempt to assess the character of the "new historical period" into which he believed mankind had passed; and an outline of the tasks confronting the Council as it pursued its policy of detached investigation in the new phase of "peculiar stress and strain."

Next day he caught a west-bound train. His eagerness to get home was unbounded. He had left one of his two watches on California time, so that he could imagine what his family was doing at any hour. His New York physician had assured him life out west would continue to keep him in good condition, provided he ate less bread and took vitamin pills. Then followed a year unbroken by serious distractions. He worked steadily on the Temple papers and began to see the story taking rough shape. In the community of scholars at the Library he found genial stimulating colleagues, gave much time to advising younger men who came there to do research, and was drawn increasingly into consultation on the problems of Library policy or administration. At "Caltech" (California Institute of Technology), which stood only a few blocks away from the Library, he conducted a seminar in economic history in his capacity as an Associate of the Institute, fostered his interest in physical science by learning what the scientists were doing there, and in return tried to explain to them the economic and social trends of the world they were doing so much to disturb. Universities and colleges became aware of his presence and invited him to give addresses at Stanford, Pomona, and elsewhere. Meanwhile he enjoyed more "leisure and outdoorness" than he had known for many decades, and delighted in the view of mountains that seemed to rise up from the end of the street — when they were visible.

During breakfast on his seventieth birthday the ringing of the front doorbell announced an unusually early caller. The man introduced himself as local representative of an automobile company, handed Gay a letter, and requested him to step out to the driveway. There stood a new car, which the letter explained was a birthday gift from three old and close friends. According to the dealer's account, "Dr. Gay was almost overcome by the gift and at first said he could not possibly accept such a present; but later he changed his mind and seemed extremely pleased, as did the other members of the family."

On more than one occasion in the past these and other friends had sought an opportunity to provide something they felt he needed. Their feelers had always been met with the reply from Mrs. Gay that a personal gift was out of the question, since her husband still felt acutely conscious of the loss he had caused them to suffer in the

*Post* venture. Now, however, faced with the *fait accompli* and a realization of the sentiments that had inspired it, he was surprised and overcome as he had never been since his "sixth Christmas morning." To the donors he wired "Kamerad, I surrender. Am overwhelmed and most grateful." He spent his spare time during the winter trying to learn to drive "Christopher" — the saint, not Morley or Robin inspired the name. He became convinced that he should have three feet and was slow in learning how to think quickly enough with two. Though he never mastered the machine, it was a source of great joy and added to the pleasure of a long period of steady-paced work and interesting leisure.

The spring and summer of 1938 were neither steady-paced nor leisurely. Invitations to lecture at the University of Buffalo, then to deliver a course of six weekly lectures under the Flexner Foundation at Bryn Mawr, made possible his second (and much longer) visit to the east coast. Having worked over his first Temple paper until he felt he was "not ashamed to print it," he departed in March for a four months' spell of hard labor. From Buffalo he moved on to New York, lectured at the New School for Social Research, was guest of honor at a dinner attended by fifty friends, was "on the go" with an unbroken round of engagements picking up old threads, was ordered by his doctor to take more vitamins and cut out his after-breakfast cigar, then escaped to Bryn Mawr.

The theme of his Flexner Lectures was the economic history of Tudor and Stuart England. As he had not taught this period since early Harvard days he was so "rusty" that he had to make "a rather frantic effort" to the very last minute before facing his Monday evening audiences. As usual he spoke from notes, brushed aside the suggestion that a reporter be engaged to take the lectures down in shorthand, and insisted that he could quickly put them in shape for publication once they had been delivered. When, however, he tried to do this, he found it impossible to recapture the mood or the material. An attempt to dictate them proved unsatisfactory and they were never printed.

When the Bryn Mawr lectures were finished he went to finish the next job on his schedule. To his wife he wrote: "If it wasn't that I really must do some work in Cambridge on that millstone round my neck, the Industrial Revolution, I should certainly come home at once." But he believed that in two months he could work through the material available in the Kress Room down to 1800 or 1815, and that this would "do well enough for [his] purpose, which is this fall to make a real start on writing the book." In that faith he drove "at forced draught" through the Kress collection. Possession of a key to the Room let him work there at any hour of day or night, and by mid-July he could write exultantly: "Yesterday I finished up what I set out to do here, examining all the books and pamphlets, noting what I needed to note, from 1700 to 1800." It was an amazing feat of endurance for a man in his seventy-first year. "But," came the next sentence as a dash of cold water, "there is still a lot to do—the Kress Library to about 1830 or 1840, and books in Widener." He left for home next day, confident of returning the following spring, thanks to an invitation to give three public lectures at Harvard. Meanwhile back in California there was only the second Temple article waiting to be finished; then the great book could be started.

This program broke down completely. Even as Gay boarded his train he slumped physically and mentally. Since the four months of "gruelling regime" at Bryn Mawr and Harvard would have exhausted a far younger man, he thought his "cave in" was only fatigue mixed with old age. When, however, a brief vacation failed to check the loss of weight and deepening debilitation, another explanation had to be sought. The doctor quickly diagnosed the trouble as diabetes. Since 1925 Gay had combatted a tendency to that complaint by care in his choice of food. When he was at home his wife was able to impose a "moderate dietary," but during the four months of eating in dining cars, hotels, and clubs, often in company and frequently as guest, he had grown careless, with the result that a cumulative situation took a definite turn for the worse.

To feel exhausted was a new experience for Gay. Since late boyhood he had rarely been ill and had always been able to draw illimitably on a bottomless well of vitality. He was, however, a good patient, submitting to the prescribed combination of light work, strict diet, and insulin, and obeying the order to abandon his Harvard lectures, though this meant the postponement of his next attack on the Kress collection. The treatment proved so efficacious that by the end of 1938 he was able to resume full-time work at the Library, potter around at home, and feel a slow but sure return of his normal vigor.

Throughout 1939 and early 1940 he pursued this steady pace. The second Temple article was published and the manuscripts yielded welcome treasure. He became increasingly enmeshed in the individual work and coöperative plans of his colleagues at the Library. His seminar for graduate students at Caltech gave him a chance to explore new interpretations of his Industrial Revolution materials, and he played a leading part in establishing an Industrial Relations Department there. Only the brewing and bursting of the storm over Europe marred the satisfaction that came with revived health and renewed zest for work.

After nearly two years of this régime in the west Gay felt fit and eager to respond to three calls from the east. The first was an invitation to preside over a conference on price history as part of the University of Pennsylvania's bicentennial celebrations. The second was from his friends in the Council on Foreign Relations. To them, as to others, American foreign relations had suddenly assumed urgent import when Germany overran the western continental countries. Gay had been concerned about the threat to the nation's vital interests since at least September 1939, and would have welcomed a declaration of war at that time. Now, in early June, when France was tottering and Britain shaking from the shock of Dunkirk, he was one of a group that issued "A Summons to Speak Out" and called for immediate declaration of war against Hitler. Since there was little likelihood the summons would be heeded, the group began to apply pressure and persuasion in the hope of procuring naval and military aid for the British.

Immediately on his arrival in New York in early September, Gay went to the Council office to learn what was happening. Two confidential memoranda were given him for critical examination. He attended meetings of the Research Committee, and on one memorable evening sat in with the handful of men who, according to his report to his wife, had "just put across the fifty destroyer deal against the opposition of the Navy and the reluctance of the President, who, they tell me, is playing politics with the whole movement. They have been acting under the screen of William Allen White's Committee for Aid to Britain 'Short of War' — in fact, dragging White along."

As he listened to their discussion of next steps — such as selling flying fortresses and new kinds of torpedo boats to Britain — and read the headlines on the progress of the Battle of Britain, Gay felt again the tension and need for prompt action of early 1918. From that time onward his mind was increasingly occupied with the part America ought to play in checkmating Germany. He voted for Willkie. He subscribed to a letter Dr. Conant and Lewis Douglas addressed to the White House urging the President to explain in a Christmas fireside chat the need for doing everything necessary to insure the defeat of the Axis. In April 1941, he told the Caltech alumni, "This is our war and the sooner we accept it as ours the wiser it will be."

The third call to the east coast had a double appeal: it was an invitation from the Rockefeller Foundation to help in exploring the feasibility of encouraging research in a large field, and the field was economic history. There had been few new research projects in the social sciences since depression ended the boom days of planning. Perhaps there had never been a proposal so broad in scope or so challenging to him as this attempt to marry economics and history, to integrate theory and economic experience. He therefore spent a week in New York considering the important unexplored areas of American economic history — it was useless to think about European history as long as war shut that continent off from the American scholar. When a conference of economic historians was convened in New York in late September "to discuss the question of what lines of work are most worthy of support and why," he started the discussion by presenting his own suggestions. The upshot of the meeting was that in late 1940 the Foundation made a substantial grant to finance research in economic history during the next four and a half years.

From this conference Gay hurried to Cambridge for one more attack on the contents of the Kress Room. He had only five weeks to spare before he must return to California; there could be no working under forced draught this time, for the doctor had banned evening work; and in addition to the usual distractions there were those attendant on the birth of the new research project. "I am sorry," he wrote, "to lose these precious days from my work at the Library, but the job has to be done for the sake of Economic History, my taskmaster." His progress along the shelves of early-nineteenth-century writings was therefore slower than in 1938, and there were many more shelves. But by watching his meals and his hours he kept well and retained, or regained, his belief that it was not too late for him to write his book — or at least to compose a series of essays on special topics. His wife was much less sure, and made it clear that she thought he was wasting his time continuing to wade through source materials. He tried to reassure her: "I know you are skeptical about the Industrial Revolution book, but I am really going to tackle it as soon as my two Temple articles are done (for which I have all the material), and these pamphlets here are essential for the Industrial Revolution job."

More things than pamphlets were essential. The determination to sit down at a desk and start writing was one; a long period of unbroken leisure for concentration was another. Gay lacked the former, for new facets or interpretations were ever coming to his mind, calling for still further exploration; and the years ahead were devoid of the latter. The months in the east had strengthened some ties that seemed to be weakening and added a new one in the economic history research venture. Other fresh interests were aroused when war came nearer to America, then arrived. The opportunity for leisure and concentration grew ever more remote; it was hard to find time even for doing the third Temple article, and the fourth was not begun. The hope of writing his version of the Industrial Revolution was never explicitly abandoned; but after 1940 no serious effort was made to get on with the work. It remained a piece of "unfinished business," to receive attention later when times were more propitious. Only a month before his death in early 1946 he returned from a physical examination cheered by the doctor's prognosis of some more years of potential working life, and began to make plans for spending part of the next summer in the Widener Library at Harvard.

If there were regrets over the delay in making his own direct contribution to the literature of economic history, there was a sense of satisfaction at the indirect contribution he had made through the scholars he had trained and stimulated, as well as over that which he could make by helping to give shape and life to the new research project. His interest in the latter was so intense that for a time he was disposed to consider leaving the Huntington Library and moving to the Institute for Advanced Study at Princeton, there to devote himself to the work of the committee of economic historians set up to initiate and direct the research. Though this plan came to naught, he did cross the continent five times to attend the committee's meetings. In great measure the plans formulated there embodied the proposals he had made when the venture was being launched, and he supervised one investigation sponsored by the committee.

There was further satisfaction to him in the formation of the Economic History Association in late 1940. As the lights went out over most of European scholarship it seemed incumbent on American economic historians to do what they could to keep the flame of research and publication burning on this side of the Atlantic. In four decades the study of economic history in the United States had reached the point where an association composed of those interested in the subject could safely and with profit be formed. Since Gay was more responsible than any other living scholar for the training of those who joined the association, he was the natural choice as first president and delivered his presidential address at the first meeting, at Princeton in September 1941. As usual he did not prepare it until the last minute, spending two days on the east-bound train painfully putting together an illegible first draft and polishing it up in spare moments up to the time of its delivery. As always he regarded the final product, entitled "The Tasks of Economic History," as "not a particularly brilliant effort — rather humdrum in fact."

Within three months the attack on Pearl Harbor swung his interest to other kinds of tasks. Though now in his seventy-fifth year, he was eager to help in shaping the conduct of the war and in creating an intelligent attitude toward the problems it would leave behind. His contribution was made on both coasts. In the west he had already spoken many times during 1940–41 about the threat to American vital interests. He had participated in discussions at Caltech on such topics as "What the defense program means for the Los Angeles area," and thereby become acquainted with managers and labor leaders in the aircraft and other industries, as well as with the problems confronting them during the mushroom growth of their plants. That acquaintance deepened when war burst out 2200 miles away, threatened to strike at the Californian coast, and gave urgency to deliberations about smoother, larger, and more varied production.

Another group of men with whom he worked was the Los Angeles Committee of the Council on Foreign Relations, in the formation of which he had played a big part in 1939. It included several present and past academics, presidents of two airplane companies, bankers, businessmen, union officials, and Hollywood producers or writers. Despite the difficulties caused by gas rationing, the committee met regularly to discuss war and postwar problems and to reach a common opinion on subjects which the Council sent out for consideration by local committees scattered throughout the country. These opinions were gathered into the central office and a digest of them was forwarded to the State Department as an indication of what people were thinking in the large cities of the nation. Gay was active in the deliberations of the Los Angeles committee, and the last document in his files contains the answers he penciled on a questionnaire about Russian-American relations, the subject to be discussed at the next meeting.

Another active group called itself the Defense Committee of the California Institute of Technology, Huntington Library, and Mount Wilson Observatory. It soon turned to the examination of wider issues than defense, and before the winter of 1941–42 was ended it had produced a "statement of war and post-war aims." Similar work by kindred groups was being done at Harvard, Columbia, and elsewhere, and Gay conceived the idea of coördinating it all in a nationwide study. The outcome of that idea will be examined in a moment. Meanwhile the war brought more work to all the scholars in the San Marino-Pasadena community. Gay's share was the teaching of a quiz section in elementary economics for the uniformed students who thronged the Caltech campus. As chairman of the research committee at the Library since Max Farrand's retirement in 1941 he carried a heavier responsibility there than formerly.

The east coast, however, claimed his chief war services. One call he resisted with the greatest difficulty. It came when in March 1942 Joseph Willits, director of the Social Sciences Division of the Rockefeller Foundation, invited him to visit England for a few months, and advanced three reasons why he ought to go. First, the desire of British scholars to have one or two Americans with whom they could study international problems that were now as much an American concern as a British. Second, the need for considering on the spot the steps the Foundation ought to take for extending or modifying its work in Europe. Third, the importance of doing something to improve Anglo-American relations. As Willits saw the situation,

> Events in the Pacific, the necessity of haggling and bargaining over each item in the Lend-Lease agenda, the ability of each country to put its worst foot forward, and our fondness for telling other people how things ought to be done — all have put the greatest strain upon our ability to work with and understand each other. Yet the growth of understanding and intimate collaboration among the Anglo-Saxon countries is the most important thing in the world. [If you will undertake this mission your] friends in the Rockefeller Foundation will rejoice. But more important, the gods of the future international order will smile too.

It took Gay a week to give his answer. "Your invitation appealed strongly to my persistent underlying spirit of adventure, physical and mental. I have always been tempted by action rather than by meditation," and the purpose of this adventure was a powerful temptation. But advancing age, his wife's frail health, and his belief that a younger man was needed for such a journey forced him to decline. "Old age has some compensations, but not enough to repay such a real affliction as the passing up of such an opportunity as this."

The reference to old age struck a new note. Hitherto there had been a certain timelessness about Gay. He did not look his age, he did not think of it, or if he did he took for granted that he could look forward to many more years and to strength adequate for filling them with hard work. But the failure to receive an immediate call for war work in Washington had stirred a suspicion that perhaps, after all, he was too old for active service and gave him a "laid off" feeling. It was therefore a momentous long distance phone call that came in early April 1942. The speaker introduced himself as Lewis Douglas, now economic adviser to Admiral Land, head of the Maritime Commission. He said he had just learned that Gay worked on shipping during World War I and would like to discuss with him the problems then faced as well as the solutions reached. Could he come to Washington for such a conference?

Gay was due to attend a meeting of the economic history research committee in Cambridge in early May. He intended to talk with the university groups engaged in studying postwar issues, and he had been requested to spend some time in New York helping the Council on Foreign Relations to make some confidential studies for the State Department. He could therefore promise Douglas that he would be in Washington shortly and routed his journey to Cambridge through the capital. There he spent a day or two with the statisticians and economists engaged in war work, many of them former students, colleagues, or such friends as Franz Schneider, his right-hand man in the battle of 1918. He quickly realized that the battle had to be fought all over again; that the allocation of ships and the management of routes was once more in the hands of the shipping people, and that commercial jealousies or international rivalries seemed to be playing a greater part in determining allocation policy and performance than did the real need for vessels.

At the end of a long conference Douglas asked Gay to write a memorandum on "some of the last war experiences," and invited him to come back for three or four days before returning home. While he was in Cambridge a wire arrived urging him to extend the three or four days to as many months. He went to Washington, interviewed Admiral Land, persuaded him to transfer the allocation of shipping to Douglas, and recommended the appointment of Schneider as director of shipping operations. By these two steps shipping policy advanced to the stage which it had not reached until the eve of the Armistice in 1918. The invitation to spend a long time in Washington was not pressed, possibly because one of Gay's friends, fearful lest he work himself to death, insisted that any appointment should be on a part-time basis. This arrangement was not deemed feasible and he therefore quietly slipped out of the proffered summer assignment, though with some regret that he was not to be once more in the thick of things.

He did not slip out of another assignment, since it was of his own making and was, in fact, the last of his grand plans. The idea of coördinated discussion of war and postwar problems in universities and colleges throughout the country grew more attractive as Gay talked it over with Professor Ralph Barton Perry, chairman of the Harvard group, Professor Philip Jessup, who headed a similar committee at Columbia, and Frank Aydelotte, head of the Institute for Advanced Study at Princeton. When therefore his engagements in Cambridge and Washington had been fulfilled he hurried home for a few days and was back in New York by the end of May.

The task he had set himself was to formulate a study plan and win sufficient support to launch it. The plan took tripartite shape: (1) The compilation of a list of problems that would have to be faced before or on the day fighting stopped; (2) the study of each problem by a small group of competent persons and the preparation of a pamphlet setting out the questions that had to be asked as well as some possible answers; (3) the distribution of these pamphlets, one each month, to university groups for discussion. The outcome of their grass-roots — or campus-roots — deliberations would be reported to the central body, which in turn would prepare a statement revealing the consensus of opinion or the conflicts of opinion, and forward it to the State Department or to some other appropriate government agency.

The first step was to ascertain what were the outstanding problems and learn what had already been written privately or publicly about them. Gay read the confidential studies which the Council on Foreign Relations was making for the State Department, as well as the relevant literature in the Council's library. Meanwhile he went out to seek coöperators. For the first month it was single-handed work without benefit of office or stenographer. He wrote all the letters and memoranda by hand and apparently paid expenses out of his own pocket. There were times when he confessed himself unable to see clearly what his enterprise was or where it might lead, and wished he were surer that it was really worth the time he was devoting to it. With Pearl Harbor still a vivid raw memory, Japanese raids on California still to be feared, and little save disaster in the headlines, it needed strong faith to plan what should be done with the unhatched chickens of victory. Yet these doubts and his strong desire to get back home were overridden by what seemed to be a bounden duty.

The duty seemed especially compelling when he read the glowing vague promises which the nation's leaders were making about the brave new postwar world, then recalled similar hopes raised and dashed in 1917–1920. That bit of history must not be repeated, and perhaps "this effort of ours may ultimately make the difference in the nation's post-war decisions between . . . Utopia (whither the Administration is leading us) and subsequent return to 'normalcy,' or . . . a realistic organization of the nations." If such a result was to be made possible, if the United States was to be fed with something better than Fourteen Points — or its current counterpart, the Atlantic Charter and enumerated "Freedoms" — and be armed with something better than "The Inquiry" of 1917–18, he must stay by his scheme for some months until it was launched or sunk.

By July a few stalwart colleagues had been enlisted, such as Professors Perry and McIlwain of Harvard and C. Reinold Noyes, a director of the National Bureau of Economic Research. The Rockefeller Foundation gave enough money to defray the costs of exploration and conference, while Aydelotte provided an office and stenographer at the Institute. Thereupon Gay moved from New York to Princeton. He tore through piles of books on the League of Nations and kindred topics, then began to draft the first problem pamphlet, and arranged several week-end conferences at which the methods of study and the list of topics to be discussed were considered.

By mid-September he felt justified in reserving a berth on a California-bound train. His project had taken definite shape; Perry had consented to take charge of its administration; one or two others had volunteered to carry part of the burden; and promises of coöperation in forming study groups had come in from some universities. Only one essential — money — was lacking, and it was with shocked dismay that the promoters learned in early November that the Rockefeller Foundation did not regard the plan as sufficiently fundamental or practicable to merit financial support. The shock was not, however, fatal. The World Peace Foundation of Boston provided both funds and clerical assistance, and "the Rockefeller" later contributed a small amount. The project therefore went ahead under the auspices of "The Universities Committee on Post-War International Problems in Association with the World Peace Foundation."

By March 1943, eighty study groups were at work and others were being formed. Twenty "Problem Analyses" were prepared and sent out before the war ended. They ranged over the whole conceivable field: the methods and stages that should be followed in reaching a peace settlement, the treatment of defeated enemies, an international security organization, relief and rehabilitation, international economic collaboration, colonial and dependent areas, post-war relations with Soviet Russia, and so forth down the predictable line. They were printed in editions of six to ten thousand and distributed to about a hundred coöperating groups, of which more than half worked steadily through the series, as well as to a considerable number of outside subscribers, journalists, and men in public life. What effect they had on the thinking of academic groups or on the course of American policy we have no way of measuring. The summaries in which the central office analyzed the reports of discussions revealed wide diversities of opinion and proposals, of nescience and prescience, of knowledge and naïveté, of efforts to be realistic in tempering the demands of abstract justice or of devotion to any such single principle as self-determination. They also betrayed a tendency to overload an infant international organization with too many burdens. Yet it is certain that those who studied the score of problems became far better aware of the complexities and difficulties of making peace than their fathers had been.[2]

Having spent a third of 1942 on the east coast Gay stayed on his own side of the continent during most of 1943. An attack of influenza, only slowly shaken off, made him more reluctant than ever to do any writing and it was only by dint of dropping literally everything else that he "managed to crawl over the deadline" with the third Temple article between his teeth. He thought much about the currently popular Beveridge Plan and schemes for social security and "full employment." On the first two closely related topics he delivered addresses, and while his desire to write an article on "The prevailing illusion about 'full employment'" remained unfulfilled he gave the gist of his conclusions in a letter to a friend:

I think the system of private enterprise, modified as experience has shown necessary by some governmental regulation, is essential to progress in material wellbeing. But a system of private enterprise involves necessarily periodic up and down swings. I say "necessarily" because some readjustments are essential to reduce the excesses of over-confidence and speculative activity.

As a matter of fact, despite all the individual and class suffering which has been caused by the down swing of business cycles, a fair appraisal, I think, would show that out of these depressions have come undoubted advantages in invention, business management, and government action.

The present generation is living too much under the shadow of the distresses engendered by the exceptionally heavy depression following 1929. A great extension of government activity in the sphere of private enterprise in order to obtain the leverage required for a program of "full employment" will, I fear, prove illusive in the long-run. It will be something like putting a corporation into a receiver's hands — only permanently.

[2] The summaries were printed in *International Conciliation* (New York: Carnegie Endowment for International Peace), Numbers 401, 405, 410, 414, June 1944–October 1945.

If he was doubtful about the panaceas of the planners, he was equally skeptical of the utterances of those who lauded "The American System of Private Enterprise," especially if they seemed to imply that American entrepreneurs had been blissfully free from government attention until the Great Divide of March 1933, and the enthronement of the New Deal. It was at his suggestion that the committee on research in economic history had chosen "The role of government in American economic development" as one of its chief fields for investigation. As economic historian he knew that laissez faire was an unusual rather than a normal governmental attitude; that the undertaking of enterprises by local or central governments had been going on for thousands of years; and that the present phase in the rhythm of history was one in which public regulation and public enterprise were inevitably bound to increase.

When therefore in 1944 he was invited by Irving Fisher to join "a new movement, with an entirely new method, to combat the attacks on our American System of Private Enterprise," he replied:

> I have strong sympathy . . . with any worth while movement to promote a continuance and strengthening of our private enterprise system. I believe, however, that we must look forward to a mixed system which recognizes an extension of governmental enterprise and, at the same time, an open field for private enterprise. The difficulty is to delimit these spheres and to insure the coöperation of both forms of enterprise. Private initiative, I believe, will find its place, provided it continues and increases its willingness for risk-taking and can demonstrate its strength by its own efforts.

Though he asked for more information before filling out the membership card, the whole tone of the letter revealed his belief that the venture was not "a worth while movement," and the correspondence went no further.

The only cross-continent journey of 1943 was a hurried trip caused by the news that his mother, now ninety-seven years old, was dying. On the way back he contracted virus pneumonia and was laid low for some weeks. As he emerged from "what the English call a rather 'dim' time" and prepared for a quiet Christmas, three letters arrived from the east coast. Their dates were so close together and their purport so similar that collusion would have been suspected had the authors not confessed it.

The first was from the chairman of the economic history research committee, expressing the hope that Gay would be in the east before long, as the committee must soon consider its postwar plans. The second was from Walter Mallory, executive director of the Council on Foreign Relations, inviting him to spend three months in New York during early 1944, "not to undertake any specific work" but to serve as general counselor and critic of plans the Council had to formulate because of an increased grant for its confidential studies and the receipt of a much more exacting and arduous assignment from the State Department.

The third, from Wesley Mitchell, supported Mallory's invitation on the ground that the National Bureau of Economic Research also needed Gay's help in solving "a very puzzling problem." One of its directors had urged it to explore the difficulties likely to arise from America's prospective position as the world's chief creditor but bound up in a protective policy, and had contended that a thorough study of international trade could be undertaken without weakening the Bureau's devotion to "basic research." Would Gay therefore come, examine the problem, and advise whether this venture should be undertaken or left alone?

The reader of these letters is prompted to exclaim, "Why couldn't those easterners leave the grand old man alone?" The answer is that they believed he was eager to come east again; that he was chafing under his exclusion from important war work; and that the appeals for advice were, in part at least, hatched in order to make his migration feasible. His reply suggests that he saw through the stratagem. He said he was not sure he could be of appreciable service to either Council or Bureau; he could not come before early March, which might be too late; but he did feel obliged to attend the meeting of the research committee. He therefore asked that matters be left fluid until he arrived and was able to see whether it was worth while keeping him three months on the other jobs.

Both organizations said they would wait — "a conclusion that represents the premium we put on your counsel" (Mitchell). He arrived on the last day of February and left three weeks later. Of most of that period he wrote, "I feel the rotation — I had better say spinning — of the squirrel cage here. It is literally true that every moment of the day and late evening has been in demand." By way of reward he was a little surprised and pleased to discover anew that people valued his opinion.

> I am undoubtedly a "has been," but although I cannot aspire to the dignity of an "elder statesman" in my narrow field, I find my judgment still sought; and even though I am increasingly unwilling to give it, being ever more conscious of the vast sea of ignorance and fallibility in which I swim, it is not without a tickle to my vanity that I find some of my contemporaries and their juniors still harboring that illusion.

The investigations he needed to make before framing his recommendations were soon finished and he was able to hasten home. By mid-April he had written his two reports. That to the National Bureau set forth reasons why the study of international trade ought to become one of its major interests and suggested aspects most worthy of exploration. The report to the Council surveyed the policies and methods pursued since the early twenties, appraised their success or failure, and indicated the places at which new advances could be made or existing practices and facilities improved. It left nothing untouched, from the operations of local committees to the appointment of research fellows and the purchase of microfilms.

There were no more journeys. Mrs. Gay's health was now failing fast and for the eighteen months before her death in late 1945 all Gay's hours that were not spent at the Library or in Caltech classrooms were devoted to her. Nurses were scarce, especially good ones. For much of this period he therefore assumed her care throughout the night as well as during the late afternoon and evening. Only near the end, when the impossibility of keeping a good day-nurse made it absolutely essential, would he consider entrusting her to a nursing home.

Though always far from robust, she had for more than half a century been his caretaker, companion, and confidante. As the first, she packed his bag whenever he went away, saw to his laundry when he sent it home, and did all his shopping, so that when on his journeys he needed to buy haberdashery he had to write her, "Please send me the sizes I wear of everything I need." As companion, her critique of whatever he wrote was always incisive and constructive. Though the plan of 1892 to make her into a professional historian had come to naught she continued to be a very good amateur one, and her tastes in literature, music, and art matched his. As confidante, she was a good listener to his plans and problems. He was never really a self-sufficient man and the self-doubting of his adolescence continued in some measure all through his life. She sought to combat it on every possible occasion, to make him conscious of his achievements, and to persuade him that his fear of inadequacy was unfounded. It was no easy task.

When the news of her death reached Gay's friends they immediately thought he might find welcome relief in the distractions and interests of the east. The Council on Foreign Relations, having reluctantly accepted his resignation from the board in mid-1945, now considered inviting him to come and supervise the preparation of a report for the State Department. His son, consulted on the matter, felt the suggestion might be beneficial rather than harmful, so long as the burden of actual writing was borne by a competent assistant. He knew that his father's mind was working as keenly as ever, that his physique seemed to be holding up fairly well, that his heart was in the east, and that he intended to hurry there during the next summer to resume his research.

This time, however, the plans which others made for steering Gay's course of action, like those he was making of his own accord, went astray. Late in January he was stricken with pneumonia and on February 8 he died. Sixty years before, his father had told him that "reading is part of the training for life." The training continued to the very end. Throughout recent years he had always read some "between minute" book as he walked through the grounds between the Library and his home, even though latterly he sometimes became so dizzy that he fell on the way. During his last days in hospital, whenever the nurse would allow him to sit up, he read the life of Sir James Mackintosh (1765–1832). The career of that wise and widely learned Scots physician, lawyer, professor, historian, civil servant, parliamentary reformer, and liberal philosopher, whose life spanned the decades of the Industrial Revolution, absorbed Gay's interest until he lost consciousness.

# INDEX

# INDEX


Acheson, Dean, 137
Adams, F. P., 157–158
Adams, T. S., 94, 159
Agricultural History Society, 222
Allied Maritime Transport Council, 106, 109, 116, 117, 118, 121, 141
American Economic Association, Gay and, 217, 222
American Shipping Mission, 109, 113, 116, 117, 118, 121, 130, 138
Angell, James Rowland, 25, 187, 188, 232
Ann Arbor, Gay in, 20–30
Antioch College, 169
Armstrong, Hamilton Fish, 185n, 204, 205, 218
Ashley, W. J., 53, 60, 69
Aydelotte, Frank, 244

Baker, Newton D., 104, 108, 123, 126
Barth, Carl G., 73
Barton, Bruce, 145
Baruch, Bernard, 114, 124, 127, 133
Bates, Henry M., 44, 68, 69, 70
Benét, William Rose, 158–159, 181
Berlin, University of, Gay at, 30, 34–41, 53–57; and women students, 36, 37, 41
Beveridge, Sir William, 213, 214, 221
Bezanson, Anne, 213
Bliss, General Tasker, 105, 108, 118
Boston Chamber of Commerce, 80, 89, 90, 98
Bowman, Isaiah, 206
Bryn Mawr, Flexner Lectures, 234
Bullock, Charles J., 97, 188, 224
Business History, professorship of, 194; Society, 194; *Journal of Economic and Business History*, 194, 212

California Institute of Technology, 233, 236, 237, 240, 241, 250
Canby, Henry Seidel, 159, 181, 182, 185n
Canfield, Cass, 181
Carnegie Foundation, 65, 197, 198, 200
Carver, T. N., 61, 63, 64, 66, 188
Cecil, Lord Robert, 149
Census, of 1920, advisory committee on, 168–169, 189, 190; of distribution, 190, 214–215
Central Bureau of Planning and Statistics, 124–136; conspectus, 126, 127, 129, 136; statistical clearing house, 128, 132; post-armistice work, 129, 131–136; and peace conference, 132–135; possible peacetime services, 135–136
Chamberlain, Austen, 149
Cherington, Paul T., 74
"Christopher," 233–234
Civil Service Reform League, 169
Clay, Henry, 151, 157, 172, 212
Cole, Arthur H., 214
Cole, G. D. H., 151
Cole, William Morse, 71
Commercial Economy Board, 98–102, 125
Committee on National Income, 94, 196
Committee on Research in Economic History, 237–238, 239, 243, 249
Commons, John R., 94
Conant, President J. B., 232, 237
Coolidge, Archibald C., 97, 134, 159, 187, 188, 205, 206, 218
Copeland, Melvin T., 78, 81, 98, 99, 101, 125
Council of Learned Societies, 208, 222
Council on Foreign Relations, 5, 7, 168, 195, 203–206, 211, 216, 232; and World War II, 236–237, 240, 241, 243, 249, 250; Los Angeles Committee of, 240
Cox, James M., and 1920 election, 165, 166, 167, 168
Cunningham, W. J., 74, 79, 159
Curtis, Cyrus H. K., 155, 180, 184, 185n
Czechoslovak soldiers, repatriation of, 130

Daniels, Josephus, 127, 131
Davis, John W., 204
Davis, Joseph S., 116, 117
Davis, Norman H., 175
Davis, Royal, 159

Day, Clive, 207–208
Delano, Frederick A., 82
Dennison, Henry S., 89, 90–91, 98, 111, 114, 127, 129, 136–137, 149, 151, 160, 170, 175, 211, 212
Department of Agriculture, 131, 215–216
Department of Commerce, reorganization of, 169, 189–191, 215–216
Department of Labor, 124
Dewey, John, 25, 48
Dodge, Cleveland, 175
Donham, Dean W., 212
Douglas, Lewis W., 237, 242–243
Dulles, John Foster, 134, 206

Economic History Association, 239–240
Economic interpretation of history, Gay on, 33, 44–45
Eliot, President Charles W., 1, 3, 53, 54, 55, 60, 63, 64, 66, 67, 68, 70, 74, 82, 84, 87, 95, 140, 144, 159, 170
Elliott, Howard, 82, 84
Elsas, Moritz, 214
*Encyclopaedia of the Social Sciences*, 207–208
English Speaking Union, 169

*Facts and Factors in Economic History*, 220
Fahey, John H., 179
Farrand, Max, 227, 241
Federal Farm Board, 215–216
*Festschrift* to Gay, 63, 218, 220
Field, James A., 116
Fisher, Irving, 98, 248
Ford, Guy Stanton, 210
*Foreign Affairs*, 5, 185n, 205, 206
Foundations and research, 6, 197, 199, 200, 203, 207, 209, 214
Franklin, P. A. S., 109, 115, 118, 119, 120–123, 124

Garfield, Harry A., 133
Garrett, Paul Willard, 181, 185n
Gay, Aaron Francis, 2, 13–17, 23, 27, 30, 70, 142
Gay, Mrs. Aaron F., 13, 14, 17–19, 23, 70, 248
Gay, Edith, 15
Gay, Edward, 43, 102, 136, 251
Gay, Edwin Francis, survey of career and characteristics, Introduction; boyhood, 13–20; youth, 20–25; college days, 25–30; graduate study in Europe, 1, 2, 30–57; marriage, 35–37; religious experiences, 24, 25, 29, 35; search for vocation, 2, 20, 25, 26–28, 31, 140–141; view of history, 28, 31–34, 38–39, 44–45, 47–49; "rhythm of history," 47–49, 192, 222–223, 232, 248; becomes economic historian, 33, 38–41, 44–47, 52–53, 55–57; as teacher, 2, 4, 9, 58–66, 75, 192–194, 233, 236, 237, 241; dean of Business School, 67–87, 95–96, 194, 195; extracurricular activities before 1917, 87–95; labor law agitation, 88–90; concept of research institutions, 92–93, 94, 195, 201, 205–206; Washington war work, 3, 4, chap. iii; on Commercial Economy Board, 98–102; on Shipping Board, 109–110, 123, 129–130; work of Shipping Board's Division of Planning and Statistics, 109, 110–115, 116, 117, 118, 119, 124; on War Trade Board, 110, 124, 125, 130–131; work for War Industries Board, 124, 125–126; Central Bureau of Planning and Statistics, 124, 126–128, 131–136; in charge of New York *Evening Post*, chap. iv; and National Bureau of Economic Research, 5, 7, 168, 188, 197–203, 249, 250; and Council on Foreign Relations, 5, 7, 168, 203–206, 232, 237, 241, 243, 249, 250, 251; and reorganization of federal agencies, 135–136, 168–169, 189–191, 214–216; second Harvard period, chap. v; sabbatical leave, 220–222; Henry Lee Professorship, 223; and Social Science Research Council, 208–214; and New Deal, 221, 222–223; at Huntington Library, chap. vi; work on Temple family, 228–231, 235; and World War II, 236–237, 241–247; plan for study of postwar problems, 241, 244–247; publications, 6, 11, 12, 53, 56, 64, 65, 91, 192, 199, 202, 205–206, 208, 217, 228, 229, 230,

233, 236, 239, 240, 247; self-appraisal, 6, 22, 23, 26–27, 30, 31, 34–35, 56, 63–64, 68, 69, 140–141, 185, 220, 224, 250; appraisals of, 1–2, 3, 8, 9, 10, 12, 21, 26, 53, 54, 56, 61, 63, 64, 66, 67, 74, 81, 87, 95, 114, 137–138, 145–146, 147, 176, 181–182, 183, 205–206, 220, 232; view of position of United States in world (1898), 50–51; concept of economics as science, 27, 39, 196; views on "future of private enterprise," 248; views on "full employment," 247. *See also* Central Bureau of Planning and Statistics; Council on Foreign Relations; Harvard Graduate School of Business Administration; Industrial Revolution; National Bureau of Economic Research; New York *Evening Post*
Gay, Mrs. Edwin F. (née Louise Fitz Randolph), 1, 7, 29–30, 35–38, 41–43, 44, 53, 54, 59, 136, 220, 224, 225, 231, 233, 238, 250–251
Gay, John, 13, 54
Gay, Mary, 15, 19
Gayley, Charles Mills, 25–26
Germany, Gay in, 2, 15, 26, 30–41, 53–57
Glass, Carter, 139
Godkin, E. L., 142–143
Goethals, Major General George W., 102, 126
Gras, N. S. B., 194
Greene, Jerome D., 66, 67, 91, 109
Gross, Charles, 52, 53, 63

Hall, Arnold Bennett, 210, 211
Hall, Hubert, 52, 65, 151
Hamilton, Earl J., 213
Harding, Warren G., on League of Nations, 164, 165, 166, 167
Harnack, Adolf von, 34, 45
Hart, Schaffner, and Marx prize competition, 91, 216–217
Harvard Graduate School of Business Administration, 3, 67–87; establishment of, 67–75; early faculty, 71–74, 78–79; aim, curriculum, and teaching methods, 76–81; and scientific management, 72–73, 79–80; finances, 70, 84–86; early endowments, 85–86; Bureau of Business Research, 80–81; Visiting Committee, 82–85; postwar growth, 192, 194
Haskins, Charles, 52, 63, 97, 134, 159, 188
Hatfield, H. R., 125, 126, 128, 137
Hauser, Henri, 213
Heilman, Ralph E., 90–91
Hoover, Herbert, 5, 101, 102, 114, 120, 166, 169, 186; as Secretary of Commerce, 189–191, 198, 202
Hosmer, Jane, 15, 18
House, Colonel E. M., 132, 134, 149
Hudson, Richard, 28
Hughes, Charles Evans, 97, 169
Huntington Library and Art Gallery, Gay at, 7, 223–224, 226–228, 233, 236, 239, 241, 250, 252
Hurley, Edward N., 102, 107, 108, 115, 117, 118, 123, 124

Imports, wartime restriction of, 106, 107, 108, 109–116, 121, 125
Industrial Revolution, Gay's work on, 7, 11, 60, 68, 75, 151, 192–193, 219, 220–222, 223, 224, 226, 231, 235, 236, 238, 252
"Inquiry, The," 132, 133, 134, 245
International Labour Office, 201, 212, 213
Italy, Gay in, 2, 15, 42–43

Johnson, Alvin, 208
Johnson, General Hugh S., 125
*Journal of Economic and Business History*, 194, 212
Jusserand, Jean Jules, 99

Kemmerer, E. W., 159
King, W. L. Mackenzie, 67, 71
Klein, Julius, 190

Labor legislation, agitation for, 88–90
Lamont, Hammond, 144
Lamont, Thomas W., and Business School, 82–83, 84–85, 96, 133, 144; and N. Y. *Evening Post*, 139–175; contract with Gay, 146–148; critique of editorials, 161–163; and 1920 election, 164–168; sells *Evening Post*, 174–175, 180

Land, Admiral, 242, 243
Lane, C. Chester, 156, 181, 182, 185n
Langer, William L., 219
Laughlin, J. Laurence, 216
Laura Spelman Rockefeller Memorial Fund, 200, 209
Leadam, I. S., 52, 53
League of Nations, Gay and, 4, 141–142, 149, 164–168, 181, 221
Leffingwell, Russell C., 206
Legge, Alexander, 215
Leipzig, study in, 30–34
Leith, C. K., 110, 134, 141, 187, 218
Lewisohn, S., 175
Libraries Association, 169
Lippmann, Walter, 206
London, Gay's years in, 43–53, 220–222
Loud, Rev. Henry, 13–14, 27
Loveman, Amy, 152, 159, 181
Lowell, President A. L., 66, 85, 95, 140, 188, 195

Mallory, Walter H., 249
Mantoux, Paul, 149
March, General Peyton C., 113, 120, 122, 123
Marx, Gay on, 33
May, George O., 160, 175
McCormick, Vance C., 122, 124, 129, 133
McIlwain, Charles H., 245
Merriam, Charles E., 208
Mezes, Sidney E., 134
Michigan, lumber industry, 14, 15
Michigan, University of, 20, 25–30
Migration, international, study of, 201, 210–211
Mitchell, Wesley C., 5, 10, 93, 94, 142, 159, 168, 188, 196–199, 205, 206, 208, 218–219, 249, 250
Morgan, Arthur, 169
Morgan, J. P., 140, 165
Morley, Christopher, 158, 159, 181, 184, 185n, 192
Morrow, Dwight W., 140, 144, 145, 160
Moulton, H. G., 207, 210
Munsey, Frank A., 174

National Bureau of Economic Research, 5, 7, 95, 168, 188, 189, 195, 196–203, 211, 249, 250
Navy Department, 127, 131, 138
Nevins, Allan, 159, 181, 185n
New School of Social Research, 234
New York *Evening Post*, Gay and, 4, chap. iv; early history of, 142–143; bought by T. W. Lamont, 143–144; Gay's appointment to, 145–148; condition of, 143, 148, 149, 151–154; Gay's policies of expansion, 155–160, 170–171; editorial policies, 160–168; Literary Review, 152, 157–159, 170, 181, 185n; in 1920 election, 164–168; financial troubles, 170–173, 176–178, 179–180; purchase by new corporation, 174–176; sale to Cyrus H. K. Curtis, 155, 180, 182, 184–185
Northcliffe, Lord, 149–150
Noyes, Alexander, 156
Noyes, C. Reinold, 245

Ochs, Adolph S., 187
Ogden, Rollo, 144

Parker, Judge Edwin, 125
Peace Conference (1918–19), U. S. delegation, 132–135, 140, 141, 164, 203–204
Perry, Ralph Barton, 244, 245
Pershing, General John J., 104, 107, 118, 120
Polk, Frank L., 176
Postwar problems, study of, 7, 8, 241, 244–247
Potter, Z. L., 153–154, 156, 184
Pribram, A. F., 214
Prices, history of, 65; international study of, 213–214, 221
Profit-sharing study, 90–91
Puckette, Charles, 156, 181, 185n

Questionnaires, plague of wartime, 127–128

*Recent Economic Changes*, 202, 219
Ripley, W. Z., 63
Rockefeller Foundation, 209, 214, 237–238, 241–242, 245, 246; plan for economic research institute, 91–93, 96

Roosevelt, Franklin D., 127, 131, 138, 165, 166, 167, 168, 170, 176, 183, 222, 237
Root, Elihu, 204
Rorty, Malcolm C., 93–94, 168, 196, 197
Rossiter, W. S., 169, 189
Royal Historical Society, 52, 64
Rublee, George, 98, 102, 109, 117, 118, 141–142, 149, 166, 206
Ruml, Beardsley, 209
Russian-American relations, Gay on, 50–51, 131, 241

Salter, J. A., 141–142, 150
*Saturday Review of Literature*, 4, 185n
Schaffner, Joseph, 91
Schaffner, Joseph Halle, 176
Scheffer-Boichorst, Paul, 34, 37
Schmoller, Gustav, 38–40, 54, 55, 56, 61, 64, 196, 213
Schneider, Franz, 120–122, 181, 206, 243
Schwab, Charles M., 115
Scientific management, 72–73, 79–80
Scott, Donald, 111, 115, 119, 156
Scroggs, O. W., 181
Secrist, Horace, 118
Sedgwick, Ellery, 144, 146, 170
Selden, Charles, 157, 172
Seligman, E. R. A., 207–208
Shaw, Arch W., 78, 78n, 80, 98, 99, 125
Ship Control Committee, 109, 115, 116–123
Ship Tonnage Conferences, 120–123
Shipping Board, 105, 107, 108, 109, 115, 118, 123, 124, 125, 129–130, 138, 139; Division of Planning and Statistics of, 109, 110–115, 116, 117, 118, 119, 124
Shipping problem, in World War I, 102–107; in World War II, 242–243
Simmons, W. D., 98
Slocum, Thomas, 111
Social Science Research Council, 6, 10, 200, 208–214; Problems and Policy Committee of, 209–211
Social scientists, coöperation between, 206–214
Sprague, O. M. W., 71
State Department, 108, 113, 114, 121, 130, 131, 169
Steed, H. Wickham, 149
Stevens, R. B., 109
Stone, N. I., 94
Straight, Mrs. Willard, 176
Strunsky, Simeon, 151–153, 156, 160, 181, 184, 206
Sullivan, Mark, 157, 185n
Swanson, A. E., 110, 124, 128
Switzerland, Gay in, 2, 15, 41–42

Tardieu, André, 150
Taussig, F. W., 60, 63, 66, 67, 70, 91–92, 188, 223
Tawney, R. H., 56n, 151
Taylor, Frederick Winslow, 72–73, 79
Temple family records, work on, 228–231
Tower, Walter S., 110, 113, 120, 130, 134, 190, 206
Towse, John R., 156, 181
Treasury, 131, 132, 133, 137, 139; Bureau of Budget, 136n

Unemployment, conference on, 190, 198; research on, 198
Universities Committee on Post-War International Problems, 245–247

Vanderlip, Frank A., 170, 199
Villard, Oswald Garrison, 143, 153
Vogel, Martin, 176

Wages, international study of, 211–213, 214
Wagner, Adolf, 38, 39
War Department, 107, 126, 127, 129, 130, 131
War Emergency Fleet Corporation, 102, 104, 105, 123
War Food Administration, 101, 102, 114, 130
War Industries Board, 100, 103, 114, 121, 125–126, 129; Division of Planning and Statistics, 124, 125, 126, 129; Conservation Division, 125–126; Industrial Adjustment (Snickersnee) Committee, 125–126

War Trade Board, 103, 105, 109, 110, 113, 119, 121, 122, 123, 125, 130; statistical bureau, 24, 129; decontrol, 130–131, 136
Warburg, Paul, 176
Webb, Sydney and Beatrice, 49, 151
White, William Allen, 178, 237
Wickersham, George, 166, 176, 187
Willcox, W. F., 201
Williamstown Institute of Politics, 217–218
Willits, Joseph H., 241–242
Wilson, President Woodrow, 97, 98, 108, 109, 118, 124, 125, 127, 131, 135–136, 170; and U. S. Peace Commission, 132–134; and League of Nations, 166–167
Wolman, Leo, 134, 159, 212
Woodrow Wilson Foundation, 170
Woolley, Clarence M., 176
World Peace Foundation, 246

Young, Allyn, 94, 132, 133, 134, 186
Young, Owen D., 176, 177, 178, 179, 232

Zurich, study in, 30, 41–42